S0-BZB-171

Nutshell Series
Hornbook Series
and
Black Letter Series
of
WEST PUBLISHING COMPANY
P.O. Box 64526
St. Paul, Minnesota 55164–0526

Accounting
FARIS' ACCOUNTING AND LAW IN A NUTSHELL, 377 pages, 1984. Softcover. (Text)

Administrative Law
GELLHORN AND LEVIN'S ADMINISTRATIVE LAW AND PROCESS IN A NUTSHELL, Third Edition, 479 pages, 1990. Softcover. (Text)

Admiralty
MARAIST'S ADMIRALTY IN A NUTSHELL, Second Edition, 379 pages, 1988. Softcover. (Text)

SCHOENBAUM'S HORNBOOK ON ADMIRALTY AND MARITIME LAW, Student Edition, 692 pages, 1987 with 1989 pocket part. (Text)

Agency—Partnership
REUSCHLEIN AND GREGORY'S HORNBOOK ON THE LAW OF AGENCY AND PARTNERSHIP, Second Edition, 683 pages, 1990. (Text)

STEFFEN'S AGENCY-PARTNERSHIP IN A NUTSHELL, 364 pages, 1977. Softcover. (Text)

American Indian Law
CANBY'S AMERICAN INDIAN LAW IN A NUTSHELL, Second Edition, 336 pages, 1988. Softcover. (Text)

Antitrust—see also Regulated Industries, Trade Regulation
GELLHORN'S ANTITRUST LAW AND ECONOMICS IN A NUTSHELL, Third Edition, 472

Antitrust—Continued pages, 1986. Softcover. (Text)

HOVENKAMP'S BLACK LETTER ON ANTITRUST, 323 pages, 1986. Softcover. (Review)

HOVENKAMP'S HORNBOOK ON ECONOMICS AND FEDERAL ANTITRUST LAW, Student Edition, 414 pages, 1985. (Text)

SULLIVAN'S HORNBOOK OF THE LAW OF ANTITRUST, 886 pages, 1977. (Text)

Appellate Advocacy—see Trial and Appellate Advocacy

Art Law

DUBOFF'S ART LAW IN A NUTSHELL, 335 pages, 1984. Softcover. (Text)

Banking Law

BANKING LAW: SELECTED STATUTES AND REGULATIONS. Softcover. Approximately 265 pages, 1991.

LOVETT'S BANKING AND FINANCIAL INSTITUTIONS LAW IN A NUTSHELL, Second Edition, 464 pages, 1988. Softcover. (Text)

Civil Procedure—see also Federal Jurisdiction and Procedure

CLERMONT'S BLACK LETTER ON CIVIL PROCEDURE, Second Edition, 332 pages, 1988. Softcover. (Review)

FRIEDENTHAL, KANE AND MILLER'S HORNBOOK ON CIVIL PROCEDURE, 876 pages, 1985. (Text)

KANE'S CIVIL PROCEDURE IN A NUTSHELL, Second Edition, 306 pages, 1986. Softcover. (Text)

KOFFLER AND REPPY'S HORNBOOK ON COMMON LAW PLEADING, 663 pages, 1969. (Text)

SIEGEL'S HORNBOOK ON NEW YORK PRACTICE, Second Edition, Student Edition, approximately 900 pages, 1991. (Text)

Commercial Law

BAILEY AND HAGEDORN'S SECURED TRANSACTIONS IN A NUTSHELL, Third Edition, 390 pages, 1988. Softcover. (Text)

HENSON'S HORNBOOK ON SECURED TRANSACTIONS UNDER THE U.C.C., Second Edition, 504 pages, 1979, with 1979 pocket part. (Text)

NICKLES' BLACK LETTER ON

Commercial Law—Continued

COMMERCIAL PAPER, 450 pages, 1988. Softcover. (Review)

SPEIDEL'S BLACK LETTER ON SALES AND SALES FINANCING, 363 pages, 1984. Softcover. (Review)

STOCKTON'S SALES IN A NUT-SHELL, Second Edition, 370 pages, 1981. Softcover. (Text)

STONE'S UNIFORM COMMERCIAL CODE IN A NUTSHELL, Third Edition, 580 pages, 1989. Softcover. (Text)

WEBER AND SPEIDEL'S COMMER-CIAL PAPER IN A NUTSHELL, Third Edition, 404 pages, 1982. Softcover. (Text)

WHITE AND SUMMERS' HORN-BOOK ON THE UNIFORM COM-MERCIAL CODE, Third Edition, Student Edition, 1386 pages, 1988. (Text)

Community Property

MENNELL AND BOYKOFF'S COM-MUNITY PROPERTY IN A NUT-SHELL, Second Edition, 432 pages, 1988. Softcover. (Text)

Comparative Law

GLENDON, GORDON AND OSAKWE'S COMPARATIVE LEGAL TRADITIONS IN A NUTSHELL.

402 pages, 1982. Softcover. (Text)

Conflict of Laws

HAY'S BLACK LETTER ON CON-FLICT OF LAWS, 330 pages, 1989. Softcover. (Review)

SCOLES AND HAY'S HORNBOOK ON CONFLICT OF LAWS, Student Edition, 1085 pages, 1982, with 1988–89 pocket part. (Text)

SIEGEL'S CONFLICTS IN A NUT-SHELL, 470 pages, 1982. Soft-cover. (Text)

Constitutional Law—Civil Rights

BARRON AND DIENES' BLACK LETTER ON CONSTITUTIONAL LAW, Third Edition, approximately 400 pages, 1991. Soft-cover. (Review)

BARRON AND DIENES' CONSTITU-TIONAL LAW IN A NUTSHELL, Second Edition, approximately 475 pages, 1991. Softcover. (Text)

ENGDAHL'S CONSTITUTIONAL FEDERALISM IN A NUTSHELL, Second Edition, 411 pages, 1987. Softcover. (Text)

MARKS AND COOPER'S STATE CONSTITUTIONAL LAW IN A NUT-SHELL, 329 pages, 1988. Soft-cover. (Text)

Constitutional Law—Civil Rights—Continued

NOWAK, ROTUNDA AND YOUNG'S HORNBOOK ON CONSTITUTIONAL LAW, Third Edition, 1191 pages, 1986 with 1988 pocket part. (Text)

VIEIRA'S CONSTITUTIONAL CIVIL RIGHTS IN A NUTSHELL, Second Edition, 322 pages, 1990. Softcover. (Text)

WILLIAMS' CONSTITUTIONAL ANALYSIS IN A NUTSHELL, 388 pages, 1979. Softcover. (Text)

Consumer Law—see also Commercial Law

EPSTEIN AND NICKLES' CONSUMER LAW IN A NUTSHELL, Second Edition, 418 pages, 1981. Softcover. (Text)

Contracts

CALAMARI AND PERILLO'S BLACK LETTER ON CONTRACTS, Second Edition, 462 pages, 1990. Softcover. (Review)

CALAMARI AND PERILLO'S HORNBOOK ON CONTRACTS, Third Edition, 1049 pages, 1987. (Text)

CORBIN'S TEXT ON CONTRACTS, One Volume Student Edition, 1224 pages, 1952. (Text)

FRIEDMAN'S CONTRACT REME-

DIES IN A NUTSHELL, 323 pages, 1981. Softcover. (Text)

KEYES' GOVERNMENT CONTRACTS IN A NUTSHELL, Second Edition, 557 pages, 1990. Softcover. (Text)

SCHABER AND ROHWER'S CONTRACTS IN A NUTSHELL, Third Edition, 457 pages, 1990. Softcover. (Text)

Copyright—see Patent and Copyright Law

Corporations

HAMILTON'S BLACK LETTER ON CORPORATIONS, Second Edition, 513 pages, 1986. Softcover. (Review)

HAMILTON'S THE LAW OF CORPORATIONS IN A NUTSHELL, Third Edition, approximately 500 pages, 1991. Softcover. (Text)

HENN AND ALEXANDER'S HORNBOOK ON LAWS OF CORPORATIONS, Third Edition, Student Edition, 1371 pages, 1983, with 1986 pocket part. (Text)

Corrections

KRANTZ' THE LAW OF CORRECTIONS AND PRISONERS' RIGHTS IN A NUTSHELL, Third Edition, 407 pages, 1988. Softcover. (Text)

Creditors' Rights

EPSTEIN'S DEBTOR-CREDITOR LAW IN A NUTSHELL, Fourth Edition, approximately 400 pages, 1991. Softcover. (Text)

NICKLES AND EPSTEIN'S BLACK LETTER ON CREDITORS' RIGHTS AND BANKRUPTCY, 576 pages, 1989. (Review)

Criminal Law and Criminal Procedure—see also Corrections, Juvenile Justice

ISRAEL AND LAFAVE'S CRIMINAL PROCEDURE—CONSTITUTIONAL LIMITATIONS IN A NUTSHELL, Fourth Edition, 461 pages, 1988. Softcover. (Text)

LAFAVE AND ISRAEL'S HORNBOOK ON CRIMINAL PROCEDURE, Second Edition, Student Edition, approximately 1200 pages, June, 1991 Pub. (Text)

LAFAVE AND SCOTT'S HORNBOOK ON CRIMINAL LAW, Second Edition, 918 pages, 1986. (Text)

LOEWY'S CRIMINAL LAW IN A NUTSHELL, Second Edition, 321 pages, 1987. Softcover. (Text)

LOW'S BLACK LETTER ON CRIMINAL LAW, Revised First Edition, 443 pages, 1990. Soft-cover. (Review)

Decedents' Estates—see Trusts and Estates

Domestic Relations

CLARK'S HORNBOOK ON DOMESTIC RELATIONS, Second Edition, Student Edition, 1050 pages, 1988. (Text)

KRAUSE'S BLACK LETTER ON FAMILY LAW, 314 pages, 1988. Softcover. (Review)

KRAUSE'S FAMILY LAW IN A NUTSHELL, Second Edition, 444 pages, 1986. Softcover. (Text)

MALLOY'S LAW AND ECONOMICS: A COMPARATIVE APPROACH TO THEORY AND PRACTICE, 166 pages, 1990. Softcover. (Text)

Education Law

ALEXANDER AND ALEXANDER'S THE LAW OF SCHOOLS, STUDENTS AND TEACHERS IN A NUTSHELL, 409 pages, 1984. Softcover. (Text)

Employment Discrimination— see also Women and the Law

PLAYER'S FEDERAL LAW OF EMPLOYMENT DISCRIMINATION IN A NUTSHELL, Second Edition, 402 pages, 1981. Softcover. (Text)

Labor and Employment Law— see also Employment Discrimination, Social Legislation

LESLIE'S LABOR LAW IN A NUTSHELL, Second Edition, 397 pages, 1986. Softcover. (Text)

NOLAN'S LABOR ARBITRATION LAW AND PRACTICE IN A NUTSHELL, 358 pages, 1979. Softcover. (Text)

Land Finance—Property Security—see Real Estate Transactions

Land Use

HAGMAN AND JUERGENS-MEYER'S HORNBOOK ON URBAN PLANNING AND LAND DEVELOPMENT CONTROL LAW, Second Edition, Student Edition, 680 pages, 1986. (Text)

WRIGHT AND WRIGHT'S LAND USE IN A NUTSHELL, Second Edition, 356 pages, 1985. Softcover. (Text)

Legal Method and Legal System—see also Legal Research, Legal Writing

KEMPIN'S HISTORICAL INTRODUCTION TO ANGLO-AMERICAN LAW IN A NUTSHELL, Third Edition, 323 pages, 1990. Softcover. (Text)

REYNOLDS' JUDICIAL PROCESS IN A NUTSHELL, 292 pages, 1980. Softcover. (Text)

Legal Research

COHEN'S LEGAL RESEARCH IN A NUTSHELL, Fourth Edition, 452 pages, 1985. Softcover. (Text)

COHEN, BERRING AND OLSON'S HOW TO FIND THE LAW, Ninth Edition, 716 pages, 1989. (Text)

Legal Writing

SQUIRES AND ROMBAUER'S LEGAL WRITING IN A NUTSHELL, 294 pages, 1982. Softcover. (Text)

Legislation

DAVIES' LEGISLATIVE LAW AND PROCESS IN A NUTSHELL, Second Edition, 346 pages, 1986. Softcover. (Text)

Local Government

MCCARTHY'S LOCAL GOVERNMENT LAW IN A NUTSHELL, Third Edition, 435 pages, 1990. Softcover. (Text)

REYNOLDS' HORNBOOK ON LOCAL GOVERNMENT LAW, 860 pages, 1982, with 1990 pocket part. (Text)

Mass Communication Law

ZUCKMAN, GAYNES, CARTER AND DEE'S MASS COMMUNICA-

Mass Communication Law—
Continued

TIONS LAW IN A NUTSHELL, Third Edition, 538 pages, 1988. Softcover. (Text)

Medicine, Law and

HALL AND ELLMAN'S HEALTH CARE LAW AND ETHICS IN A NUTSHELL, 401 pages, 1990. Softcover (Text)

JARVIS, CLOSEN, HERMANN AND LEONARD'S AIDS LAW IN A NUTSHELL, Approximately 350 pages, 1991. Softcover. (Text)

KING'S THE LAW OF MEDICAL MALPRACTICE IN A NUTSHELL, Second Edition, 342 pages, 1986. Softcover. (Text)

Military Law

SHANOR AND TERRELL'S MILITARY LAW IN A NUTSHELL, 378 pages, 1980. Softcover. (Text)

Mortgages—see Real Estate Transactions

Natural Resources Law—see Energy and Natural Resources Law, Environmental Law

Office Practice—see also Computers and Law, Interviewing and Counseling, Negotiation

HEGLAND'S TRIAL AND PRACTICE SKILLS IN A NUTSHELL, 346 pages, 1978. Softcover (Text)

Oil and Gas—see also Energy and Natural Resources Law

HEMINGWAY'S HORNBOOK ON OIL AND GAS, Second Edition, Student Edition, 543 pages, 1983, with 1989 pocket part. (Text)

LOWE'S OIL AND GAS LAW IN A NUTSHELL, Second Edition, 465 pages, 1988. Softcover. (Text)

Partnership—see Agency— Partnership

Patent and Copyright Law

MILLER AND DAVIS' INTELLECTUAL PROPERTY—PATENTS, TRADEMARKS AND COPYRIGHT IN A NUTSHELL, Second Edition, 437 pages, 1990. Softcover. (Text)

Products Liability

PHILLIPS' PRODUCTS LIABILITY IN A NUTSHELL, Third Edition, 307 pages, 1988. Softcover. (Text)

Professional Responsibility

ARONSON AND WECKSTEIN'S PROFESSIONAL RESPONSIBILITY IN A NUTSHELL, Second Edition, approximately 500 pages, April, 1991 Pub. Softcover. (Text)

ROTUNDA'S BLACK LETTER ON PROFESSIONAL RESPONSIBILITY, Second Edition, 414 pages, 1988. Softcover. (Review)

WOLFRAM'S HORNBOOK ON MODERN LEGAL ETHICS, Student Edition, 1120 pages, 1986. (Text)

Property—see also Real Estate Transactions, Land Use, Trusts and Estates

BERNHARDT'S BLACK LETTER ON PROPERTY, 318 pages, 1983. Softcover. (Review)

BERNHARDT'S REAL PROPERTY IN A NUTSHELL, Second Edition, 448 pages, 1981. Softcover. (Text)

BURKE'S PERSONAL PROPERTY IN A NUTSHELL, 322 pages, 1983. Softcover. (Text)

CUNNINGHAM, STOEBUCK AND WHITMAN'S HORNBOOK ON THE LAW OF PROPERTY, Student Edition, 916 pages, 1984, with 1987 pocket part. (Text)

HILL'S LANDLORD AND TENANT LAW IN A NUTSHELL, Second Edition, 311 pages, 1986. Softcover. (Text)

Real Estate Transactions

BRUCE'S REAL ESTATE FINANCE IN A NUTSHELL, Second Edition, 262 pages, 1985. Softcover. (Text)

NELSON AND WHITMAN'S BLACK LETTER ON LAND TRANSACTIONS AND FINANCE, Second Edition, 466 pages, 1988. Softcover. (Review)

NELSON AND WHITMAN'S HORNBOOK ON REAL ESTATE FINANCE LAW, Second Edition, 941 pages, 1985 with 1989 pocket part. (Text)

Regulated Industries—see also Mass Communication Law, Banking Law

GELLHORN AND PIERCE'S REGULATED INDUSTRIES IN A NUTSHELL, Second Edition, 389 pages, 1987. Softcover. (Text)

Remedies

DOBBS' HORNBOOK ON REMEDIES, 1067 pages, 1973. (Text)

DOBBYN'S INJUNCTIONS IN A NUTSHELL, 264 pages, 1974. Softcover. (Text)

FRIEDMAN'S CONTRACT REMEDIES IN A NUTSHELL, 323 pages, 1981. Softcover. (Text)

Remedies—Continued

McCormick's Hornbook on Damages, 811 pages, 1935. (Text)

O'Connell's Remedies in a Nutshell, Second Edition, 320 pages, 1985. Softcover. (Text)

Sea, Law of

Sohn and Gustafson's The Law of the Sea in a Nutshell, 264 pages, 1984. Softcover. (Text)

Securities Regulation

Hazen's Hornbook on the Law of Securities Regulation, Second Edition, Student Edition, 1082 pages, 1990. (Text)

Ratner's Securities Regulation in a Nutshell, Third Edition, 316 pages, 1988. Softcover. (Text)

Securities Regulation, Selected Statutes, Rules, and Forms. Softcover. Approximately 1,300 pages, 1991.

Social Legislation—see Workers' Compensation

Sports Law

Schubert, Smith and Trentadue's Sports Law, 395 pages, 1986. (Text)

Tax Practice and Procedure

Morgan's Tax Procedure and Tax Fraud in a Nutshell, 400 pages, 1990. Softcover. (Text)

Taxation—Corporate

Weidenbruch and Burke's Federal Income Taxation of Corporations and Stockholders in a Nutshell, Third Edition, 309 pages, 1989. Softcover. (Text)

Taxation—Estate & Gift—see also Estate Planning, Trusts and Estates

McNulty's Federal Estate and Gift Taxation in a Nutshell, Fourth Edition, 496 pages, 1989. Softcover. (Text)

Taxation—Individual

Hudson and Lind's Black Letter on Federal Income Taxation, Third Edition, 406 pages, 1990. Softcover. (Review)

McNulty's Federal Income Taxation of Individuals in a Nutshell, Fourth Edition, 503 pages, 1988. Softcover. (Text)

Posin's Hornbook on Federal Income Taxation, Student Edition, 491 pages, 1983, with 1989 pocket part. (Text)

Trial and Appellate Advocacy—Continued
(Text)

HORNSTEIN'S APPELLATE ADVOCACY IN A NUTSHELL, 325 pages, 1984. Softcover. (Text)

JEANS' HANDBOOK ON TRIAL ADVOCACY, Student Edition, 473 pages, 1975. Softcover. (Text)

Trusts and Estates

ATKINSON'S HORNBOOK ON WILLS, Second Edition, 975 pages, 1953. (Text)

AVERILL'S UNIFORM PROBATE CODE IN A NUTSHELL, Second Edition, 454 pages, 1987. Softcover. (Text)

BOGERT'S HORNBOOK ON TRUSTS, Sixth Edition, Student Edition, 794 pages, 1987. (Text)

MCGOVERN, KURTZ AND REIN'S HORNBOOK ON WILLS, TRUSTS AND ESTATES–INCLUDING TAXATION AND FUTURE INTERESTS, 996 pages, 1988. (Text)

MENNELL'S WILLS AND TRUSTS IN A NUTSHELL, 392 pages, 1979. Softcover. (Text)

SIMES' HORNBOOK ON FUTURE INTERESTS, Second Edition, 355 pages, 1966. (Text)

TURANO AND RADIGAN'S HORNBOOK ON NEW YORK ESTATE ADMINISTRATION, 676 pages, 1986. (Text)

WAGGONER'S FUTURE INTERESTS IN A NUTSHELL, 361 pages, 1981. Softcover. (Text)

Water Law—see also Environmental Law

GETCHES' WATER LAW IN A NUTSHELL, Second Edition, 459 pages, 1990. Softcover. (Text)

Wills—see Trusts and Estates

Women and the Law—see also Employment Discrimination

THOMAS' SEX DISCRIMINATION IN A NUTSHELL, 399 pages, 1982. Softcover. (Text)

Workers' Compensation

HOOD, HARDY AND LEWIS' WORKERS' COMPENSATION AND EMPLOYEE PROTECTION LAWS IN A NUTSHELL, Second Edition, 361 pages, 1990. Softcover. (Text)

Advisory Board

XIV

LEGAL
INTERVIEWING
AND COUNSELING

IN A NUTSHELL

Second Edition

By

THOMAS L. SHAFFER

Professor of Law

Washington and Lee University

and

JAMES R. ELKINS

Professor of Law

West Virginia University

ST. PAUL, MINN.

WEST PUBLISHING CO.

1987

COPYRIGHT © 1976 By WEST PUBLISHING CO.
COPYRIGHT © 1987 By WEST PUBLISHING CO.
50 West Kellogg Boulevard
P.O. Box 64526
St. Paul, Minnesota 55164-0526

Library of Congress Cataloging-in-Publication Data

Shaffer, Thomas L., 1934–
  Legal interviewing and counseling in a nutshell.

  (Nutshell series)
  Includes bibliographies and index.
  1. Interviewing in law practice—United States.
2. Attorney and client—United States. I. Elkins,
James R., 1945–   . II. Title. III. Series.
KF311.S5 1987   347.73′5   87–2127
                      347.3075
ISBN 0-314-36474-9

  Shaffer & Elkins, Legal Inter. 2nd Ed. NS
  1st Reprint—1991

ACKNOWLEDGMENTS

Several sections in this book have been condensed and rewritten from our earlier work. Material which was used in the first edition, with permission, appeared originally at:

—45 Notre Dame Lawyer 197 (1970);

—57 American Bar Association Journal 123 (1970);

—18 UCLA Law Review 844 (1971);

—Sixth Annual Institute on Estate Planning, University of Miami (1972);

—17 American Journal of Jurisprudence 125 (1972);

—Seventh Annual Institute on Estate Planning, University of Miami (1973);

—Estate Tax Techniques (Lasser, ed.; Bender, 1973);

—113 Trusts and Estates 568 (1974).

Material used for the first time in this edition, used with permission:

—48 Southern California Law Review 721 (1975);

—61 American Bar Association Journal 854 (1975);

—53 Notre Dame Lawyer 229 (1977);

—64 Virginia Law Review 735 (1978);

—30 American Journal of Jurisprudence 155 (1985).

We have borrowed thoughts and other authors' ideas in a number of places from informal papers, talks, and notebook material published by the N.T.L. Institute for Applied Behavioral Science. Most of this material is acknowledged as it appears in the text. However, some of the N.T.L. material has been so thoroughly internalized (as the psychologists say) that we have not attempted to acknowledge it directly. We are grateful for that material; for the inspiration of those who worked with Shaffer in N.T.L.; and for David Bradford, at the Stanford Graduate School of Business, who worked with Elkins.

We are grateful for permission to use copyrighted material, as follows:

From Professor Gerald P. Lopez, permission to use unpublished material that appears, in this book, in Chapter Two.

From Pantheon Books, permission to use excerpts from David Hilfiker's "Healing the Wounds," copyrighted by Pantheon Books, a division of Random House, Inc.

From Houghton Mifflin Company permission to use excerpts from the short story, "Equitable Awards," from the volume entitled "Narcissa and Other Fables," by Louis Auchincloss; copyright 1983 by Houghton Mifflin Company.

At places in the text, we quote from diaries compiled by legal counseling students and from tape recordings made of counseling sessions (some by students, some by practitioners). These sources are necessarily confidential and, in some cases, are rewritten slightly to preserve confidentiality.

John Schaperkotter, of the Class of 1977, University of Virginia School of Law, assisted on the first edition, and Nancy J. Shaffer assisted with both editions. Brenda Waugh, at West Virginia, read the manuscript of the second edition and provided many helpful suggestions, and Andrew P. Shaffer assisted with research on the second edition. Our thanks to them.

                                        T.L.S.
                                        J.R.E.
April, 1976
February, 1987

*

CONTENTS

OUTLINE

LEGAL INTERVIEWING AND COUNSELING

IN A NUTSHELL

*

CHAPTER ONE

INTRODUCTION

People deal with lawyers out of necessity. And when people deal with lawyers, they often complain that lawyers are not people-oriented, that lawyers are out of touch with the clients they serve. One of the practical criticisms of legal education is that it does not teach human-relations skills. Many lawyers and law students find that there is something in the study and the practice of law that leads us to know more and more about legal strategies and techniques, and less and less about the people law serves. We lawyers tend to become identified more with law and less with people, the public interest, social welfare, the common good.

This characterization of lawyers suggests something about who we are as lawyers, who we are as a profession, and what happens to us when we study and practice law. It is a characterization that presents a truth about lawyering, but it is not the entire truth of the matter. Many lawyers are sensitive, people-oriented professionals who relate to their clients as persons rather than problems. There are law-school courses on interviewing and counseling, negotiation, and mediation; there are clinical courses that involve one-on-one human relations skills training; and there is in legal education a growing contingent of teachers who support and practice people-oriented humanistic lawyering. And we suspect that there are tough-minded lawyers who, from years of practice and exposure to clients, courts, and the law, become more rather than less sensitive to the feelings of participants in the legal system. Even these lawyers find a need for commitment to real people in contrast to the abstraction called law. So it would not be accurate to paint lawyers (and law students) as uncaring, insensitive, or unreceptive to the idea that the practice of law is the practice of human relations.

To talk about legal counseling is to talk about lawyers as they appear to those they serve, and that image is crucial. We argue that counseling is the heart and soul of lawyering. The practice of law is *not*, for most lawyers, a mechanical, repetitive, routine activity. One becomes a student of law, and makes a life of the practice of law, to escape the confinements and restrictions found in much contemporary work. One of the attractive ideals of professional life in law, medicine, ministry, or teaching is that it offers work that is meaningful and fulfilling. If that ideal is to be more than rhetoric followed by disappointment, disillusionment, and burnout, though, it must describe the truth about lawyering, the truth that makes it worthwhile to search for the intrinsic value in lawyering, and that intrinsic value is, we think, encoded in the image of the lawyer as a counselor.

We are aware that some lawyers and law teachers and law students have a different image of lawyers and a different sense of what lawyers do with clients. Some law teachers believe that knowledge of the law and the ability to apply substantive rules of law constitute the core activities of lawyering. We find no reason to reject such a claim outright. The knowledge, skills, and attitudes of the lawyer as counselor are not in conflict with the acquisition of legal knowledge and the technical skills practiced by an able lawyer. The counseling orientation to lawyering complements legal knowledge and the skills of planning, drafting, and argument. Being both a counselor and a lawyer may, of course, create conflicts; most adventures in life are children of conflict, and, in some instances, the adventure of being a lawyer makes life difficult. Being a lawyer, in any adequate sense of the word, is a life of knowledge, craftsmanship, skill, and virtue, but ultimately it is a life lived with those we serve.

The legal profession in America is not and never has been a homogeneous entity. We have never had a single model or image to portray the good lawyer, or, for that matter, the bad lawyer. American lawyers are as diverse in taste and personality as Americans in general and are therefore diverse as lawyers and as counselors. This does not mean that anything goes in the practice of law, or that all lawyers agree on what is good lawyering and good counseling. Our point is that lawyering in America is not a uniform enterprise.

Still, lawyers learn a body of knowledge and practice their craft within prescribed limits, within an interpretative community. You (as a law student) learn a language and a way of thinking that feels different. This won't make you exactly like other lawyers, but it can set you apart from non-lawyers.

We believe that there are certain persistent notions, attitudes, beliefs, and values that can be identified and associated with American lawyers. The lawyering ethos and ethic give rise to a legal *persona,* a way of being a lawyer (and a person) that identifies a law student with the craft and craftiness of lawyering. Clients and community form perceptions of lawyers based on their interaction with lawyers, as lawyers assume the professional mask. And as members of a profession which is not an entity but is a community of sorts, lawyers form images of themselves. The images others have of lawyers, and the images lawyers have of themselves, cohere into the persona lawyers use in their interactions with clients.

The presence of a legal persona does not mean that we cannot recognize and celebrate our diversity, the enormous difference in styles found in the legal profession. The truth is that lawyers are citizens, neighbors, spouses, parents. They are as diverse as the plumbers, or the stockbrokers, or the checkout clerks at the Kroger store. It is when we

try to talk with clients and help them respond to
their problems that we *become lawyers* (that is, we
put on the persona).[1] When we are conscious of
putting on the mask, we learn how professionalism
and the craft of lawyering set us apart—a distanc-
ing that is in part our own doing and in part the
effort of others. In being apart—in being behind
the mask—we gain power, power to serve those
who need our help and power to make our own
way with autonomy and dignity, gaining along the
way prestige, status, and financial well-being. An
inevitable side effect of this persona is our feeling
of disease and disquietude about our work. Alienation and burnout are common maladies of professional life.

Counseling is one way of addressing the issues
associated with our professional persona and the
odd way our profession both prepares us for and

1. We need to pause over this word *persona;* it will be an
important word in this book. Psychology borrows the word
from the classical theatre: A persona is a mask worn by an
actor. It is, in psychology, "what one passes for and what one
appears to be, in contrast to one's real individual nature." It
"corresponds to one's personal environment, and to the community," in this case, both the professional community, and the
broader community that enfranchises and makes demands on
the professional community. "The persona is the cloak and the
shell, the armour and the uniform, behind and within which the
individual conceals himself—from himself, often enough, as well
as from the world. It is the self-control which hides what is
uncontrolled and uncontrollable, the acceptable facade behind
which the dark and the strange, eccentric, secret and uncanny
side of our nature remains invisible." Erich Neumann, *Depth
Psychology and a New Ethic* 37–38 (1973). (*See* Chapter Three,
and Exercise One in the Appendix.)

impoverishes our relations with those who seek our services. Counseling is one of several ways of focusing on these issues in law school. Every course subject in law school involves issues of human relations. Law schools are now mandated to offer instruction in what is called "professional responsibility" (or, as we prefer, "legal ethics"), a subject that ought to be closely related to counseling, dealing as it does (or should deal) with the moral dimensions of the relationship of attorney and client. We recognize that a lawyer's moral outlook is crucial to counseling, and we make references throughout this book to counseling as a moral art.

The ethical issues in counseling, and the concerns of the public and the profession about the human dimension of lawyering, raise social and political issues for lawyers. Some critics suggest that a counseling orientation based on a psychological model gives an asocial, apolitical cast to lawyering. William Simon, among others, argues that legal educators (especially those who emphasize human-relations skills) tend to ignore the social and political dimensions of client problems. We agree that a counseling orientation grounded exclusively in psychology would be problematic. But it is false and misleading to behave as if psychology, the study of the interior world of feeling and emotions, of the "felt experience" of what is going on around us and to us, is separate from the social, political, and professional world in which we live.

A counseling orientation and a sense of the psychological dynamics of lawyering, crucial as these are, do not address every concern raised by critics of law and legal education. (That is part of Simon's point.) There is a tendency, which should be resisted, to see in counseling (as in ethics, economics, or any other discipline) an answer to all that ails the legal profession and the study of law.

DESCRIBING THE LAWYER AS COUNSELOR

Counseling, narrowly defined, is the activity in which one person seeks and pays for help from another person. It is characterized by need on one side of the relationship, by willingness to help on the other, and by an interpersonal contract based on mutual attraction.

Counseling exists in all professional disciplines—in the traditional professions of law, medicine, and the pastorate; in education (both in the teacher-student relationship and in specialized educational and vocational counseling); and in a wide array of business, industrial, and service occupations. Insurance underwriters, bartenders, appliance salespeople, employment security officers, and clerks in the courthouse all spend time counseling, as do social workers, nurses, physicians, geneticists, and ministers.

Surveys suggest that lawyers spend most of their time in activities the lawyers themselves describe as "counseling." One study says that lawyers spend more time "interviewing" clients than in any other professional activity. Lawyers spend less time in court or in the library than one would think; many lawyers spend no time in either place, and the average lawyer time spent in each place is less than ten percent of a work week. It is probably the case that an average lawyer spends more than half of her time influencing, facilitating, and implementing choices that are made not by courts but by individuals or small organic communities (families, boards of directors, neighbors—people who love one another and people who don't). That professional activity—influencing, facilitating, and implementing choices in the law office—is a sufficient working definition for "legal interviewing and counseling."

For the most part this professional activity will not require other professional activity (drafting, advocacy, research), or, if it does, the other professional activity will take less time and energy than counseling. Another way to put this is to say that the "problem" (or, as we prefer, the situation) in legal counseling is often more non-legal than legal.

Counseling decisions are as awesome, as authoritative, as binding, and often as final as decisions of courts or legislatures; they are much influenced by what is loosely called "legal thinking" but are not confined to it. They proceed from whatever makes it possible to relate to another person, to listen to his or her story, to respond to the needs of that person. Law office decisions proceed as much from subjective emotional factors as from rules of law. This is also, often, the case with decisions by judges or legislators—but the subjective in counseling decisions is more obvious, because it is not hidden in procedure and rational explanation. Counseling decisions often clearly proceed from love and hate—so much so that any accurate assessment of law office decisions must begin with the proposition that feelings are to law office decisions what facts—facts in the record—are to common-law appellate decisions.

FEELINGS ARE FACTS

Counseling decisions themselves are more important, more awesome, more binding, more directly pertinent to the human lives they affect than decisions of courts or legislatures. The settlement of a serious personal-injury claim asserted by a client will mean more to him and to his family than the entire product of this session of the Congress. A decision taken tomorrow morning, in a law office, by the president of a business enterprise who makes his decision in concert with his lawyer, and no one else, may mean more in the next year, to thousands of employees, investors, and families, than all of the law you will learn this semester.

Law student readers will want to get some theories for legal counseling. This book tries to provide some. Law students and lawyers will want to know about the skills necessary to become competent at counseling. Competence in counseling be-

gins with two immediate questions, both directed
to the lawyer: "What am I doing?" and "Where
am I going?" It asks these questions in reference
to two crucial dramatis personae: I (lawyer) and
Thou (client). The I-Thou reference is frightening
and complicated and turns on self-awareness and
the ability to become aware of others. We argue
that the avenue into competence in counseling is to
recognize self-awareness as a primary skill for it.
We are convinced that knowledge about people, as
a necessary avenue to competence in counseling,
has to recognize that (1) the best resource for
learning about people is you; and (2) the next best
resource is another person, a person you care
about, the other whom Martin Buber called Thou.
These resources for learning are intertwined.
That is one of the landmark discoveries of psycho-
analytical psychology: I can learn about myself
with the help of another.

Those who say that this subject is business for
psychologists, not lawyers, are being defensive and
short-sighted. They deserve E. M. Forster's bit of
invective: "Man is an odd, sad creature as yet,
intent on pilfering the earth, and heedless of the
growths within himself. He cannot be bored about
psychology. He leaves it to the specialist, which is
as if he should leave his dinner to be eaten by a
steam-engine. He cannot be bothered to digest his
own soul."

IMAGINING THE LAWYER AS INTERVIEWER AND COUNSELOR

How are we to imagine the lawyer as counselor? The lawyer is a counselor when she listens to and talks with a client. When a lawyer talks and a client listens, or a client talks and a lawyer listens, is this talking and listening *always* the kind of activity to be imagined as counseling? Our answer is a radical *yes;* we follow the view that all talking and listening is a kind of counseling, and that any conversation between client and lawyer involves counseling. All lawyers are therefore counselors. Counseling is therefore inherent in the talking and listening that lawyers do when they are with clients. Counseling is so fundamental to lawyering that all lawyers do it, which means that counseling is something that every lawyer knows something about. And it is something that law students already know about. (When students talk and listen to each other, even in conversations about law, about their teachers, about the kind of summer jobs they had, they are counseling. They are being counselors for each other.) It requires no psychological training or a special degree or a license to be a counselor. Counseling is an ordinary activity that we all engage in, an activity inherent in the conversations that go on in law offices and law schools.

Counseling as a course subject in law school accepts this generic view of what counseling is;

legal counseling is counseling in this generic view. What counseling as a subject of study then seeks to do is to avoid the imposition of an instrumental view of the lawyer-client (human) relationship. An instrumental view of the relationship is the one we usually find imposed on the people who are described in law school casebooks. Counseling as a subject seeks to avoid the imposition, to hold on to the ordinary, generic, friendly notion of what being helpful is, but to add to that view the information and skills needed when a lawyer sets out to treat her clients as persons rather than as problems.

The problem with the casebook, instrumental notion about legal counseling is that it describes only the limited and obvious purposes and goals both of client and lawyer. The instrumental relationship takes account of words going back and forth, but it does not really involve talking and listening and does not address the needs and possibilities inherent in a professional relationship. The risk and the deficiency—the lost opportunity— is that the client's concern is recast, by the lawyer, into narrow and manageable categories—manageable in the sense that the client's concern is restated as a problem that can be channelled into the legal system for solution: Interviewing is getting the facts; counseling is telling the client what the law is. The lawyer then serves and disserves the client; the deficiency that shows up is that the lawyer perceives the client as a problem rather than as a person; that's what we mean by *instrumental*.

The interviewing and counseling that goes on in this narrowly defined, instrumental relationship consists of: (1) gathering the appropriate facts for the limited and obvious purpose of determining the nature of a *problem* ; (2) securing the client's aid in gathering additional facts and obtaining necessary documents; (3) explaining the nature of the *problem* in legal terms; (4) exploring alternative resolutions of the *problem* ; and (5) determining how to proceed. By this description the lawyer's role is straightforward, if not simple: Get the facts, define the situation as a problem, present alternatives, solve the problem (as defined). More specifically, the counseling in such an instrumental view of lawyering consists of heeding the client's words only as needed for what law school casebooks call the facts, telling the client what the legal problem is and how the law regards it, and then presenting alternatives and consequences and the lawyer's evaluation of an appropriate course of action.

There is little need for collaboration with the client in this instrumental model of interviewing and counseling. There is only a sort of mechanical necessity to encourage the client to present "all" the facts (interviewing) so that the lawyer can tell the client what to do (counseling). The lawyer doesn't need training as a counselor to accomplish these tasks. Law school training in "issue spotting" (interviewing) and reciting the law (counseling) are the skills for this kind of lawyering. The activities that are ordinary and inherent in lawyering, in this view, are (1) eliciting facts, (2) reciting law, (3) minimized interaction with clients (and other people), and (4) presentations to decision-making tribunals.

The instrumental theory of lawyer-client relationships regards the client as a necessary nuisance. The special skills a lawyer needs are skills for abating a nuisance. One client comes in talking; maybe he is all talk. The problem for the lawyer is to cut through the talk to see if there is a problem she can do something about. Or perhaps the lawyer has trouble getting the facts: A client schedules an appointment to talk about a problem. He enters the office and is silent. He answers questions but volunteers little information on his own. (We pray for courtroom witnesses who will conduct themselves in this fashion, but this is not a witness.) The client has trouble talking about his problem. Both clients are nuisances, but in both cases things get better once the lawyer gets the facts. Then she can get to work.

The lawyer with counseling skills has a radically different perspective when talking and listening to clients. One client's talking too much and another's silence are not obstacles to be overcome. The way we (lawyers and clients, students and teachers) talk and listen tells us—if we notice—how we see the world and how we try to cope with the world we see. The judgment that some clients talk too much and other clients don't talk enough illustrates a point about the lawyer-client relationship.

When the relationship is healthy, it is not a matter
of the client talking and the lawyer listening.
Maybe the client does not share the lawyer's ideas
of how conversation should go. Maybe the client is
hurt, angry, vengeful; the legal consultation is a
vehicle for reconciling the hurt or finding a target
for anger and vengeance. One way to see this is to
turn the instrumental metaphor around: Suppose
the client uses the lawyer, or attempts to use the
lawyer, for ends other than what the lawyer sees
as the legal resolution of the problem. The point
is this: The client wants to be a person as much as
the lawyer does. The client wants to be somebody
(too). A lawyer either promotes or obstructs his
client's need to be somebody.

For examples: A financially secure husband in a
divorce case may seek custody of his children to
punish his wife; or he may feel guilty, want to
concede or confess, pay money, avoid litigation.
Another client is terrified at the thought of being
in a trial, or being interrogated in a discovery
deposition; he misrepresents the facts, trying
(sometimes successfully) to deceive the lawyer. A
third client cannot decide whether to settle or
proceed to trial; her feelings are in conflict as she
tries to protect some individuals, knowing that
pursuit of the case will reveal information that
everyone concerned would prefer to keep secret. It
is in situations such as these that the distinction
between either lawyer or client talking while either lawyer or client is listening breaks down;

these ordinary cases are the most interesting ones from a counseling perspective: If the lawyer continues to talk, even when the client appears to listen, the lawyer is probably dealing with the situation defensively. When the lawyer acts defensively, responding to needs of his own that are not admitted, or are even unknown, the client is less likely to get what she needs. The lawyer is not getting the job done. He is avoiding the issue, manipulating the client to serve his own needs. It is a case of impoverished skills.

THE ISSUE OF TRUST

We claim that the talking and listening that lawyers do is the kind of talking and listening that anyone does. But there are, as the tendency to instrumental lawyering shows, complications with this view. The most obvious complication is that lawyers are talkers, not only verbally aggressive but often eloquent and usually articulate. They have to be if they are to speak for others, convincingly, in a variety of settings. Lawyers are advocates. An advocate speaks for another—speaks out. Lawyers are hired speakers. Clients hire lawyers to do their talking for them, and that presents an occasion of conflict when the client wants to say something about what the lawyer will say. Some clients take the image of the lawyer as a "hired speaker" seriously. "I hire you to speak for me, and this is what I want you to say." But that is not exactly what the lawyer has in mind.

She is tempted to respond to her client: "In this relationship, there are times for you to talk for yourself, and times for me to decide how it is best to speak for you. Yes, it is true that you are to decide what you want to do, what is in your own interest. But as we try to secure what you want (and need), to promote your interest, you must remember that I am the final arbiter of what I will say, and how it will be said. There is some limited part of our talking that is left to me, that is mine, an area of responsibility that I have to you, but which I must execute on my own."

Another case is presented by the client who hires the lawyer not only to speak for him, but to make his decisions. A client may be ambivalent, confused, or otherwise unable to make a decision on her own. Our clients depend on us: "Mr. Shaffer, what would you do in this situation?" ("Doctor, would you have the operation if you were me?") Some lawyers make decisions for clients because their clients ask them to. Others make decisions for clients because they *assume* that is what the client wants. Still others make decisions for clients because it makes life easier than trying to find out what the client wants. Other lawyers simply do not trust clients enough to let clients make decisions for themselves.

In each of these situations, the client who tries to dictate to the lawyer and the lawyer who makes decisions for the client, there appears to be an imbalance in talking and listening; but underneath the imbalance is an issue of trust. Clients sometimes learn that they cannot trust their lawyers. Lawyers sometimes learn that their clients are not to be trusted. In the worst of cases, both client and lawyer engage in active deception, each mistrusting the other. Usually the problem of trust is as much a matter of who we are as of what we are doing. By that we mean that the issue of trust, a client's trust of the lawyer, and the lawyer's trust of the client, is present from the very beginning. Some of us (lawyers and clients) have trouble trusting anyone. If we have difficulty with trust, it is going to present itself as a snag in our relationships, including relationships among clients and lawyers. We bring the issue of trust with us into such relationships. The issue of trust calls for more than ordinary talking and listening. And it is when we experience the need to learn more about ordinary law office conversations, the need to transcend ordinary talking and listening, that we develop counseling skills, a way of listening and talking that is responsive—as instrumental legal thinking is not—to the needs of both clients and lawyers.

BIBLIOGRAPHY

The idea of teaching counseling as an integral part of legal education, and consequently the image of the lawyer as a psychological counselor, came during the late 1950's as part of a critique of legal education and the professional training of lawyers. For a review of the early literature on counseling and human relations skills training see Elkins, A Humanistic Perspective in Legal Education, 62 Nebraska Law Review 494 (1983).

On the psychological basis for legal counseling: See Watson, Psychiatry for Lawyers (1978), and The Lawyer in the Interviewing and Counseling Process (1977); Elkins, "A Counseling Model for Lawyering in Divorce Cases," 53 Notre Dame Lawyer 229 (1977); Freeman and Weihofen, Clinical Law Training: Interviewing and Counseling (1976); Goodpaster, "The Human Arts of Lawyering: Interviewing and Counseling," 27 Journal of Legal Education 5 (1975); Saxe and Kuvin, "The Attorney-Client Relationship: A Psychoanalytic Overview," 9 New England Law Review 395 (1974); Watson, "Professionalizing the Lawyer's Role as Counselor: Risk Taking for Rewards," 1969 Arizona State Law Journal 17; Appel and Van Atta, "The Attorney-Client Dyad: An Outsider's View," 22 Oklahoma Law Review 243 (1969); Watson, "The Lawyer as Counselor," 5 Journal of Family Law 7 (1965); Redmount, "Attorney Personalities and Some Psychological Aspects of Legal Consultation," 109 University of Pennsylvania Law Review 972 (1961), and "Perception and Strategy in Divorce Counseling," 35 Connecticut Bar Journal 249 (1960).

On teaching the skill and ideal of counseling: Barkai and Fine, "Empathy Training for Lawyers and Law Students," 13 Southwestern Law Review

505 (1983); Greenebaum, "Lawyers' Relationship to Their Work: The Importance of Understanding Attorneys' Behavior," 53 New York University Law Review 651 (1978); Greenebaum and Parsloe, "Roles and Relations in Legal Practice," 28 Journal of Legal Education 228 (1976); Watson, "Some Psychological Aspects of Teaching Professional Responsibility," 16 Journal of Legal Education 1 (1963); Sacks, "Human-Relations Training for Law Students and Lawyers," 11 Journal of Legal Education 316 (1959).

The image of the lawyer as counselor is grounded in a conception of legal education that is best described as humanistic. See Dvorkin, Himmelstein, and Lesnick, Becoming a Lawyer: A Humanistic Perspective on Legal Education and Professionalism (1980); Himmelstein, "Reassessing Law Schooling: An Inquiry into the Application of Humanistic Education Psychology to the Teaching of Law," 53 New York University Law Review 514 (1978); Reich, "Toward the Humanistic Study of Law," 74 Yale Law Journal 1402 (1965).

For the broader criticism of law, legal practice, legal philosophy, and legal education within which these humanistic-oriented views appear: Lehman, "The Pursuit of a Client's Interest," 77 Michigan Law Review 1078 (1979); Elkins, "The Paradox of a Life in Law," 40 University of Pittsburgh Law Review 129 (1979); Shaffer, "The Practice of Law as Moral Discourse," 55 Notre Dame Lawyer 231 (1979); Simon, "The Ideology of Advocacy: Procedural Justice and Professional Ethics," 1978 Wisconsin Law Review 30; D'Errico, "The Law is Terror Put into Words," 2 Learning and the Law 39 (1975); Kennedy, "How the Law School Fails: A Polemic," 1 Yale Review of Law and Social Action 71 (1970); Savoy, "Toward a New Politics of Legal Education," 79 Yale Law Journal 444 (1970).

For a critique of the psychological perspective and (implicitly) the ideas expressed in this chapter Simon, "Homo Psychologicus," 32 Stanford Law Review 487 (1980); Schur, The Awareness Trap: Self-Absorption Instead of Social Change (1977); Botein, "Reflections on the New Humanism in Law," 22 Wayne Law Review 1295 (1976); Stone, "Legal Education on the Couch," 85 Harvard Law Review 392 (1971); Elkins, " 'All My Friends Are Becoming Strangers': The Psychological Perspective in Legal Education," 84 West Virginia Law Review 161 (1981).

CHAPTER TWO

SOLVING PROBLEMS AND TELLING STORIES

The work day of most lawyers and doctors is a busy one, so busy that we have difficulty slowing down to think about what we do. But whether we think about what we do, or do the work automatically (at times almost unconsciously), there are interruptions of many sorts. Our clients interrupt us with new information or with telephone calls to find out what has happened in their cases; our families and friends interrupt the course of the day needing attention or care, or just someone to talk with; one of the other lawyers in the office interrupts to talk about a case that she is working on. These interruptions in the well-organized, planned day of the professional are important; they are the "little" bits of telling and listening that we call conversation, an activity that we engage in so readily that we place no significance on it.

But conversations differ, from the slight and insignificant to those in which we exchange needed information (or give and get directions in how to do something, or how to proceed) to those in which we actively listen to what a client is saying and say something to the client that will be responsive to her concerns. The work that lawyers do with clients depends upon conversation, the talking and

listening that we have called counseling. From
the counseling perspective, conversations matter.
Alasdair MacIntyre, a philosopher, suggests that
"a conversation is a dramatic work, even if a very
short one, in which the participants are not only
the actors, but also the joint authors, working out
in agreement or disagreement the mode of their
production. For it is not just that conversations
belong to genres in just the way that plays and
novels do; but they have beginnings, middles and
endings just as do literary works. They embody
reversals and recognitions; they move towards and
away from climaxes. There may within a longer
conversation be digressions and subplots, indeed
digressions within digressions and subplots within
subplots." MacIntyre focuses on conversations as
narratives, as stories in progress.

It is one of those hectic days, the phone ringing,
a settlement conference that lasted two days, and a
trial to prepare for at the end of the week. Your
secretary reminds you that you have an appointment at 3 o'clock with Ron Barrett, a young man
that you have not previously met. When you meet
with Barrett you ask him what you can do to be of
help. He tells, in outline form, the following story:
He owns a small print shop that keeps prices low
by hiring motivated high school kids and offering a
training program in small business administration
in conjunction with the local high school. The
program is innovative and educational, and it
helps the kids financially. The customers know

the kids and patronize his shop because they support what he is doing. The problem, as Ron Barrett describes it, is that one of the kids, who had helped manage the store, working the cash register and taking customers' orders, is now threatening him. Ron fired the student because he thought he was taking money from the cash register. The student has now threatened to file a complaint with the state wages-and-hours authority, claiming that he was not paid overtime wages, as the law requires, unless the print shop owner pays him two months' severance pay. There was, of course, no mention of overtime or of severance pay in the student's contract of employment.

The story that Ron Barrett tells you interrupts your day, but you realize that without such interruptions you wouldn't have new clients, and without new clients you would be stuck with "old" cases and "old" clients and that that would eventually drive you crazy. So there is something pleasureable in seeing a new client, in starting at the beginning, in listening to what the client has to say and trying to figure out what the legal problem is and how it can be resolved.

Lawyers work for clients. We (and they) sometimes think of what lawyers do as problem solving. Ron Barrett has a problem and the lawyer knows how to solve it (or knows who can), or knows that it isn't the kind of problem that lawyers try to solve. This view of what lawyers do is descriptive, accurate, and incomplete. Lawyers do work with certain kinds of problems and not others, seeking particular kinds of resolutions, in particular kinds of places; but the description and the images of the lawyer this implies don't go as far as a lawyer's professional life goes. The traditional image of the lawyer in court, or the lawyer drawing up a legal document, or even the lawyer listening to an individual client like Ron Barrett, is not detailed enough. The variety of things that lawyers do is so broad that we are not comprehensive when we say that lawyers are problem solvers. Your life as a lawyer is not going to be appealing even to yourself if you view what you do within the framework of that traditional job description. There is more going on in this meeting with Ron Barrett, for example, than the description of a legal problem (which is *one* of the things going on), and the counselor in you intuitively knows that Ron Barrett is not *just* a legal problem, not *just* a new client.

There are tough-minded lawyers, law teachers, and law students who argue with us on this point, maintaining that their image of the lawyer is indeed that of a problem-solver. Our response is that this image of the lawyer and others which follow from seemingly straightforward descriptions of lawyers tell us something about the way lawyers work, but not enough.

The lawyer sitting at a desk, a pile of papers and books before her, looking for an answer in the law books, is an image of the lawyer as problem-solver.

It is an image rooted in experience. Our first association with problem solving is doing math problems when we were kids in school. The problems were what followed the explanations and examples in the math book. We came home from school at night and tried to solve the problems. Sometimes we asked for help from our parents; more often, solving problems was something we did in our rooms alone. In solving math problems, we were doing something relatively technical, or at least that is what our fathers told us when we asked for help. As they put it: "You just have to read the book and learn to do them yourself." The earliest idea we have of problem-solving is the use of technical rules or technical skills to find an answer.

Louis Auchincloss is a lawyer and a teller of stories about modern, big-firm lawyers in America. His novel "The Great World and Timothy Colt" tells a story about a problem solver, a lawyer who came to legal education and then to law practice as one who had learned to work alone, and to solve problems alone:

"All his youth he worked, at night, during summers, in laundries and restaurants, in banks and garages; he put himself through Columbia with only a minimum of unexpected aid from a Colt cousin." Tim lived with his mother (his father was dead) and, of course, had to take into account this other person in his life: "It was as if she were an actual part of him, the looser, lighter side of his own nature, the one that he had to make up for before the great golden eye of a demanding God. . . . Only in the spare neatness of his own small room, under the green lamp with his law books, was there rest from the pressure of his imagined overseer, as in childhood at the same desk he had sought the solace of the solved equation, the translated stanza. What Genevieve threatened to upset . . . had to be righted by remorseless application of himself."

Tim becomes a senior associate in his law firm, a deal-maker and a competent engineer at the complexities of corporate mergers. Auchincloss tells particularly the story of Tim and a demanding corporate magnate who resents the fact that the firm has assigned a young lawyer to do his work. The great advantage of Timothy Colt's temperament, of his seeing his legal work as he saw his law books and, before that, his math books, in his room, alone, is that the obnoxious client need not be known—his story, as we put it in this chapter, need not be known. "Timmy's defense was . . . inflexible courtesy and unvarying patience, and if these sometimes formed the grey panes and lattices behind which an equally inflexible dislike could be just detected, he did not care. The client was entitled to the job done and the job done well. . . . If George wanted a friend, George would have to be more friendly; if he wanted an admirer, he would have to be admirable."

This is one way to look at problem solving by lawyers. It is technical in the sense that you have to know the formal rules of a system so that you can apply those rules and get what the system tells you is the answer. In solving math problems we were looking for an answer and knew it when we got it. In problem-solving there was (and is) the right answer (and there are wrong answers). What emerges from all this is the idea that the problem-solver is doing something technical and by being technical is able to find an answer and verify it as the answer. It was and is all very cut and dried when you know what you're doing. Ron Barrett's "legal problem" may thus be a simple one, but only when it is narrowly described—it is a simple problem only from the perspective of the lawyer who likes his problems to be like math problems.

This notion of the lawyer as problem-solver brings to mind the image of a highly trained technician who can examine a situation, name the problem, and take whatever corrective means are necessary to get things going again: The lawyer as technician. The work is technical because it involves a high level of specificity, *i.e.,* some legal rules rather than others apply and you have to know what you are doing when you apply rules; the application of rules to specific facts takes practice, as every law student learns. When the rules are known and the facts are presented, an answer should be available.

In legal education, this image of the lawyer as technician is given credibility and at the same time systematically undermined. Becoming a lawyer is not as simple as learning rules and applying them, and virtually every law student either learns this is true or suffers for failing to learn that it is. Both the credibility and the doubt abound in our learning law and becoming lawyers, but there is something more going on in the work that lawyers do with clients. What, one might ask, is going on, when a man like Ron Barrett goes to a lawyer with the story that he is telling? The images of Ron Barrett as a legal problem and his lawyer as technician are law-school images, one kind of truth about the work that lawyers do. They are valid and dangerous; the danger is that they overwhelm other images, including good, useful images that each of us brought to law school, the kind of images that professionals secretly harbor during their hectic days in the office.

In this book we are suggesting a way to think about lawyering that (we hope) includes and honors the problem-solving element of lawyering—counselors at law solve problems—and provides an alternative set of images, drawn from the other counseling professions, that have more to do with being a companion for someone like Ron Barrett than with solving the technical legal problem he seems to bring with him.

In Chapter One we suggested that counseling is a form of talking and listening, the kind of talking and listening that we are engaged in in everyday conversations, the kind of exchange that we would have with Ron Barrett if he was our friend or our brother. But counseling is more than just talking (free advice is readily available) and listening (also free but in short supply). The talking and listening that we associate with counseling takes place when the counselor knows the limits of advice (talking at the client) and has learned something of the art of listening (hearing what is said and more than what is said). Another way to look at counseling is that it is a highly skilled, artful way of talking and listening. One image (or metaphor) of counseling is that it is an intense and purposeful conversation. The conversation can be directed (and is, regardless of the image) to problem-solving, and it can become a source of still other images that help us understand what we do with a client like Ron Barrett.

The conversation with clients is both like and different from other conversations. If there were no difference, law school would consist of technical training that would be completed in one year instead of three and practitioners of law would make far less money than many of them earn today. The point is that our conversations in the law office are different and they are different because law itself influences what you will say to Ron Barrett and how his story will unfold and be told, how his problem will turn out (if not be resolved).

James Boyd White has written extensively about conversations between lawyers and their clients. "[L]aw," White argues, "establishes roles and relations and voices, positions from which and audiences to which one may speak, and it gives us as speakers the materials and methods of a discourse. It is a way of creating a rhetorical community over time." *Law* is a kind of conversation, one in which the way we speak, the audience, and the nature of the responses of those who participate are distinctive, but not limited to the legal system. This is a focus, like MacIntyre's on conversation (rather than fixing things), but here *law* is the conversation.

The conversation between the lawyer and Ron Barrett, and the lawyer and the discharged employee (or his attorney) may be sufficient to deal with the problem and to satisfy Barrett that he is getting what he wants from the lawyer. But conversation may not be enough, and a lawyer is educated (and trained) to get the kind of facts and structure the relationship in such a way that Barrett can use the law, to the fullest extent possible, to get what he wants. But even if informal conversations (and how is a conversation in a law office ever to be viewed as really informal, at least by the client?) fail to resolve the issue, and there is a resort to litigation, conversation does not stop. White tells us that a litigated legal case "proceeds by a conversation in which each speaker is invited to present an ideal version of himself, speaking to

an ideal audience." A litigated legal case, like the
case of a client whose concerns are resolved by
informal conversation (sometimes a little talk and
a letter are enough) begins as a story and over time
is presented to a decision-maker in the form of a
narrative, one that places special demands on judges. If the law is a conversational process, a narrative, then the judge, White observes, "will have to
speak in an extraordinarily rich and complex way,
not in a voice that is merely bureaucratic and
official. To be true to the actual difficulties of a
real legal case, an opinion must be full of the kind
of life that comes from a set of acknowledged
tensions: between the two versions of the story
before the court; between the stories so told and
the language of legal conclusion; between the demand that like cases be treated alike and the
recognition that cases never are 'alike'; between
the fidelities owed to the past and the future;
between an awareness that the case is a particular
dispute between individual persons and a sense
that it is typical as well; and so on. . . . In the
complexity and formality of his speech, its meta-
phoric character and its openness to uncertainty,
in its tension between the general and the particular, the judge must indeed be something of a poet."

White speaks of lawsuits, but he could speak as
well of the more common kind of legal decision
that is made by and with a counselor at law, in a
law office; of what a lawyer might do with Ron
Barrett. In White's view of the law as narrative,

the client plays an integral role. We contend that the client is a resource, the best resource that the lawyer has available, for finding out what the situation is and (this is less obvious) the resolution that will work best. Ron Barrett's problem is with the law, but it is also a problem with himself, and the situation that he has made that brings law into the story. For Barrett, White says, "the case is, at its heart, an occasion and a method in which he can tell his story and have it heard." Ultimately, Ron even "has the right to a jury, to insure that he will have an audience that will understand his story and speak his language. The presence of a jury requires that the entire story, on both sides, be told in ordinary language and made intelligible to the ordinary person. This is a promise to the citizen that the law will ultimately speak to him, and for him, in the language that he speaks, not in a technical or special jargon."

Barrett has a legal problem, a problem that you as his lawyer may help resolve. But Ron Barrett also has a story to tell. It is a story about success (the print shop is doing well); the American dream (the client wants to get the legal matter cleared up so that he can take his wife on their first trip to Europe); short-cuts (everybody in this business makes under-the-table arrangements with employees); betrayal (putting trust in employees and having trust violated); and fear (what will happen to me now). Ron Barrett comes to the lawyer as a person who may, it is true, even see himself as a

legal problem. He can be a print-shop owner with
a legal problem; he can be reduced to his problem
and encased in a file folder; he can become just
another part of a hectic day. Barrett's problem—
this person *as* a problem—is, when you are a
lawyer, legal. Your role is to *solve* legal *problems*.
But the client has a story to tell, and in the
enactment of the story now seeks to involve you as
his lawyer. It is now your story, for you will stand
beside him. You will hear his story. Maybe you
will tell his story for him. Maybe what you will
tell is some story that you and he will create
together.

Gerald Lopez, who teaches law at Stanford,
writes eloquently and persuasively of the centrality of legal stories to a lawyer's problem-solving
task. What follows is Lopez's description of the
lawyer storyteller. We find the description rich
with possibilities and an image of the lawyer that
stands along with, if not against, the image of the
lawyer as a technician, as a problem-solver. "A
lawyer is a storyteller. To be sure, she is an
instrumental storyteller—she wants something
from her audience. But every storyteller wants
something from her audience—attention certainly,
but also a reaction—laughter, tears, shock, joy.
Lawyers want attention, too, but usually in order
to obtain remedies (some desired outcome) from
their audience for their clients. They must therefore learn to tell a story that will persuade the
audience (whether judge, jury, opposing party, gov-

ernment official, or other person in control of the
desired remedy) to grant whatever it is the client
desires or needs. The story may be a simple one—
'X hurt my client, X was careless, X must pay the
damage'—or a much more complicated one—'The
language in this agreement may appear to mean X,
but once I tell you about the context of the agreement, the expectations of the parties, the customs
of the industry, the nature of the technology involved, and the consequences of a literal interpretation, you will see that the language can only
mean Y'—but it must make sense as a story. Put
differently, the story told by the lawyer must develop, both in human terms and in legal terms, a
narrative that is plausible and that suggests to the
audience some obvious, indeed necessary, conclusion—what the client wants.

"The lawyer's job, then, is to 'make sense' of the
client's problem, first to her own satisfaction, and
then in a way which will persuade the relevant
audience to grant the desired remedy. [Note that
this is as true of contracts that have to work, or of
wills that affect people not products, as it is of
lawsuits.] How does she do that? Most likely by
asking herself a series of questions: For example,
Do I really understand what happened (or is happening, or is about to happen) in my client's world?
Do I understand why whatever is happening is a
'problem' for my client? Do I understand what my
client wants in terms of solutions?"

Lopez goes on to suggest that when law students read cases they should do so from the perspective of the potential story teller, a perspective we find equally applicable to the way a lawyer might try to listen to a client. The questions suggested by Lopez are: "What is the human story here? What is at stake? Why did the client seek legal help? How did this problem come to be seen as one to be dealt with by the legal culture? What decisions by the lawyer and client in this case were made that led to litigation . . .? What other choices did the lawyer and client have? Are there other legal stories that might have been told about this human story? Are there audiences other than a judge or jury that the client or lawyer might have approached . . .? Why are the legal stories that can be told about this case so limited? Why are they shaped the way they are? What do the legal stories that apply to this problem tell us about the society which produced these stories? Can we write new stories?" Lopez suggests that this is only a small sample of the questions that can be asked about the human and legal stories reflected in a single appellate opinion, and, we might add, appellate opinions are only a tiny, tiny fraction of the stories heard and told by lawyers.

Lopez says that the job of the lawyer as story-teller involves an examination of the following:

—Professional storytelling—what it means to represent others, to tell other people's stories.

—Understanding the human story—working with (investigating, creating, shaping and so forth) what become known as "the facts" of a particular case.

—Learning the legal repertoire—what the judge needs to hear [or what needs to be expressed in an arrangement among people or in a document].

—Storytelling and argument—the relationship between these forms of persuasion, between stories and their meanings and the meanings suitable to particular legal settings and subcultures.

—Understanding audiences—what different audiences need to hear (juries, judges, arbitrators, legislators, government officials, opposing counsel, and just plain folks).

—Where legal stories come from—the psychological, philosophical, historical, social and political themes and features of legal stories.

—The art and politics of legal storytelling—using, not using, and changing the existing repertoire of legal stories.

The world of stories, of human tellings and narratives, is far greater than what can be subsumed within legal narratives. Law, from the perspective of storytelling, and from the reality of our clients as storytellers is, in James Boyd White's opinion, "best regarded not so much as a set of rules and doctrines or as a bureaucratic system or as an instrument for social control but as a culture, for

the most part a culture of argument. [White
speaks here of argument as a philosopher would;
the idea is not so much an advocate's argument as
it is the presentation of a point of view.] It is a
way of making a world with a life and a value of its
own. The conversation that it creates is at once its
method and its point, and its object is to give to the
world it creates the kind of intelligibility that
results from the simultaneous recognition of contrasting positions . . . .

"The fact that the conversation of the law is
largely argumentative has important consequences
of its own. Legal argument exposes in clarified
and self-conscious form—in slow motion, as it
were—the processes of agreement and disagreement—of persuasion—by which this part of our
culture, and our culture more generally, are defined and transformed. For in legal argument the
state of the discourse itself—how we should think
and talk—is a constant subject of conscious attention and debate. This means that the contours of
the culture are pushed to their limits and marked
with extraordinary distinctness. As the argument
proceeds, each speaker tests the limits of his language, subjecting its every term and procedure to
all the strain that it can take—that we can take—
in order to make things come out his way. And
since he must always operate within strict limits
imposed by time and the interests of his audience,
he is constantly forced to discriminate among the
arguments he might make, putting forward what

seems best, holding back what is weak or unimportant, and so on. As the materials of the legal culture are tested in this manner, are put to work—they are defined and reorganized in especially clear and reliable ways. This makes it possible to think clearly about their transformation."

Legal stories are "imaginative forms," forms derived from local knowledge, from what happens and is said, felt, thought, and experienced when law is invoked, when disputes are settled, when lawyers and clients talk about problems and how to address them. The anthropologist Clifford Geertz argues that law is a form of "local knowledge, local not just as to place, time, class and variety of issue, but as to accent—vernacular characterizations of what happens connected to vernacular imaginings of what can happen." Geertz understands "legal sensibility" as a complex of characterizations and imaginings, "stories about events cast in imagery about principles."

Lopez, writing for law students, trying to bring the image of the lawyer as storyteller to the classroom, finds that "Contrary to popular belief, law is not a lot of rules, but a set of stories and storytelling practices. Law is not simply a collection of definitions and rules to be memorized and applied, but a culture consisting of storytellers, audiences, a set of standard stories and arguments, and a variety of conventions about storywriting, storytelling, argument-making and the structure and content of legal stories. . . . In order to transform human

stories effectively and persuasively into legal stories, you must not only learn about and internalize
the conventions and values of the legal culture,
you must also be able to relate that culture to the
varied ways in which human beings perceive, interpret and represent the world.　In order to be an
effective legal storyteller, you must be able to see
all the possible meanings in legal stories and use
those meanings to persuade different audiences to
see the world as you want it seen."

Lopez presents some other observations on how
we use and embody stories that are richly suggestive for the lawyer as counselor.　"We depend on a
stock of stories to help us organize our knowledge
about people, events, objects, and their characteristic relationships."　Another way to say this is that
stories locate us in the world.　Stories show how
we find a place in the world of others and at times
how we live a life trying to escape from them.
Whatever place I find, whatever role I accept or
reject, whatever stance I take, it is ultimately in
relation to some story, a story told within the
context of a community and a culture.

Story is one way that we deal with our experience and understanding of the world and ourselves
in the world.　It is the way we engage our own
experience.　Living the story is one thing, telling it
another.　We can become the teller of stories, our
own and the stories of others.　We can also live a
life bound by the stories of others, deny our own
story, and make the stories we tell part of an on-

going self-deception (that is, some stories are not adequate).

When we see our own stories, and hear the account of the client as a story, there is a sense of human worth and value in the struggle to give meaning to what has happened and what will happen. We don't see the objects of our service as persons until we hear the story being told, until we realize the story that we live out in our work and in our interactions with our clients.

Stories reflect a fundamental human need for narrative, for the kind of telling that gets beyond routine and standard descriptions of our work and our relations with others. The daily doing that otherwise dries us out is given new meaning and purpose, in the plots of our stories. We find out who we are as lawyers and persons (as persons who are lawyers) by the story we tell, by the conversation that we have with clients and other lawyers, in court and on the street corner. Our stories about being lawyers, shaped by the way we imagine ourselves and our clients, are central to the way we understand and reflect on the way our lives unfold and interact.

Lopez suggests that "given our limited information-processing capabilities, we need stories to allow us to figure out what's going on and what we should do about it. By simplifying the world, however, stories may distort our perceptions and responses. . . . Studying our use of stories can thus help us both to improve our ability to use stories to change the world and to become aware of ways in which our stock stories constrain our views of ourselves and the world.

"Our stock stories embody our values and assumptions about the way life is and the way it ought to be. Because telling a particular story implies acceptance of a set of political, human, and social values, telling a story is always a [moral] political act. One of the important things to learn about stories is which ones you *don't* want to tell, and when, and why. A story may present the storyteller or other characters in ways that they'd rather not be presented. A story may also incorporate values that you don't want to accept, even for the moment, even if telling that story would be an effective way to achieve a short-term objective.

"If you're telling someone else's story, it's even harder to sort out good stories from bad stories. We don't often recognize how hard it is to understand someone else's life, the story someone else is living or wants to live, and we often don't appreciate how little we know about the kinds of stories that a friend or client is willing to have told about her. It's never enough just to pick any story that will compel the audience to grant the desired remedy. Responsible storytelling requires sensitivity to the needs and values of the subject of the story, and to the values embodied in the story itself.

"We learn to use stories to understand the world and to solve problems by living in a culture. We learn stories and storytelling by hearing people around us describe 'what is going on' or 'what we have always done.' Each person's practical, working knowledge includes a set of stock stories and storytelling techniques appropriate to her everyday needs, whether or not she is aware of it. People naturally absorb lawyering skills from their cultural environment, but may not recognize them as skills which may be useful out of the context in which they were learned . . . ."

BIBLIOGRAPHY

The image of the lawyer as story teller is rooted in our conception of counseling as a form of skilled listening and talking, a conversation between a person who needs help and one who is responsive to those who ask for help and can pay for the kind of talking and listening that lawyers do. The image also reflects an emerging body of jurisprudential literature that views law as a form of narrative, constitutive of a body of literature. See West, "Jurisprudence as Narrative: An Aesthetic Analysis of Modern Legal Theory," 60 New York University Law Review 145 (1985); Kennedy, "Spring Break," 63 Texas Law Review 1377 (1985); Burt, "Constitutional Law and the Teaching of Parables," 93 Yale Law Journal 455 (1984); Cover, "Nomos and Order," 97 Harvard Law Review 4 (1983).

James Boyd White is one of the leading legal scholars in this movement and has produced a series of thought-provoking scholarly works: Heracles' Bow: Essays on the Rhetoric and Poetics of the Law (1985); When Words Lose Their Meaning: Constitutions and Reconstitutions of Language, Character, and Community (1984); The Legal Imagination: Studies in the Nature of Legal Thought and Expression (1973).

The authors (Shaffer and Elkins) have written on stories and law, stories and the practice of law: Elkins, "On the Emergence of Narrative Jurisprudence: The Humanistic Perspective Finds a New Path," 9 Legal Studies Forum 123 (1985); Shaffer, "Christian Lawyer Stories and American Legal Ethics," 33 Mercer Law Review 877 (1982); "Henry Knox and the Moral Theology of Law Firms," 38 Washington and Lee Law Review 347 (1981); "The Moral Theology of Atticus Finch," 42 University of Pittsburgh Law Review 181 (1981); Hauerwas and Shaffer, "Hope in the Life of Thomas More," 54 Notre Dame Lawyer 569 (1979).

See, more generally, Randall, "Why Scholars Become Storytellers," Book Review, New York Times, January 29, 1984; Kotre, Outliving the Self: Generativity and the Interpretation of Lives (1984); MacIntyre, After Virtue: A Study in Moral Theory 190–209 (2nd ed. 1984); "From System to Story: An Alternative Pattern for Rationality in Ethics," in Hauerwas, Truthfulness and Tragedy: Further Investigations in Christian Ethics 15–39 (1977); Cottle, Private Lives and Public Accounts (1977), and Religion as Story (Wiggins, ed. 1975); Keen and Fox, Telling Your Story (1973); Novak, Experience of Nothingness 23–29 (Harper Colophon ed. 1971).

For other images of the lawyer, see Mindes, "Trickster, Hero, Helper: A Report on the Lawyer Image," 1982 American Bar Foundation Resource Journal 177.

REFERENCES

Auchincloss, The Great World and Timothy Colt (1956); Geertz, Local Knowledge: Further Essays in Interpretative Anthropology (1983); Lopez, unpublished ms., and Lopez, "Lay Lawyering," 32 UCLA Law Review 1 (1984).

CHAPTER THREE

THE LAWYER PERSONA AND THE FEELINGS IT DISGUISES

LEARNING THE MASK

There were, early in the career of most lawyers, two goals identified by law professors and older law students: Law students must learn to "think like a lawyer" and learn to "talk like a lawyer." That is the advice that was and is given to beginning law students. The assumption is that to be a lawyer, one must act like a lawyer. The message comes at a crucial time—as we begin to try to learn the law and to find a place for ourselves in the profession. The significance of this early message on the lawyer as counselor is profound. But, first, what does it mean to "talk" and "think" like a lawyer?

TALKING LIKE A LAWYER

Lawyers speak a foreign language; clients hear it as "legalese." In a vehement attack on the language of lawyers, almost 40 years ago, Fred Rodell argued that the law deals with ordinary facts and occurrences but that lawyers use "a jargon which completely baffles and befoozles the ordinary literate [person]." Rodell berated lawyers for the use of "professional pig Latin" and for their failure to relate legal concepts to clients in simple

English. "It is this fact more than any other—the fact that lawyers can't or won't tell what they are about in ordinary English—that is responsible for the hopelessness of the non-lawyer in trying to cope with or understand the so-called science of law. For the lawyers' trade is a trade built entirely on words. And so long as the lawyers carefully keep to themselves the key to what those words mean, the only way the average [person] can find out what is going on is to become a lawyer, or at least to study law, himself. All of which makes it very nice—and very secure—for the lawyers." E. B. White, the greatest of American wordsmiths, said, "I honestly worry about lawyers. They never write plain English themselves, and when you give them a bit of plain English to read, they say, 'Don't worry, it doesn't mean anything.'" When we talk to clients we must remember, as James Boyd White points out, that lawyers "still speak an inherited and traditional language with marked peculiarities of vocabulary and construction." The language of law can become a barrier between lawyers who know the language and clients who do not.

The United States Tax Court once held that a lawyer who tried to learn the English language was not acquiring a skill that is necessary to his profession. We suspected as much, but were depressed to see it become official. Steven J. McAuliffe in that case lost his claim for a deduction of $1,822 for taking English courses at Georgetown

University. He argued that the study of poetry, Victorian literature, and writing were important to his being a lawyer. Not so, said the Tax Court. "We are unwilling to declare that the study of English literature . . . bears the sort of proximate relationship to the improvement of an appellate attorney's legal skills to justify the deduction," Judge Howard A. Dawson, Jr., said. An unfortunate decision. If Judge Dawson had taken the courses Mr. McAuliffe took perhaps he wouldn't say things like "bears the sort of proximate relationship" when he means "is close enough."

It is not that lawyers speak in a single voice or utilize a unique language, for there is no special language reserved for law. From the perspective of lawyers, legal language is ordinary English (some of it very old), or foreign phrases that an educated gentleman of the 19th century was supposed to understand, to which we give special and sometimes technical meaning. It is difficult for a lawyer to talk without using these special meanings, and when we work with other lawyers there is little reason to do so. Gaining mastery of the way law uses (and abuses) language is an integral part of learning to be a lawyer. But words that mean something to lawyers can become obstacles to communication with clients. The words we use and the way we use them with (and against) our clients are of special concern to the lawyer as counselor. A counselor monitors what he or she is doing with and to the client with words. We look for the effect, and the *affect* of our words.

There is another perspective to be considered—that of clients. Clients have their ways of saying things, too; as we note in Chapter Five, in reference particularly to Alfred Kinsey's interviews, using words the client uses is often indispensable to understanding what the client wants to say. (Not just hearing those words, Kinsey says—but using them.) Failure in the art of understanding words (and, Kinsey said, understanding means using) may mean failure to understand feelings, failure to understand what the client's situation is.

THINKING LIKE A LAWYER

Social scientists, including psychologists, sociologists, and anthropologists, concur that every person has a unique way of seeing things. Bandler and Grinder write, "Each of us creates a representation of the world in which we live—that is, we create a map or model which we use to generate our behavior. Our representation of the world determines to a large degree what our experience of the world will be, how we will perceive the world, what choices we will see available to us as we live in the world."

A *Weltanschauung* (world view) consists of the underlying postulates and assumptions that an individual (and her social group and culture) uses to understand and explain the world. The legal profession has its own world view, one that functions much like the programming software of a computer; it programs our interaction with others, our way of being in the world as lawyers, and even our way of being persons outside the law. In the world of computers some computer users know enough about programming to "patch" the software to get the program and the computer to do what they want it to do. Others use existing software and use it as it permits them to use it. In a similar way, some lawyers make the practice of law into an art, one they devise, a craft to serve clients' and their own needs; they remake an existing role of the lawyer into forms and activities that fit them. Others take what the legal profession gives as standard fare; they take it on as a job, as if the law were a drill press on an assembly line, and clients were pieces of metal.

The lawyer as lawyer thinks about client problems, about clients, and about himself through a veil of legal rules and legal problems. His program tells him that he is a neutral, rational, objective problem-solver. Jerald Auerbach argues that it is the lawyer's dislike of vague generalities, the preference for case-by-case treatment of social issues, the structuring of human relations into the form of legal claims and counter-claims, that constitutes the lawyer's way of thinking—what the social scientist calls a world view. Stuart Scheingold writes, "When we accuse someone of being legalistic, we suggest an excessive zeal for purely formal details which becloud rather than clarify the real issue. The legalist is someone who is lost among the trees and cannot or will not consider the overall shape of the forest. So it is a sense of willful closure together with an obsession for procedure and minutiae that we associate with the law game."

Lawyers, it will surprise no one, become legalists and legalistic. Judith Shklar defines legalism as the ethical "attitude that holds moral conduct to be a matter of rule following and moral relationships to consist of duties and rights determined by rules." Legalism in her view is "a way of thinking about social life, a mode of consciousness." Of course, "legalism" may be an epithet, a word used to describe rigid, formal, or narrow-minded reasoning. Academic lawyers will sometimes listen to the charge of "legalism" in university faculty meetings, become reciprocally insulting, and refer to an argument as "metaphysical." Metaphysics is, like law, an ancient and respectable discipline; the word would probably not be used unless there was someone in the room who knew the discipline and could be insulted by the word, a word used to scoff at philosophers in the way "legalistic" is used to scoff at lawyers.

But Shklar's point cuts deeper; it has more to it than the identification of an insult. Legalism is, she said, characteristic of a certain way of thinking, and ways of thinking are characteristic of ways of being. Here the computer metaphor is less indicative than the deeper social science concept,

Weltanschauung, world view: Jungian psychology
has a term for ways of being—a word we use also
in Chapter One. It is a word derived from the
mask used by actors in Greek theatre: "persona."
What Shklar was talking about, and what, when
we get down to it, we are talking about in this
chapter, is the lawyer persona, the way a lawyer is
being when she or he is being a lawyer.

A persona is functional. That is why we begin to
use it in the first place. The problem is that the
persona becomes a habit; we forget we have it on,
forget about the masks we have put between us
and other people. And of course when that happens, the persona is not functional at all; we only
tell ourselves that it is. Function is not the issue;
character is the issue. It is important to understand that the lawyer persona, even when it is
functional, and especially when it is not, operates
to exclude and to screen, to limit what we see and
think. It often leads to self-deception and injustice: We may end up trying to convince ourselves
that we are not, in fact, limited by what we have
become, by what we have learned or will learn
about how to practice law. "Law professors and
lawyers," Scheingold points out, "do not believe
that they are either encumbered or enlightened by
a special view of the world. They simply feel that
their legal training has taught them to think logically. In a complex world, they have the intellectual tools to strip a problem, any problem, down to
its essentials."

Legalism as a world view, what we are calling
the lawyer persona, is promoted and maintained by
the legal profession; its roots are deep in the
pedagogy, curriculum, and everyday activities of
the law school. Law schools claim to teach a "way
of thinking," a model for seeing, diagnosing, and
resolving problems, a way of thinking that creates
(or narrows reality to) a universe of rights and
obligations, causes of action, forms and procedures.

Because of this last reality—and the demands of
those who want to deal with us when our masks
are on—the legal persona is a social phenomenon.
The activities of lawyers are, because of this demand and through these masks of ours, structured
and molded in habitual and historical ways, with
habitual and historical attributes that are usually
referred to as "professional." An association of
people calls itself a profession and then acts for the
community (or the state) in creating a sense of
obligation, in each of its members, that refers to
and gives definition to the persona. The professional role of the lawyer is represented in but is
not fully realized by assuming a professional mask.
The persona represents both an idealized legal
mind and a cover or disguise over the underlying
self, a disguise used in conspiracy with those in the
community who find it safer to deal with a mask
than with a person. As a result, the persona forms
character; it imposes a morality, and we come to
talk of the lawyer persona as having a life of its
own. We then demand status, as lawyers, within

the community; we become a community (of sorts)
ourselves, a community of people entitled to the
masks they wear.

The legal persona is the mask through which the
counselor sees the world. Our work and the effect
of our conversation are carried through the mask.
Our wishes and fears are filtered through the
mask. The mask frames the way we talk to a
client and what we hear the client say. We see the
client through the persona, the professional mask
that gives us an identity and shields us from what
we are unwilling to hear—feelings that are painful, anything we do not understand, all that we can
deny.

The lawyer persona is a world view and is significant in determining the kind of information we
call facts and excluding from awareness and consideration the kind of information we refuse to call
facts. The verbal stuff of law practice—what lawyers call facts, or legal problems, or law—is made
subjective by the legal persona. First, the facts
that we derive from our legal world view are based
upon the selection of what we hear, and how we
are able to organize, verbally, what we hear, for
use in responding to the problem. Lawyers typically obtain their facts from a client (comple-
mented in some instances by an "independent"
investigation that is organized and reported by, to,
and through the lawyer persona). The attorney
reviews, selects, organizes, and synthesizes facts to
derive a cause of action in a complaint; an affirma-

tion or denial in an answer to a complaint, or an argument, in words, to a governmental decision maker. By selecting and excluding that which is unacceptable, a coherent, organized, and orderly view of the world is maintained. We lawyers communicate with one another not only or even principally with all of these words but also with this (tacit) world view; we define reality with our masks.

FEELINGS WITHIN AND BEYOND THE PERSONA

One of the ways that we avoid strong feelings in professional relationships is to adopt, often unconsciously, a psychological and interactive "style" that we use with and on clients. When interaction with the client goes unexamined, and when we ignore or suppress our feelings about this person as a client, this client as a person, then we tend to adopt a style dictated by social role and professional mask. The interaction with the client may be adequate, or even admirable; it may be effective in soliciting facts and making the client feel secure, but it will be a style developed out of the lawyer's conflicts, anxieties, and fantasies, a style that serves all that is unconscious as well as that of which he is conscious. The problem with the style that emerges, the common, intuitive, and "natural" style that we use in interactions with clients, is that it becomes rigid and inflexible. It is one mask that we wear whenever we work with clients.

Each client is exactly that—a client. And a client is "seen" and "heard" through the mask. The mask is in large part unconscious: Remember that the lawyer feels the mask (style) as natural and intuitive, rather than constructed out of present needs and without regard to what is happening "now" for both the client and the lawyer. The mask is easy, because it is already there; efficient, because we don't have to think about it; and effective enough to lure us into ignoring it. It has its purpose, sometimes serves us well, and we pay the price (as does the client): Every client is a type; finally every client is like every other client. No one is a person. No person is an adventure.

What can a lawyer do with his feelings about the client, the client's "problem," and the problems he is having with the client? These feelings (ignored, suppressed, or admitted) are central to the way we are seen by our clients (how they see us working, talking, responding, helping, caring). Since we are not generally capable of admitting and responding to the entire range of human feelings and emotions, we tend to select some, filter out others (ignoring, suppressing, denying, compartmentalizing, partitioning and walling off). When this selective filtering process takes place, which it does whether we are conscious of it or not, a style develops, a mask is constructed, a persona (mask) is presented to the client. And it is to this business of forging a relationship with our own feelings

and becoming aware of the resulting style of interaction that we now turn our attention.

There are some general points that can be made
about feelings:

—Most human behavior expresses striving for
emotional satisfaction or the avoidance of emotional threats. We act to move toward comfort
and stay away from what we fear or dislike.

—Many of us ignore feelings as long as it is
possible to do so. The person (read "lawyer")
who pretends to himself that he is a rational
calculating machine, moved only by the business
at hand and concerned only for legal competence, suffers from a grave illusion. He may
have ceased to recognize his feelings, but emotions are still present. He cannot be whole until
he relaxes his repressions and experiences his
own feelings. It is not surprising that a person
who for years has pretended to others that he
feels what he doesn't really feel should lose his
ability to discriminate among his own emotions.

—Lawyers say, "We have work to do. Let's
lay aside feelings and buckle down to business!"
Feelings are forced to operate under the table.

—Problems arise, not because emotions are
present, but because they are denied. People get
into trouble, not because they have emotions, but
because of attempts to repress, distort, or disguise their emotions.

—The test of a good decision (tough choice), one which is carried out wholeheartedly, is not whether it has been unemotionally made, but rather whether all of the emotions involved have been expressed, recognized, and taken into account. Innumerable business decisions are bad because they have been devised on the assumption that feelings can be laid aside or ignored.

What is the lawyer to do with her feelings, in particular those about the client? One alternative: Forget them. Repress them through habitual, unconscious mechanisms, which means that she does not even become aware of them. Wall them off from the on-going relationship with the client and then find a "release" outside professional relationships: running, sailing, weaving, family life, farming, gardening, church work, building model ships. Another alternative: Channel them secretly back into the relationship, using them as tools of manipulation. A third alternative, one which we advocate: Bring them openly into the relationship with the client.

The Problem. One way, and a common one, that we relate to our feelings for a client is to put the feelings aside or ignore them, by trying to focus on the "problem" that the client presents. We do this because we select a narrow definition of lawyering, and stay close to that narrow definition; we may do that unconsciously: The lawyer is able to conceive a role of interaction that minimizes the need to take account of her feelings. In this role-oriented, instrumental approach to lawyering, feelings are devalued. Objectivity and independent judgment are emphasized. Professionalism itself comes to be defined in terms of the ability to keep the client at arm's length. The good lawyer, in this view, *controls* the client, and does so for the specific purpose of obtaining the best results. In medicine, this is translated as "the doctor knows best." It is an interactional style supported by one strain of the lawyering ethos, in fantasies and stories about lawyers and what they do for, and to, their clients; by the rules of professional ethics; and by individual psychological needs.

The interactional (psychological and professional) style that we describe here cuts the client off from her story (see Chapter Two). When we focus on the legal problem to the exclusion of the client, or on the client as a problem, attention and energy are directed outward, toward a safe zone of objectivity represented by knowledge and skill, and away from the relationship. When the lawyer encourages the client to focus on the problem, it is one way to focus his own energy and at the same time a way of restricting and limiting the range of feelings he experiences. But the lawyer, the client, and the problem are not separate entities. The problem cannot be separated from the client, and the lawyer cannot keep the energy and focus of the relationship solely on the problem. Relationships premised upon a problem fail even as they succeed. The relation of the lawyer, client, and problem are in reality too complex and overwhelm the problem-oriented focus of the lawyer. If the problem were a ball, and both lawyer and client could keep their gaze directed on the ball and its movement between them, the psychodynamics of the attorney-client relationship would be a relatively simple matter. But the client's problem is not separate from the client. The client does not experience the problem as outside him and outside the relationship, and will not experience it that way even at the behest of the most authoritarian lawyer. (See Exercise Eight, in the Appendix.)

THE AUTHORITARIAN STYLE, THE PROBLEM OF POWER, AND THE NEED TO BE HEROIC

There are lawyers who actively assert dominance over the client, letting it be known, from the beginning, that the client can take it—that is, submit—or leave it—that is, leave. Some clients want a "take it or leave it" lawyer, a lawyer that will assume control, and will get them what they want. A client may be willing to acquiesce, and pay the price of submission, in the hope that she will actually get what she wants. And it takes little imagination to speculate on the dynamics and the pathologies of such relationships. The authoritarian lawyer who dominates the client and does so routinely and as a matter of course cuts himself off from the client and the world of the client. This lawyer retreats into a world of his own and will

tend to see the world from his own Olympian
perspective. When we live in a world of self-
designed Olympian heights, we begin to act like
the Greek god Zeus, taking on an assumed power
and lofty unreachableness that calls for competition, power-plays, and the pushing and shoving
that goes with a "top-dog" mentality. The authoritarian lawyer can, and sometimes does, become a
legendary figure, renowned for his success, revered
for his exploits, a folk hero in both professional
and public circles. The heroic authoritarian lawyer is often a mesmerizing figure, a subject of
controversy and gossip, a legend to himself and in
his culture. The problem in relating to a legend,
to a heroic figure that is distant and remote, is that
we come to see the figure as a symbol, a symbol
that represents some split-off part of our own
selves.

We admire our pop-culture lawyer heroes
(whether they are heroes in the fuller sense of
what it means to be an authentic cultural hero is
another matter). They represent, symbolically,
our own struggle, and our will to compete, to
overcome mediocrity, to fight for something that
we believe in, something of significance for ourselves, our clients, our community. The popular
lawyer hero is a symbol and a projective screen for
our fantasies of prevailing, of overcoming, of securing just rewards for the injuries and damages to
ourselves and our clients. The lawyer hero is a
winner: She or he prevails against obstacles that I

confront. The hero is a version of myself. I, too, feel (or desire to feel) heroic, confronting the conflict, engaging in struggle, and having a sense of power, a knowledge that I will overcome all that stands against me. My clients will be well advised to place themselves entirely in my competent hands.

A point of clarification. We are not suggesting that it takes an authoritarian lawyer to become a cultural hero, or that popular lawyers, some of whom achieve local and national acclaim (and some of whom are real heroes), are all authoritarian. (A wonderful counter-example is the story of a southern lawyer-hero, Atticus Finch, in Harper Lee's novel To Kill a Mockingbird.) There are different kinds of heroes, as there are different kinds of lawyers. And there are limits to what one can do as a lawyer who can be acclaimed by the public as a hero. On this point, it is well to admit to a distinction between popular figures that are admired by the public, made heroes by the press and television, and the struggle of lawyers who are less well known but in quiet ways are genuinely heroic. And finally, there is the heroic quest, the mythic journey that each of us takes when he enters the world fully as a public citizen and seeks to do something significant, as we do when we take on the cause of others, advocating and professing for them.

The authoritarian lawyer style is both a caricature (as any style is) and a reality. It is one way lawyers protect themselves from their own feelings and the feelings of others, a form of protection that is associated with objectivity in professional relationships. It is one way lawyers measure their success, a success that makes some lawyers popular heroes. In the reality of the law office—which is our concern—the authoritarian lawyer points to the problem of power, of who will control a relationship, of who will feel powerful and who will experience feelings of helplessness, as clients work with lawyers. We assume that it is inevitable in the course of a professional relationship (and perhaps, any relationship) that the "helper" will feel strong or subtle pressure to take command of the situation and to wield power over the client. Power, the desire for control, is never absent from human relationships; it ebbs and flows and gives life, for example, to a friendship. In the relationship of lawyer and client, the lawyer is pushed from many directions, internal (psychological) and external (social, political, and cultural) to take charge and be in control. In Freudian and Jungian psychology, this need is analyzed from the perspective of the countertransference, a name for those strong feelings that are directed toward the client, that are linked up with other relationships (often past), needs, and feelings that are not specifically related to those of the client who is the real person before us and with us in the room.

Evidence of the need to be powerful (a need that is itself a countertransference reaction) includes

unsolicited advice, false reassurance, grandiose
claims and arguments, browbeating, insisting on
rigid compliance with the lawyer's plan on how to
proceed, frequent references to aspects of the law
that are beyond the client's understanding, trivial-
izing the work of other lawyers.   Every lawyer
knows the impulse to get and maintain control
over clients and their "cases." The need for control and power is something we take into relationships with us (a need that runs from functional to
neurotic) and is often enough exacerbated by the
client's needs and the nature of the work that we
are called on to do for and with the client. More
problematic still is the need for control that ema-
nates from the feeling that the client is making a
similar bid for power, so that lawyer and client
compete for control in and of the relationship.
Clients, no less than lawyers, have a need for
control and a wish for power. A client can take
control, assume a power position, and dominate a
lawyer—a situation that is not in the best interests
of either client or lawyer. The power issue is not
solved by giving up control or forcing the client to
make decisions that he does not feel capable to
make.

  Murray Stein is a Jungian analyst and is one of
the psychologists whose work we have drawn on
for this description of the need for power in professional relationships. He makes this useful distinction: Sometimes the need for power comes from "a
professional attitude," what we have called the

lawyer's persona. (See Chapter One.) The persona brings power with it, and so we control our clients in order to live up to, and live out, the demands of the persona. The power dynamic of the professional attitude that comes from this persona leaves the client in the position of taking it or leaving it. As Stein puts it: The client "either accepts it and adapts, or rejects it and leaves." That Olympian clarity is a possibility, but more frequently the power dynamic is set into motion *during* the relationship, as the case proceeds, or, as Stein puts it, "as the complexes of each partner become engaged with those of the other. Here the power pattern derives from the psychodynamics that operate between two specific individuals, while other areas of each person's life remain relatively free of this pattern." Stein gives an example of the patient who brings out the sadist in the analyst. This kind of person is not unknown in law offices: "They are unconsciously looking for someone to take charge and to assert power over them, to tell them what to do, to give them tough advice, to punish them for their inadequacy . . . ." In such a case, it doesn't take an overwhelming need to control, a neurotic power drive, for a lawyer to find himself controlling the client. That is, after all, what the client wants. It is in fact what the client has tricked you into doing. The effect of the power dynamic, viewed from either client or lawyer perspective, is that it creates psychological distance between two persons. It produces isolation.

THE THEORY OF
COUNTERTRANSFERENCE

When we talk about the feelings of a lawyer for and about a client (and feelings *against* the client), we have entered the realm of transference and countertransference. When Freudian and Jungian psychotherapists talk about their own feelings in relation to their patients they do so in the name of *countertransference*. This term is less familiar to lawyers. It is uncommon, in professional relations outside the therapeutic setting, for the professional ("helper") to take account of his feelings. For the most part, feelings are left to take care of themselves. They are just there, to be left alone, undisturbed. They receive little attention or conscious thought, and there is generally no effort to understand how they might influence interactions with clients (or with other lawyers, or judges), or how one might make active and affirmative use of his feelings. We take our feelings for granted. And this means we give too little thought to the question: How am I as a lawyer and a person (a Christian, a wife, a Mason, a father, a daughter) to act toward and with my clients? Do I approach all my clients with the same kind of attitude, a professional attitude that has become a legal persona? Or do I find myself responding to each client as the person he or she is or wishes to be? Do I respond to the story the client tells with its unique particulars or to the story as a genre whose plot I have memorized so well that there is no longer a need to listen?   (See Chapter Two.)

The countertransference is a prototypical form of reaction, and one that helps explain why one re-acts as he does to clients in general and to a particular client.   Beyond (or within) countertrans-ference, and in manifestations that seem more ordinary, are a number of evasive maneuvers we lawyers take to cope with or deny the feelings we have for our clients.

There are two elements of the countertransfer-ence that need to be distinguished, but first a brief comment about how we recognize a countertrans-ference and what it means in terms of our under-standing of professionalism.   The countertransfer-ence is witnessed in unexpected behavior, strong feelings (affection and hostility are common), a quick reply, a rebuke, browbeating, abruptness, verbal threats.

Here are a few clues, from Saxe and Kuvin, clues—some of them expressed, we think, too medi-cally—that are signals of countertransference in lawyer-client relationships.   They may lead to awareness of lawyer needs that are not being met, or to a recognition that the process level of the relationship needs attention.   As long as these signals are ignored, the client rather than the lawyer is made to bear the burden of them:

　　—Feelings of discomfort during or after inter-views with the client (". . . most likely indicate inability on the part of the attorney to understand and honestly deal with certain kinds of material which touch on the attorney's own problems").

—Carelessness and discourtesy toward the client, such as being late for appointments, permitting avoidable interruption, or making appointment arrangements that are inconvenient for the client. ("Despite the rationalizations . . . this is usually an . . . indication of his hostility toward his client or his fear that the coming appointment will further produce material that will cause anxiety in the attorney.")

—Strong affectionate feelings for the client, which feelings are usually recognized when the client is of the opposite sex and repressed when he or she is not.

—Inclinations to boast, to colleagues or client, on the importance of the matter the client brings in (". . . indicative of the attorney's damaged self-concept and his lowered self-esteem . . . a reparative maneuver").

—Avoidance of the client and neglect of his case (the principal source of complaint about lawyers to bar-association grievance committees) ("may indicate serious neurotic conflicts").

—Gossip with others about the client ("causations may include . . . need to associate with peer group . . . psycho-sexual pathology . . . self-defeating or self-destructive mechanism").

—A tendency to "hammer away at minutiae beyond the scope of even the most intelligent lament." Saxe and Kuvin see this as a manifestation of aggression, and note that it often occurs with a client who is perceived as dissatisfied with the lawyer. "If the attorney is blind to his vulnerability in this area, and contracts with a client who is neurotically 'pain-dependent,' the conduct of the case is usually chaotic, and the end result is usually a disaster for the client. . . ."

—Boredom or drowsiness—"the most important of all responses." Saxe and Kuvin believe this to be "almost inevitably an indicator of extreme anxiety produced in the attorney." The agenda then, of course, would be to locate the source of the anxiety.

Howard F. Stein in his work on countertransference in physician-patient relationships observes that "we discover and recognize its [countertransference] power only by stumbling on it, by feeling disturbed by it, or by having someone else identify it." There is an element of surprise (sometimes confusion, anger, or shame) that comes from this stumbling onto our own feelings. Stein puts it this way: "When we 'accidentally' let slip our feelings—through words, tone of voice, gestures, impulsive actions—we often feel surprised if not overwhelmed by such lapses in self-control." Whenever a feeling is denied or ignored and then finds its way back into the conversation or is acted

out in behavior, it is overdetermined, which means
it is differentiated from on-going reactions by having an unexpected power, a way of making itself
known that is unexpected and that takes us by
surprise. "It strikes us," Stein says, "unprepared."

The countertransference is threatening because
it is no respecter of professional status and training. In the world of feeling, a lawyer has no more
expertise or knowledge than the client. The compartmentalization of role and self collapse in professional life when we recognize and work with
countertransference feelings. Role is a way to
institutionalize, that is, regularize and routinize,
the professional's response in confusing and threatening situations. But feelings are embedded in
even the most routinized response. By gaining
insight into the law office countertransference, we
see the subjectivity (an essential aspect of human
caring) operating inside the mask of professionalism.

We mean to imply, in all of this discussion of
countertransference, a healthier and more truthful
way to work through the three-cornered reality of
client, lawyer, and problem. Murray Stein describes this in a mode of countertransference in
which the client and "helper" move closer to one
another and into an interaction that accepts the
reality of psychological identification and distanc-
ing. Instead of allowing power to create distance,
the lawyer and client become partners, in meetings
and between meetings. The lawyer and client

work together. The work (the work of being together and the work that is the legal problem) bring them together. It is like Robert Frost's farmer (in the poem "Tuft of Flowers") who begins the day feeling alone but comes in his work to say, "We work together when we work apart."

BIBLIOGRAPHY

On the persona, legal and otherwise: Jolande Jacobi, Masks of the Soul (1976); John Noonan, Persons and Masks of the Law (1976); Judith Shklar, Legalism (1964).

On feelings: Callwood, Emotions (1986); Parker, Emotional Common Sense (revised ed. 1981); Gaylin, Feelings (1979); Viscott, The Language of Feelings (Pocket Book ed. 1977); Solomon, The Passions (1976); Goldberg, The Hazards of Being Male: Surviving the Myth of Masculine Privilege 42–60 (1976).

On anger: Travis, Anger (1982); Rubin, The Angry Book (Collier 1970).

On anxiety: Sheehan, Anxiety Disease (1986); McCullough and Mann, Managing Your Anxiety (1985); May, The Meaning of Anxiety (1950).

On narcissism: Lowen, Narcissism: Denial of the True Self (Collier 1985).

On compassion and self-hate: Rubin, Compassion and Self-Hate (1986).

On jealousy: Friday, Jealousy (1985).

For a social and political perspective on feelings: Unger, Passion: An Essay on Personality (1984); Bailey, The Tactical Uses of Passion: An Essay on Power, Reason, and Reality (1983); Sennett, The Uses of Disorder: Personal Identity and City Life (Vintage, 1971).

On countertransference: Shaffer, "Undue Influence, Confidential Relationship, and the Psychology of Transference," 45 Notre Dame Lawyer 197 (1970), in Death, Property, and Lawyers (1970).

REFERENCES

Bandler and Grinder, The Structure of Magic: A Book About Language and Therapy (vol. 1, 1975); Rodell, Woe Unto You, Lawyers! (1939); White (James Boyd), The Legal Imagination: Studies in the Nature of Legal Thought and Expression (1973); Saxe and Kuvin, Notes on the Attorney-Client Relationship, 2 Journal of Psychiatry and Law 209 (1974); Scheingold, The Politics of Rights: Lawyers, Public Policy, and Political Change (1974); Shklar, Legalism (1964); Stein (Murray), "Power, Shamanism, and Maieutics in the Countertransference," Chiron: A Review of Jungian Analysis 67 (1984); Stein (Howard), The Psycho-Dynamics of Medical Practice: Unconscious Factors in Patient Care (1985).

CHAPTER FOUR

ESTABLISHING A WORKING RELATIONSHIP

PERSONAL CLIMATE

The key to tough decisions in law offices, to client choices that work, is the climate lawyers provide. The heart of counseling effectiveness, wherever it falls on the spectrum from information (advice) to therapy, is the client's ability to trust the counselor. A climate of trust involves acceptance, understanding, and empathy. The issues of trust, dependence, choice, personal growth, and client choice turn on the climate that the counselor creates. Many legal counselors are poor at building a healthy, constructive, non-manipulative office climate for the people who come to them with worry and trouble and doubt.

It is obvious that two people who propose to work together have to come to a working agreement, a sense about how they will proceed, how they will talk and listen to each other, and how the stories they tell each other will be reconciled. Life is filled with working agreements, from the resolution of who is to go through the door first to comity among the three branches of the federal government. The working agreement between a lawyer and client will develop quickly in most cases, may-

73

be too quickly, and will reflect factors such as these:

—Each party's view of the law. Lawyers tend to regard law as something sacred; clients may regard it as oppressive, intrusive, or tyrannical.

—Each party's philosophy of human worth. This sometimes shows up in clients who look upon a lawyer the way some people look upon a clerk in a drugstore—as an instrument.

—Each party's view of lawyers. Research indicates that most citizens have a low regard for lawyers. People who have dealt with lawyers retain this low regard for the profession but tend to have a higher regard for the lawyers who represented them. The client who expects his lawyer to file a lawsuit, immediately, has a different feeling about what lawyers do than the client who appears to seek personal guidance. And the lawyer who thinks that his expertise is litigation will tend to encourage lawsuits where personal guidance is more appropriate and is the professional service the client seeks.

—Each party's view of the client's situation. Virginia Anne Church puts it well: "The fact that a client first seeks you, an attorney, rather than a minister, marriage counselor, psychologist, therapist, or doctor, may have little to do with the nature of his underlying problem (or even with the best means of effectively resolving it). Most likely he will choose a lawyer because of his stereotypes of the other helping professions in relation to his self image, or his view of the lawyer as an authoritative, rational, and respectable power source." In his work with divorced spouses, Robert Weiss, a sociologist, found that individuals with marital difficulties seek lawyers for a variety of reasons: "Some retain a lawyer because they want a specific legal service: a separation agreement to be negotiated, legal pressure to be brought on a nonsupporting husband or on a wife who refuses visitation, or simply a divorce. But others retain a lawyer for all sorts of non-legal reasons. They may want to demonstrate to themselves and their spouse that they are seriously dissatisfied with their marriage: 'I saw a lawyer today' can be of decided dramatic value when dropped into an evening's dispute. Or they may be unhappy and confused, and perhaps fearful of the future, and want the reassurance of having talked with someone knowledgeable. Many among the separated see a lawyer initially just for information regarding their legal situation, without any immediate desire to proceed beyond this. Some retain a lawyer almost against their will, because their spouse has insisted that they do so, or because their spouse has retained one and they believe that in self-protection they must follow suit."

—From the other side of the desk, some lawyers see themselves as available for warfare (they even speak of themselves as "hired guns") and are not very interested in anything else. Some see themselves as society's keepers of the peace and will go to extraordinary lengths to avoid warfare. Some see themselves as sources of wisdom, and some see themselves as vindicators of justice.

Experts seem to agree that an open, reflective, supportive atmosphere in the office, as soon as the client settles into it, is likely to produce both good rapport and the minimum level of interpersonal negotiation that is necessary for rapport and for a good working arrangement between the parties. Such an atmosphere suggests the use of these devices as soon as the client arrives: (1) "active listening," (2) evidence of empathic regard for the client's feelings, and (3) acceptance (what Carl Rogers calls "unconditional positive regard"). These are useful devices for the development of interpersonal arrangements (they may or may not be good for other purposes). They are effective in preventing an early and troubling emotional dependence on the lawyer (of which more in a later chapter). They are also likely to avoid a dependence based on inappropriate perceptions of expertise. Our professional ideals, the dynamics of interpersonal relationships, and a decent respect for human persons require that clients remain active in the development of their own legal relationships. This client activity varies from the drafting of a complaint to the language of a routine letter written on the client's behalf, from the provisions of the client's will to conducting a trial. It is astounding, though, how many clients say, "Why do I want to read the draft of my will? What do I have a lawyer for?" Such questions (remarks) are evidence of a bad working relationship, one in which the lawyer's technical expertise is being made to carry more than it can bear.

The best working arrangement is one founded on an understanding of the client and of his situation, and that suggests a strategy in which the client is encouraged to talk freely, to become a working member of the relationship. The recommended approach is to aim one's responses toward acceptance, and away from leading or interpretation, in the early stages of the relationship.

The dialogue between lawyer and client, early in their association, has much to do with how the working agreement is formed. Consider for a moment the words of an initial dialogue: Appel and Van Atta report communication research that suggests that the more leading the professional's words are, the more likely the resulting contract will be a contract based on undue reliance. They report a continuum which ranges from a category of Acceptance Remark (illustrated by a simple, "Uh huh" or "I see") to Rejection Responses ("I'm sure you don't mean that" or "I'm afraid you're wrong about that"), a category of maximum lead. To encourage client talk, they recommended fewer leading techniques. When leading is necessary they suggest "general leads": "Could you talk a bit more about. . . ." Conversely, if he wants to assume responsibility, the counselor will employ techniques that involve a high degree of lead, such as interpretation remarks: "It appears to me that your situation boils down to" or urging remarks, such as "It seems to me that what you need is. . . ."

Here is part of an initial interview of the owner of a photography studio who consults a lawyer because she thinks she is being (unfairly? wrongly? illegally? corruptly?) excluded from taking pictures of high school students. She has been describing how competing studios that are given yearbook contracts provide free services, or outright cash, to the schools involved:

1 C: . . . But I know the time that I bid, I had given the best bid. I know. But the studio that ended up getting it did both. They gave both money and services.

2 L: I see.

3 C: But the actual work that the studio did, or the prices that we were going to charge the seniors—it really was not important.

4 L: The studio—the charges to them—was—were—presumably, high.

5 C: Oh, yes. Well, you have to—what else are we going to do? You know, somewhere the money—

6 L: Umm.

7   C: It's going to come out of somewhere. You take a yearbook—I don't know whether you were on a yearbook committee when you were in school—I don't know—

8   L: No. But I had my picture taken.

9   C: That you had done. But the yearbook committee—when you consider that they have a printer. The printer doesn't donate his work. They don't go to the printer and say, "Okay, sir, you print up the book for us, and then you can come in and sell them. And if you sell a few, you can get some money, you can cover your printing expenses." No. The printer charges. You know it's going to cost so much to get those books printed up.

10 L: Right.

11 C: But the only one in this whole area of professional people, that has to give free things, is the photographer. And this seems wrong to me.

The lawyer's responses here do not interrupt flow. The client's story is not diverted or interrupted by what the lawyer says. The responses are, in the argot of counseling, acceptance remarks. However, the client needs more than the absence of interruption (although the restraint necessary to provide even that would be difficult for many lawyers). She also needs some encouragement, and that is most naturally provided by responses that demonstrate that the lawyer feels some empathy with her. The difference between acceptance and empathy is that empathy brings the lawyer's feelings into the interview. What, for example, would have been a good response to the last-quoted client remark?

(1) I can understand that you feel strongly about that.

(2) You really feel that that is wrong.

(3) Yes, and this probably reflects the fact that business has been a struggle for you.

(4) Oh? Why is that?

The second response—from the standpoint both of rapport and working arrangement—is, in our opinion, preferable. It expresses both acceptance of the feeling and empathy for it. But, to be effective, it must be sincere, and some lawyers would probably not have received and shared the feeling well enough to express themselves empathically; they would not have experienced empathy, and it would be false for them to attempt to express it. In that case, the first answer, which shows understanding, seems best. The third answer would fit the category of interpretative remarks; it comes across, here, as arrogant. The fourth answer is probing and, even if it might be appropriate later in the interview, is likely here to throw the client off course.

This lawyer in fact responded: "And the reason you have come to see me is—?" That seems to us a poor response. It does not demonstrate acceptance of the client's strong feeling. Silence on the issue of acceptance, as here, is rejection (of the feeling and, inevitably, of the client too). This lawyer's response was also abrupt and premature. The remainder of the interview demonstrates that the client had more to say, including facts crucial to her claim, and it also demonstrates that these two did not, that day, get to a sound working arrangement. If the lawyer were experiencing time pressures, it would have been more honest and much less damaging to say so and to arrange for a second interview. Response "10" is an earlier indication of this—what? impatience?—and is also an inappropriate response; client statement "9" presented an occasion for acceptance of feeling. The lawyer mistook agreement for acceptance of feeling, which is not the same at all. If the client says (as she, in a way, was saying), "I'm damned mad," an accepting response would be something like "Yes, you really are mad," said with feeling; the response, "Right," fails to reflect the feeling and also implies that client feelings are presented for agreement or disagreement by the lawyer.

Evidence that a working agreement was not being developed in the most effective manner occurs in two statements that followed:

11 C: . . . And this seems wrong to me.

12 L: And the reason you've come to me is—?

13 C: I don't know. (Laughter.) That's what you're supposed to decide. I don't know.

There's [such] a lot of problems that I don't know that you can do anything for me.

Here, by way of contrast, is a short dialogue between Carl Rogers and a young woman who came to see him about problems in her family:

14 C: I mean I hate the idea of everybody telling me what to do. Even my husband, he'll tell me what to do. Even though I'm young and I'm married, I mean I'm a human being and I like to run my life myself.

15 R: M-hm.

16 C: I mean I don't want to feel like I'm still in a baby buggy or something like that.

17 R: You feel that your mother and your husband and everybody tries to run your life.

18 C: Yes, that's why I feel that I was old enough to bear a baby and that's surely a lot of pain but yet they won't leave me make up my mind for myself.

19 R: M-hm. M-hm. (Pause; the client might have continued, but did not; Rogers apparently decided he had to say something.) Here I was old enough to have a child and yet nobody thinks I can make my decisions or run my own life. Is that what you're saying?

20 C: Yes.

21 R: M-hm. M-hm.

22 C: I mean, like, uh, now this is when my husband and I went to California with my little boy. I mean we were happier out there. He didn't have to run home to his mother all the time, and his mother is another one that, that we just don't get along. She hated me right from the day she saw me. But when we went to California, we had a good time out there.

23 R: I guess you're saying that kind of shows that when we're just by ourselves, we really get along better.

24 C: Yes, we get along better. . . .

Notice several things about these exchanges: (1) They probably took less than a minute, but, in them, Rogers learned about the significant effects on the marital relationship of the client's mother-in-law. (2) Rogers uses very slight non-verbal sounds of encouragement to keep the client talking. When the client stops talking, he uses reflective statements that carry much of the client's feeling, and therefore encourage her to go on. (3) Rogers checks with the client to see if his understanding is correct ("Is that what you're saying?" "I guess you're saying that. . . .") (See Exercise Eight, in the Appendix.)

CONTENT AND PROCESS

The relationship between a person and her lawyer reflects both content and process. Content includes advice (information about the law or about realities in the world in which the client proposes to act). Process includes the feelings of lawyer and client toward one another, and each toward herself, and all of the ways they act toward one another that do not pertain in words to the business they transact. Content is the reason a person seeks legal assistance; process may explain how she chose the lawyer she came to see. Content in a law-office consultation can usually be taken down on a yellow pad. But process can be captured only by a perceptive human being.

Process includes gestures, sounds that are not words, posture, and inflection. Non-verbal ways of communicating often give better clues to process than words do. (See Exercise Eleven, in the Appendix.) They show how process is as pervasive as content, and how it has more to do than content with the way things turn out. Process follows the twists and turns in the professional relationship. It reflects the depth of attraction, the feeling, and the understanding between the client and the lawyer. Process reaches further into the depths of a person's life than content does—and this is true of both persons in the relationship. "The gestures which we sometimes call empty are perhaps in fact the fullest things of all," as Erving Goffman put it.

Law office process relates—at least initially—to a lawyer's persona and role. Lawyers try to be lawyers. Lawyers groom themselves (in more than one sense) to be lawyers, rather than themselves. "In considering the individual's participation in social action," Goffman says, "we must understand that in a sense he does not participate as a total person but rather in terms of a special capacity or status; in short, in terms of special self." Law-office conversation illustrates both sides of this; here is an example of good manners in the law office. It is, in process terms, an example of deference on the part of lay clients to the chairmanship of their lawyer. Clients do not try to be themselves in law offices; they try to be clients. This occurred during a real-estate-closing conference in which both buyers, husband and wife (H & W), and seller (S) were present:

W: We gotta go home and get our things.

L: Yeah.   Yeah.

W: All that way, and—

L: Yeah.

W: It's too darned cold there now.

L: Where you from?

W: Decatur, Illinois.

L: Yeah.   That's sorta in my neck of the woods.   I come from Iowa originally.

W: Iowa.   That's right.   We've lived there about 45 years.

L: Come to the Sunny South, huh?

W: Yes.   We're not taking no more of that cold weather.   (Laughter.)

S: You'll love it down here.

W: Oh, I know.   We been down here—

S: The people are just marvelous.

L: Yes. They are.

S: You have no idea how marvelous they are.

W: No. Well, I have my—

L: Oh! I didn't—

W: Have my sister here.

L: I didn't finish—uh—my sentence with you there. In that you were asking how much the deposit would be.

S: Yes.

L: At ten per cent, it would be. . . .

And here is an example of bad manners in a law office, bad manners which suggest that there is much more to this three-cornered relationship than the words convey. A husband and wife are talking to a lawyer about wills:

L: My secretary has told me that you would like to discuss a will, so I sent you a small form to fill out. A couple of basic questions. Did you—uh—fill it out? Bring it with you?

H: Uh. I didn't fill it out because I didn't think you needed that information.

L: Didn't need it. You didn't think I'd need it.

H: I mean, what relevance does it have?

L: Well—really—

H: I mean, how much do you need for a will? My wife tells me we need a will. But do we really need a will?

L: Well, let's find out. Why don't you tell me something about yourself and your wife, and—uh—your background.

H: Go ahead, Mary. You're the one who wanted to come down here.

W: I think everybody needs a will—and I think he probably needs to know as much information as is relevant, if we really need a will.

H: Why?

L: Well, there's a certain amount of information that an attorney needs to know. . . .

At the process (or what the late Dr. Eric Berne called the ulterior) level, both of these transactions are rituals in which chairmanship is being worked out. In the first case, the clients accede to the lawyer's demand for control; in the second the husband challenges both the lawyer's control of the transaction and his wife's position in a transaction which should make apparent the husband's strong feelings (as yet undetermined as to nature and source).

Deference. Process in lawyer-client relationships involves questions of deference; Goffman points out that all human relationships involve deference. It is illustrated in daily transactions in the elevator, the dining room, the board room, the law-office waiting room, and the classroom. It reveals itself in the way people greet one another, the invitations—express and implicit—that they issue, the compliments they pay, and the minor services they render. If these daily rituals are, in process terms, symmetrical, what they say to the world is that the actors regard themselves as equals. If they are asymmetrical, they say that one actor is expected to defer to the other. Law-office deference rituals are usually asymmetrical. A client is not likely to address his lawyer by the lawyer's given name unless the lawyer indicates that this conduct is acceptable (and maybe not even then); certain territory in the office (behind the desk; in front of the filing cabinet) is restricted to occupancy by the lawyer; certain facilities are available only for his use (the telephone and intercom equipment, the dictating machine). The deferred-to member in a professional relationship usually has implicit permission to inquire into the private life of the deferring member, and the deferring member is expected to honor the inquiry. (See Exercise Six, in the Appendix.) Goffman says:

> To ask after an individual's health, his family's well-being, or the state of his affairs, is to present him with a sign of sympathetic concern; but in a certain way to make this presentation is to invade the individual's personal reserve, as will be made clear if an actor of wrong status asks him these questions, or if a recent event has made such a question painful to answer.

He gives several examples from a hospital. Physicians there, for instance, are permitted to touch patients (pat them on the back, grip their arms, etc.), but it is not usual for patients to touch doctors:

Medical doctors had the privilege of swearing, changing the topic of conversation, and sitting in undignified positions; attendants, on the other hand, had the right to attend staff meetings and to ask questions during them . . . but were implicitly expected to conduct themselves with greater circumspection than was required of doctors. . . . Similarly, doctors had the right to saunter into the nurses' station, lounge on the station's dispensing counter, and engage in joking with the nurses; other ranks participated in this informal interaction with doctors, but only after doctors had initiated it.

The lawyer in the property-closing conference, quoted above, behaved as the doctor at the nurses' station behaves; he directed the conversation away from the business at hand ("Where you from?") and then, seconds later, when the two clients began to talk to one another rather than to him, he ordered a return to business ("I didn't finish my sentence") and the clients respected the call to order.

Deference of this sort is illustrated in formal law-office rituals, such as will-execution conferences—where the lawyer acts as a master of ceremonies in a sort of liturgy (or as a judge) would act—and in informal ceremonies such as explicit directions to clients on which chair to sit in, and implicit directions on whether clients may cross their legs, smoke, or argue with what the lawyer says, and on whether male clients may take off their suit jackets. All of this behavior awaits stage directions from the lawyer; it often does not appear in the content of the transaction, but it always has a significant influence on the content.

Demeanor. A similar process occurs in matters of demeanor. Clients who work with their hands will normally put on "Sunday" clothes to come to a law office (but may not when they go to a physician's office); they will be at some pains to demonstrate—by the way they sit, the tone of voice they use, and the way they open and close doors—that they wish to show deference. Their behavior will indicate whether or not they wish to be thought of as comfortable in the lawyer's world or confused about it and therefore specially dependent on the lawyer to guide them. "Good demeanor is what is required of an actor if he is to be transformed into someone who can be relied upon to maintain himself as an interactant, poised for communication, and to act so that others do not endanger themselves by presenting themselves as interactants to him" (Goffman).

Openness. From the lawyer's side, signals indicating relative levels of openness to the client will determine the course of an hour in the law office or even of the entire professional relationship. If the lawyer says, "What is your problem?" he reduces his client to a thing. If the lawyer says, "What can I do for you?" he limits his client to the

client's preconceived idea of the range of the lawyer's usefulness. Here, by contrast, is the way
Carl Rogers greeted one of his clients:

R: Now, what I would like would be for you to
     tell me anything you're willing to tell me
     about yourself and your situation, how you
     feel about yourself. Or I guess another way
     of putting it is that anything you are willing
     to tell me that would help me to know you
     better, I'd be very glad to hear.

C: Where do you want me to start?

R: Wherever you would like to.

Many lawyers feel unprepared to begin the relationship on so broad a basis. But the psychotherapist's approach does illustrate, by way of contrast
to "What is your problem?" or "What can I do for
you?" an effort to be open to as much of the client's
person as the client is willing to bring into the
relationship. Another example from Carl Rogers's
practice illustrates an interpersonal expression of
his perception that the client came into his office
angry:

Do you look kind of angry this morning, or is
that just my imagination? (Client shakes head
but says nothing.) Not angry, huh? (Long silence.) I kind of feel like saying that, if it would
be of any help at all, I'd like to come in. On the
other hand if it's something you'd rather—if you
just feel more like being within yourself, feeling
whatever you're feeling within yourself, why,

that's okay too . . . . I guess another thing I'm saying, really, in saying that, is, "I do care. I'm not just sitting here like a stick."

Lawyers often attempt to fashion a similar communication of openness by beginning the conversation with small talk, or offering the client coffee. These are sometimes effective—that is, the client sometimes responds to them with relaxation and freedom—but the more direct way to go about this is to state simply an openness to whatever is on the client's mind. Here is a young lawyer who attempted to do that:

L: Come in.

C: Hi. Are you Mr. Harris?

L: Yes, I am. Have a seat.

C: Sit here?

L: Fine.

C: How are you today?

L: Fine. How are you?

C: Oh, good.

L: I would like to offer you coffee, but our new offices don't have a coffee machine yet.

C: No problem. I don't drink coffee anyway. So we're all set. Let me think a second.

L: Okay.

C: I came right from work and I have not had a chance to sit down and think about this.

L: Fine. I don't know anything about why
    you're here, but perhaps you can tell me a
    little about it, and a little about yourself.

A sadder example is the public defender, ap-
pointed to represent a juvenile offender, who first
met the client in an interview room at the jail.
These were her opening remarks:

L: Would you like to tell me about your past
    record? I have some notes here that you've
    been in trouble before. If you think there's
    anything that's relevant, and want to tell me
    what happened—

C: Yeah. I been in trouble. A lot of trouble.

L: What for?

This relationship was thus characterized, at the
beginning, as the relationship between a criminal
and a defender of criminals. The process, in these
few seconds, seems to make the lawyer say, "I have
no interest in you aside from the fact that you are
in trouble."

Of course, process shifts and changes. A poor
beginning does not limit the relationship forever—
or even for five minutes. And a good beginning
can narrow quickly, as it tends to do, for example,
when a lawyer receives "irrelevant" personal information from the client with indifference, or when
he rejects the client's curiosity about the lawyer as
a person. The relationship between lawyer and
client—the way they are together—warms and
cools, moves forward and regresses, opens and

closes constantly. The principal objective in learning to attend to process is to be aware of these shifts and changes and of their implications for professional service for helping the client and serving her interests. The objective, in a phrase, is to choose the process in lawyer-client relationships as consciously (and as self-consciously) as lawyers choose words in drafting instruments, or strategies in litigation. (See Exercise Two in the Appendix.)

INITIAL THREATS TO A WORKING RELATIONSHIP

It is comfortable to be one who helps others. It is comfortable to deal with other people who come seeking help, who are willing to pay for it, who admire our learning and composure, and who listen with respect to what we say about what we think. Helping is such a comfortable thing to do, in fact, that it may end up blocking awareness of the process that underlies the on-going interaction in the relationship.

Jack Gibb has a test for whether one's image of himself as a helper is useful to the client or harmful to him: Does the help lead to *growth* in the client? There is a chance that it may not, a chance illustrated by the array of motives within the helper, who may seek "to reduce his own guilt, obtain gratitude, make someone happy, or give meaning to his own life. He may wish to demonstrate his superior skill or knowledge, induce indebtedness, control others, establish dependency, punish others, or simply meet a job description."

The growth test would not ignore these things, but it would ask whether the client was becoming more helpless (more in need of a helper), "less able to make his own decisions or initiate his own actions, less self-sufficient, more apathetic and passive, less willing to take risks, more concerned about propriety and conformity, and less creative and venturesome." Gibb suggests that some orientations in the helper lead to creativity and growth, and some don't. Those that do, he notes, include reciprocal trust, cooperative learning, mutual growth (the helper also has a right to grow and helper traps will hold him back even more than they will hold the client back), reciprocal openness, shared problem-solving, freedom, and experimentation (which includes a willingness to be, of all things, playful). Orientations that retard growth include distrust, the need to teach the client a lesson, the need to evaluate and judge, gamesmanship in the relationship, coaching (molding, steering, controlling), and a disposition to pattern—to set standards. The question is: What is this client *becoming* because of me?

In terms of content, the object of a lawyer-client relationship is a mutually satisfactory resolution of the business that the client brings to the lawyer. In terms of process, the object is a healthy relationship between the lawyer and the client. Process affects content. As R. S. Hunt puts it, the "prob-

lem" orientation in the relationship is evaluated
(by lawyer, client, and others) in terms of whether
the client will follow the course of action that has
been worked out in the law office—whether he
will, as it is commonly put, "take the lawyer's
advice." That result depends on how the client
feels about the lawyer. Process also affects itself;
it affects the relationship. The way two persons in
the law office feel toward one another today affects
the way they will act toward one another next
week.

Both content and process are affected by process.
A significant and initial issue in law-office process
is the identification of dangers to the working
relationship. Identifying these dangers resembles
wariness about the Internal Revenue Code or the
rule against perpetuities when the lawyer is drafting a will; of wariness about due process of law
when defending someone accused of a crime. Two
principal dangers are identified in this section—
the danger of competition, and the danger of domineering paternalism.

Competition and domineering paternalism are
threats to the process of a working relationship.
Both are most likely to become serious when they
are ignored or neglected. Time and energy spent
in attending to them—in preventing them—are
time and energy spent in developing and protecting the working relationship itself. Neglect of
them is likely, at worst, to end in a bad professional result—advice the client will not follow, or a

decision by the client not to return for further legal assistance. At best, neglect of competition and domination is likely to lead to a crisis in the relationship that will cost more time, energy, and emotional stress to resolve than it would have cost to prevent their development in the first place. The point is illustrated by a favorite story of the late Dean Joseph O'Meara: A hiker came upon a man chopping wood. The hiker noticed that the chopper's ax was dull. He said to the chopper, "You should sharpen your ax." And the chopper said, "I can't. I have to chop all this wood."

What must be attended to are (1) our tendency, and the tendency of our clients, to adopt strategies of competition, rather than strategies of collaboration, in the law office; and (2) our tendency to invite dependence from clients, and clients' tendency to emotional reliance on us. Both forces are subtle. Each tends to destroy the working relationship.

Competition. Competition is built into law offices. Law-office interviews can be games that lawyers prepare in advance to win. The typical prosperous law office suite is an engine of one-upmanship, from decor to copies of Barrons and rooms lined with the English Reports. Some law offices are only a trifle more subtle than the chair Mr. Tutt kept for unwelcome visitors; it had an inch cut off each of the front legs. Lawyers meet people in coat and tie, sit behind massive desks in massive chairs, and barricade themselves with superior demeanors, yellow pads fourteen inches long, and gadgets such as computer terminals and "squawk box" telephones. Our heady language suggests that all communication is what Eric Berne would have called from parent to child. The atmosphere—the process in the atmosphere—is a mighty nonverbal claxon directed at clients: "SIT UP AND PAY ATTENTION; I'M IN CHARGE HERE."

Lawyers are trained in law school to be competitive; in fact we are selected, and we select ourselves for legal education, because of competitive talents. The educational atmosphere professors and students live in, and practicing lawyers are nostalgic about, is a jungle atmosphere—more of a jungle than the practice of law. Lawyers are people who need to win arguments; many of us have only one way to deal with our own internal conflict, our doubt, our hurt—and that way is to slug it out with somebody else.

The alternative is to learn non-competitive strategies, as a valid and important professional preparation for dealing with clients. What we have to be able to say, verbally and nonverbally, to clients is: "There is no need to compete in this office. I am your companion on a journey which I know to be strange and anxious for you. I will prove that I am your companion by being willing to tell you how I feel; I am going to try to take down the barriers that I and my law teachers and my colleagues in the practice have built between me and the people I care about." (See Exercise Three, in the Appendix.)

Dependence. A working relationship is as seriously threatened from the other direction, from dependence in the client. In response to client expectations and psychological needs, the attorney is often cast in a directive role. Feelings of dependence on the client's part may arise from a variety of factors: the client's expectation that the lawyer will step in and straighten things out; the client's attempt to avoid responsibility for making a decision; the client's expectation that the lawyer is able to manipulate the legal system or people in the client's world so as to achieve what the client desires; the client's inflated view of the legal profession; the client's low self-esteem or sense of failure; and, finally, the attorney's psychological need to occupy a dominant role in the interaction.

A lawyer cannot properly regard his client unless he can grant the client dignity and self-determination. The threat to counseling may be that the lawyer treats the client as a child, and the client treats the lawyer as a domineering parent. Psychiatry warns of a dangerous possibility here, in what it calls transference. The idea is that the client is reliving an emotional relationship from the past, and is casting his lawyer in an inappropriate role. The lawyer is being made to stand in for an important person in the client's life—typically, in the Freudian view of things, the client's tyrannical father. The result is a distorted dependence on the lawyer—not only the normal dependence common in people who think that lawyers know a lot, but a focused, emotional dependence. Critical choices and biases are then likely to come from the lawyer—or, rather, from the way in which the client regards the lawyer—rather than from the client. It is a well accepted tenet of Freudian psychology (one accepted by various "schools" of counseling) that this distortion in relationships is a common occurrence, that it happens in law offices, and that decisions apparently made by clients are in fact made by lawyers, because clients are too dependent on lawyers. It is likely that transference feelings are a significant feature of most lawyer-client relationships. (See Chapter Six.)

The lawyer's reaction to those client feelings that are the product of transference—of emotional distortion, in other words—either advances or retards the incipient dependence that occurs in most professional relationships. The lawyer's reaction, in other words, is critical. It is not possible not to react. Some lawyers may think they can say to clients, "Okay, whatever you want," but, as a matter of fact, they cannot. The lawyer has feelings, and his feelings are picked up by the client; they matter to the client, especially as the client moves toward emotional dependence. The client may not understand the lawyer's feelings accurately, but he will act as if he does. Lawyers tend, as everyone does, to feel moral disapproval, or rebellion, or panic, or a lack of control, or a need to protect the client from himself. The present point is that clients perceive and guess at these feelings and, often, conclude that they are more negative than they are. The lawyer's feelings, and the client's perception of them—or guesses at them—have everything to do with whether the dependence issue will be resolved in a productive way.

If the lawyer reacts as a domineering parent would react (or if the client believes that the lawyer is reacting that way)—with judgmental approval or disapproval—she will encourage dependence. Dependence will sometimes be expressed in submission (and a fantasy of rescue), sometimes in rebellion, but it will be dependence, however expressed. It will be a situation in which the client is being led to believe, or is leading himself to believe, that he is not old enough, not wise enough, to act for himself. He has to have a parent who will tell him what to do.

Dependence in those situations where the client abdicates to the lawyer decision-making responsibility sometimes plays what transactional therapy analysts call "rescue." Strong negative feelings develop from low self-esteem and dependency on the lawyer which give rise to a perception of helplessness and the need for a rescuer. The lawyer fits the role perfectly. In the language of transactional analysis: What some therapists have called "the victim's position" is "I'm not OK, you're OK (I am helpless and hopeless, try and help me)." The rescuer's position matches the victim's; "I'm OK, you're not OK (you are helpless and hopeless; nevertheless, I'll try to help you)."

Claude Steiner, a therapist who practices transactional analysis, explains the pleasures and danger of this rescue game. "No one enjoys being one-down, but it is pleasurable to let go and have others take over. One can let others take over for short periods of time without playing the game, especially if one has agreements to reverse the situation later on. The feeling of being a powerless victim, however, is hellish and is only made worse by rescuing. No matter how we feel, it is good to hear that we are not completely powerless; and it is energizing to be asked and expected to take our power and do our part by someone who is willing to help."

How should the attorney approach the client who has the victim's attitude? Carl Rogers points out that the natural tendency in such a situation is to try to convince the client that feelings of powerlessness and low self-esteem are exaggerated, and that there is no logical reason for him to feel that way. This attempt, however, may not be successful. "The client feels worthless, no matter how many good qualities may be objectively pointed out to him.. . . . The counselor is giving more genuine help if he assists the client to face these feelings openly, recognize them for what they are, and admit that he has them."

There is an alternative to the game of rescue and to other forms of client dependence. The alternative is to sort out the feelings involved, to discover with the client where the boundaries are between his feelings and the feelings of his lawyer. This requires that the lawyer level with the client about the *lawyer's* feelings. It requires honesty, self-awareness; genuineness (what Rogers calls *congruence*); and a level of openness that may be uncomfortable for the lawyer. But locating boundaries in the relationship is not a matter that can safely be left to the client's guesses. If, for example, the client's attitude toward his wife is something which annoys the lawyer, the lawyer would be best advised to express annoyance.

Another part of the alternative is to accept the client's feelings, whatever they are. The idea, put negatively, is that the lawyer refuses to be a judge. He can be annoyed without being a judge, and is in fact entitled to have his own feelings without having them draped in a judicial mantle. He says to the client, in effect: "I hear what you are saying; I understand your feelings, but I refuse to judge them, one way or another, because it is you who are important to me."

Nancy K. Schlossberg gives this example: A client says, "Sometimes I just get so depressed I don't know what to do." She hypothesizes four possible responses:

   1. Sometimes you feel like you're never going to get up again.

2. When was the last time this happened?

3. Everyone feels that way once in a while.

4. Well, you know it's a critical time for you.

She then evaluates these responses in terms of their process communication: "In the first exchange the [lawyer] reflected with accuracy the feelings and mood of the client by respecting the client's right to be frustrated. The second [lawyer] response raised a question that was irrelevant. In the third response, the [lawyer], rather than trying to get into the client's shoes, subtly undercut the client by minimizing the client's feelings. The fourth example is unfortunately typical of many advisers and helpers. They jump to conclusions, do not listen to or feel with the client. . . . Very few counselors [stick] to the goal of helping the client explore; very few [focus] on the feeling and content expressed by the . . . client." Very few, in other words, avoid dependence by efforts for a working relationship. A relationship in which the lawyer and client work together means a relationship in which each treats the other as a competent adult.

It sounds hard to be open and accepting at the same time, but that is what is required if one wants to avoid becoming the judge of his clients—if one wants to insist on maintaining a working relationship, on being a companion rather than a censor. The key to it, in Carl Rogers's phrase, is to enter into the client's world. To feel it as he feels it. It is a subtle and difficult skill; Rogers relates it to empathy. The empathic response to people is acceptance without judgment—what Rogers calls "unconditional positive regard"—and an affirmation of the client's dignity and ability to choose for himself. (See Exercises Eight and Nine, in the Appendix.)

In addition to facing the client's (and our own) need for dependence (and feelings of powerlessness), the attorney is in a position—by virtue of professional status, knowledge of the legal process, and previous experience with clients—to function in a strong supportive role towards the client. Support is not the same as parental approval. Support is a matter of saying, as advocates have always said, "I am on your side; my knowledge, and what I can do, are on your side. You are not alone." Attorneys should consider support as an integral and specific part of the lawyer's "helping" function, especially for clients in crisis. A strong supportive stance is what advocacy is all about. It is not always appropriate, but, when it is, it helps reduce debilitating anxiety for clients and the discomfort of dealing with a professional and the legal system.

CONTINUING THREATS TO A WORKING RELATIONSHIP: PROJECTION AND TRANSFERENCE

One way to live with ourselves, and those aspects of self that we find unacceptable, is to see in others what we cannot see in ourselves. Unable to tolerate the possibility of our own weakness, vulnerability, fear, we see these things in others. It is comforting to find you crabby when it is I who am crabby. Freudians (and psychologists from other schools of counseling) call this ego defense *projection*. Projection is common in those relations in which we stand, psychologically, as if we were relating to a parent. Strong negative or positive feelings for a parent are transferred, projected onto the person of the lawyer, the judge, the client. The root meaning of projection is "casting out" or projecting from self to others. Psychology regards the maneuver as defensive, as an unconscious process by which the ego defends the conscious self.

A similar process, and another way that the ego protects the conscious self, is in the displacement of feelings. For example, hostility toward one partner in the firm can be displaced and expressed against another. The experience of frustration in the office is directed toward one's spouse who had no part in producing the frustration. The feelings that a client has for her lawyer can be displaced from feelings she has for her husband. Displacement is defensive, as are projections; by displacing feelings a person may avoid confronting in a realistic way relationships with significant people in her life.

By bringing together these two ways that the ego works to defend itself—projection and displacement—we can begin to understand the psychology of a professional relationship that gives rise to strong feelings of attachment and anger. These

feelings are often a product not of the ongoing
interaction but an unconscious psychological need
that lies outside the immediate relationship.
Freud called this phenomenon *transference* (the
strong feelings of the client for the helper). (The
name *countertransference* is given to the strong
feelings of the helper for the client).

Transference is not limited to psychotherapeutic
relationships. It may occur in any relationship in
which one person becomes dependent on another,
or where one person in a relationship is viewed as
an authority figure (one to be accepted or rejected).
Andrew S. Watson suggests that transference is an
essential "tool" in the relationship between lawyer
and client. Transference is, he says, an "ubiquitous phenomenon"; lawyers who bother to understand the phenomenon "can profit immensely."
He quotes the late Justice Abe Fortas and sociologist Talcott Parsons in support of the proposition
that transference and countertransference are
commonplace in law office, client-attorney relationships and often develop between young lawyers
and senior partners. "The capacity to accept the
possibility that one's feelings about another may be
due to unconscious and unrealistic coloring rather
than to the other's reality traits," he says, "is a
major step toward understanding relations among
lawyers and in lawyer-client encounters."

Jung spoke of this with a characteristic avuncu-
lar chuckle, but he had important words to say to
lawyers about transference:

So, if a patient [client] projects the saviour complex into you, for instance, you have to give back to him nothing less than a saviour. . . .

So he [the professional] begins to feel, "If there are saviours, well, perhaps it is just possible that I am one," and he will fall for it, at first hesitantly, and then it will become more and more plain to him that he really is a sort of extraordinary individual.

Transference is likely to exist in any professional relationship in which rapport has been attempted and dependence permitted (or required); one psychiatrist even attempted to gauge transference between students and their teachers in an engineering class.

Transference and countertransference are pervasive in everyday living, especially in "helping" relationships. But professional helpers are given little opportunity in the course of their training to work out principles of relatedness (attachment, dependence, authority, awe, disgust) in their interaction with those they help. The problem of "relatedness," however, is present everywhere. "Early experiences in interpersonal relatedness," Frieda Fromm-Reichmann said, "affect . . . later relationships with [a] family doctor, dentist, minister, etc. Even the mere anticipation of consulting any kind of qualified helper . . . may pave the way for the development of transference reactions." She added that "as a result, present-day persons and interpersonal situations will be misjudged, incorrectly evaluated, and . . . distorted along the lines of the patients' unrevised, early, dissociated experiences." "The transference itself," Jung said, "is a perfectly natural phenomenon which does not by any means happen only in the consulting room—it can be seen everywhere and may lead to all sorts of nonsense. . . ."

Transference is treated in one fashion or another in all schools of psychotherapy and is fundamental in Freudian psychoanalysis and Jungian analytical psychology. Carl Rogers reports similar discoveries about transference in counseling. Rogers believes that transference in his "client-centered therapy" develops to some extent in almost all cases. In each situation, he sees four indications that transference is present: (1) "a desire for dependence upon the counselor, accompanied by deep affect [feeling]"; (2) "fear of the counselor, which is . . . related to fear of parents"; (3) "attitudes of hostility . . . beyond the attitudes . . . realistically related to the experience"; and (4) "expressions of affection, and a desire for a love relationship."

Rogers believes that the milder—and more common—transference disappears as the client is led to rely on his own judgment rather than that of his counselor. He reports the case of a young woman who wanted to drop her sessions with her therapist because of a dream:

I was up for trial, and you were the judge. . . . I didn't see how I could come back into the situation. I mean the circumstances, you already judged me, and therefore I didn't really see how I could possibly talk any more. . . . I suppose in my own way I was judging myself.

In the process of talking about the dream, Rogers believes, this woman came to see that she was projecting her assessment of herself. She was seeing in Rogers a disapproval which did not come from him, but from her. She was doing that because Rogers had come to occupy a parental position in her feelings. The source of disapproval was parental disapproval within herself (and that may have come from her parents). She came to understand, Rogers reports, that she was capable of recognizing that there were other "sensory evidences" that she had not admitted into consciousness, or had admitted but interpreted inaccurately. When this happens:

the "transference attitudes" . . . simply disappear because experience has been reperceived in a way which makes them meaningless. It is analogous to the way in which one attitude drops out and another entirely different one takes its place when I turn to watch the large plane I have dimly glimpsed out of the corner of my eye, and find it to be a gnat flying by a few inches from my face.

C. G. Jung's treatment of transference is at the center of his view of psychology and psychotherapy. Jung regarded transference as a natural phenomenon, rather than a manipulative device to be used by the analyst. When it occurs, he said, it poses a delicate and sometimes insurmountable obstacle to the physician:

> What seems to be so easily won by the transfer-
> ence always turns out in the end to be a loss; for
> a patient who gets rid of a system [of symptoms]
> by transferring it to the analyst always makes
> the analyst the guarantor of this miracle and so
> binds himself to him more closely than ever.

Jung seems to be fundamentally at odds with Freud, who viewed psychoanalytic treatment of the "transference neurosis" as the central task of the psychoanalyst and the focal point of healing in the psychoanalytic relationship. Moreover, mental disorders that interfere with the formation of the "transference neurosis" were, in Freud's view, un-suitable "to a greater or lesser extent" for psycho-analysis (a view that has been modified in recent developments in psychoanalytic theory). This idea leads the Freudian and his patient to work for transference, a venture Jung believed to be futile: "Transference is only another word for 'projection.' No one can voluntarily make projections, they just happen. They are illusions which merely make the treatment more difficult." When transference does occur it is delicate, time-consuming, and not easily or methodically erased. Jung's insight is valuable for the lawyer who is often puzzled over the way clients seem to become "hung up" on him. Jung would say the "hang-up" is the most natural thing in the world.

Psychotherapeutic relations rest, in Jung's view, on a rapport which is coextensive with transference, although his discussion suggests that transference overwhelms rapport. Transference, when it occurs, is a projection; and projections are dissociative—they are unintegrated bits of the personality wrongly seen as belonging outside the self. The cure for them is integration—individuation—and this involves two or three features that are noteworthy for present purposes. First, honest rapport minimizes transference:

> The transference is the patient's attempt to get into psychological rapport with the doctor. He needs this relationship if he is to overcome the dissociation. The feebler the rapport . . . the more intensely will the transference be fostered and the more sexual will be its form.

Another feature is that the physician's personality is unavoidably involved in the transference. The very survival of the patient may depend on "the doctor's knowledge, like a flickering lamp . . . the one dim light in the darkness." The physician then has an opportunity to lead his patient to the integration of personality—"[n]o longer a mere selection of suitable fictions, but a string of hard facts, which together make up the cross we all have to carry or the fate we ourselves are." This idea is central:

> So long as the patient can think that somebody else (his father or mother) is responsible for his difficulties, he can save some semblance of uni-

ty. . . . But once he realizes that he himself
has a shadow, that his enemy is in his own heart,
then the conflict begins and one becomes two.
Since the "other" will eventually prove to be yet
another duality, a compound of opposites, the ego
soon becomes a shuttlecock tossed between a mul-
titude of "velleities," with the result that there is
an obfuscation of the light, i.e., consciousness is
depotentiated and the patient is at a loss to know
where his personality begins or ends.

But Jung is at some pains to make it clear that
this "therapeutic," helping process is not a matter
of manipulation; it is the result of dealing honestly
with the client.

Both Freud and Jung took account of the sexual
element of transference and countertransference.
Freud linked it to the infantile Oedipus complex,
the child's desire to replace his father in his mother's life. Transference to a female therapist by a
male patient would therefore involve these sexual
feelings. (Not all modern Freudians would agree.)
Jung thought that the projection was fundamentally of the contrasexual element within the patient
himself. A man tends to project the female within
him—the anima. In childhood he has made this
projection on his mother and sisters; he later
projects it on other women, but it often retains a
certain incestuous character. (He also projects
homo-erotic feelings from within himself on his
father, his brothers, his male physician.) This
anima projection in its purest form involves the

incest taboo; but it affords also the therapeutic opportunity for a "spiritual marriage" in which the projected and unprojected elements of the patient's personality are integrated into a renewed, conscious self. This process, insofar as it is therapeutic, is a process that needs some substitute for the biological unity of the family—"family" here in the sense of ancient, archetypal "kinship." An important insight of Jung's is that the sexual element in transference is archetypal—that is, rooted in the "collective unconscious" we all share. His idea was that integration (cure) takes place in a human association that is libidinal but not sexual. That idea is complex—almost mystical—but it is obviously central to what Jung says about transference in everyday life:

> Everyone is now a stranger among strangers. Kinship libido . . . has long been deprived of its object. But, being an instinct, it is not to be satisfied by any mere substitute such as a creed, party, nation, or state. It wants the human connection. That is the core of the whole transference phenomenon, and it is impossible to argue it away, because relationship to the self is at once relationship to our fellow man, and no one can be related to the latter until he is related to himself.

Jung used a medieval book on alchemy to explain transference. He built his explanation around woodcuts that illustrated the conjunction between symbolic, mythical male and female figures. His theory was that transference involves the projection of contrasexual contents (the anima of a man, the animus of a woman) in the unconscious of the transferring person. Although he did not confine transference to this sort of projection—it was possible, he said, to have a transference even onto inanimate objects—it is clear that the Jungian prototype of transference is contrasexual.

Freud's view of transference, in contrast to Jung's, was tied to his view of the Oedipus complex. Feelings transferred by the patient originated in competition between the patient and his father for the love of the patient's mother—a necessarily contrasexual relationship.

It is possible to exaggerate the importance of the sexual element in transference. Fromm-Reichmann appears to disagree with Freud's view on the Oedipus complex in transference; she regards the affective, or feeling element, in the transference as a "wish for closeness and tenderness with the beloved parent . . . without recognizable sexual roots," and attributes the apparently contrasexual character of transference to the fact that people in our culture find it easier to talk about sex than about "friendly, tender, asexually loving aspects of . . . interpersonal relationships." However, the evidence for some contrasexual tendency in transference is at least strong enough to justify seeking a parallel between clinical experience with the phenomenon and the incidence of contrasexual transference in the law office.

* * *

Transference relationships may become exceptionally strong. Examples from Freud and Jung illustrate the point. Freud's case involved a Herr P who had developed a strong positive transference for Freud. Freud had decided he could not help Herr P and had told him so, but Herr P wanted to continue therapy for some few weeks until his duties at a university began. Freud agreed, although he recognized that his only link to the patient was that Herr P "felt comfortable in a well-tempered father-transference to me," and that this indefinite arrangement was "in disregard of the strict rules of medical practice." The relationship became so intense that the patient seemed to know facts—most notably the name of a foreign visitor to Freud's office—which were, objectively, hidden from him. Freud was tempted to believe that the relationship between him and Herr P caused a transfer of thought.

Jung's examples are even more candid; one of them involved Freud, older than Jung, with whom Jung had a strong father-son relationship, which Freud also experienced. Before Jung's break with Freud, Jung had a dream that signaled to him their forthcoming break and that represented both aspects of the ambivalent transference relationship:

He still meant to me a superior personality, upon whom I had projected the father, and at the time of the dream this projection was still far from eliminated. Where such a projection occurs, we are no longer objective; we persist in a state of divided judgment. On the one hand we are dependent, and on the other we have resistances. When the dream took place I still thought highly of Freud, but at the same time I was critical of him. This divided attitude is a sign that I was still unconscious of the situation and had not come to any resolution of it. This is characteristic of all projections.

Jung cited another example in explanation of parapsychological phenomena. A patient, with whom Jung had formed a strong transference, was progressing toward cure when he discovered that his wife resented Jung. In the face of stress between wife and surrogate father the patient relapsed into depression. One night Jung was awakened as if someone were in his room. While awake he felt a dull pain at the back of his skull. The next day he learned that his patient had shot himself in the head, at the time of Jung's experience. "The collective unconscious is common to all," Jung said of this experience. "It is the foundation of what the ancients call the 'empathy of all things.' In this case the unconscious had knowledge of the patient's condition."

BIBLIOGRAPHY

What we have called conversation, the talking and listening of lawyers and clients in law offices, others describe in more formal, academic terms as *communication.* One of the ways we assess the health of a relationship, and the way we see failure in working relationships, is in patterns of communication, the relational climate (the "felt experience") created by the way talking and listening takes place. See Patton and Giffin, Interpersonal Communication in Action: Basic Text and Readings (1980); Watzlawick, The Language of Change: Elements of Therapeutic Communication (1978); Smith and Nester, "Lawyers, Clients, and Communication Skill," 1977 Brigham Young University Law Review 275; Ruesch, Disturbed Communication (1972); Probert, Law, Language and Communication (1972); Sacks, "Talking with Clients," Student Lawyer Journal (December, 1967); The Human Dialogue: Perspectives on Communication (Matson and Montagu eds. 1967); Ruesch, Therapeutic Communication (1961).

Studies of how language works in therapy: Havens, Making Contact: Uses of Language in Psychotherapy (1986); Bandler and Grinder, The Structure of Magic (Volume I, 1975; Volume II, 1976).

The literature on human relationships is extensive. We have found useful: Brammer, The Helping Relationship: Process and Skills (1985); Johnson, Reaching Out: Interpersonal Effectiveness and Self-Actualization (2nd ed. 1981); Cassell, The Healer's Art: A New Approach to the Doctor-Patient Relationship (Penguin, 1979) (about our physician colleagues but richly suggestive for lawyers); Perlman, Relationship: The Heart of Helping People (1979); McCall and Simmons, Identities and Interactions (1978); Dyer, The Sensitive Manipulator (1972); Schlossberg, "Liberated Counseling: A Question Mark," Journal of N.A.W.D.A.C., Fall 1974, p. 3; Spelman, "On Treating Persons as Persons," 88 Ethics 150 (1978); Satir, Making Contact (1976).

The counseling relationship, viewed from a professional and psychological perspective, is surveyed in Sharma, The Therapeutic Dialogue: A Theoretical and Practical Guide to Psychotherapy (1986); Hobson, Forms of Feeling: The Heart of Psychotherapy (1985); Weinberg, The Heart of Psychotherapy: A Journey into the Mind and Office of the Therapist at Work (1984); Nelson-Jones, The Theory and Practice of Counseling Psychology (1984); Carkhuff and Berenson, Beyond Counseling and Therapy (1977); Upham, Ego Analysis in the Helping Professions (1973); and Rogers, Counseling and Psychotherapy (1942).

For a broader perspective on the counseling relationship see, Dass and Gorman, How Can I Help? (1985); Awakening the Heart: East/West Approaches to Psychotherapy and the Healing Relationship (Welwood ed. 1983); May, Psychology and the Human Dilemma (1980); Mayeroff, On Caring (Perennial Library ed. 1972).

Power and authority are working elements of every professional relationship. They are also elements of professional encounters that create an initial and continuing threat to a working relationship. Power and authority in human relations are explored in Steiner, The Other Side of Power (1981); Sennett, Authority (1980); Guggenbuhl-Craig, Power in the Helping Professions (1978); Kipnis, The Powerholders (1976); Sampson, The Psychology of Power (Vintage, 1968); and Lasswell, Power and Personality (Viking Compass, 1962).

REFERENCES

Appel and Van Atta, "The Attorney-Client Dyad: An Outsider's View," 22 Oklahoma Law Review 243 (1969); Berne, Transactional Analysis in Psychotherapy (1961), and Games People Play (1967); Church, "Counselor-at-Law: A Game of Chess?" Trial, Sept.-Oct. 1972, p. 271, and "People Come to Lawyers Wanting a Good Parent, Magical Bodyguard, and Political Ally with Muscle," Student Lawyer, Dec. 1973, p. 10; Freud, Dora: Analysis of a Case of Hysteria (Collier ed. 1963); Fromm-Reichmann, Principles of Intensive Psychotherapy (Phoenix ed. 1951); Goffman, "The Nature of Deference and Demeanor," 58 American Anthropologist 453 (1956); Hunt, "Problems and Processes in the Legal Interview," 50 Illinois Bar Journal 726 (1962); Jung, The Psychology of the Transference in the Practice of Psychotherapy, in 16 Collected Works (Bollingen, 2nd ed. 1966), and Analytical Psychology (1968); Rogers, Client-Centered Therapy (1951), and On Becoming a Person (1961); Steiner, Scripts People Live: Transactional Analysis of Life Scripts (Bantam, 1975).

CHAPTER FIVE

GETTING THE FACTS (INTERVIEWING)

FACTS: LAW–OFFICE FACTS AND LITIGATION FACTS

Neat packages of fact are a predicate for problem-solving by lawyers. Law students learn to state facts in a sentence or two, almost as soon as they enter law school. Facts are stated concisely at the beginning of case briefs for study, on the first pages of briefs in litigation, as the opening paragraphs in appellate opinions, and at the beginning of examination answers.

Facts in law-office practice are similar. Lawyers in law offices need to find out the objective dimensions of their clients' situations, in order to help the clients, or to help the clients help themselves, just as lawyers in litigation need to learn the facts required by the logic of litigation, or appellate judges, whose function in government it is to consider, shape, and proclaim legal doctrine, need to learn the facts required by the logic of policy.

There are three critical differences between fact-finding in litigation or policy making and fact-finding in the law office:

1. *Relevance.* Relevance in litigation is expressed, more or less, in the rules of evidence.

Rules of evidence (and of pleading) are political limitations on the operation of the law in courts. (Courts are part of the government; law offices are not.) Feelings and perceptions are usually excluded from proof in litigation—so that statements that begin "I feel" or "I think" are not proper in courts, and statements which begin "I saw," "I heard," or "I smelled" are proper there. Relevance in law offices is not bounded by external politics; if political considerations limit what is said there, they are political considerations imposed not by the law but by lawyers. (See Exercise Three, in the Appendix.)

2. *Malleability.* Louis M. Brown refers to facts in law offices as "hot facts." Judge-made law turns on "cold facts," that is, facts as historical. (This is true only more or less; facts in judge-made law are also made as they are presented, as they are embodied in stories.) Or, as Brown puts it, law follows facts in judge-made law; facts follow law in office-made law. An example occurs early in the movie "Anatomy of a Murder," when the defense lawyer (James Stewart) sees his client for the first time (in jail) and tells the client he does not want to hear the "facts" until the client has an opportunity to consider the law of temporary insanity. The novel gives an example of fraudulent use of the principle of hot facts. Office practice abounds with more righteous examples. Whether a contract or declaration of trust is oral or written, for example, makes a legal difference. That fact is within the client's control in the law office; it is

beyond control—is a cold fact—once litigation is brought on the contract or the trust.

3. *Organization.* Facts in litigation come when they are supposed to—at the beginning of a brief, oral argument, or judicial opinion, or with controlled precision during an evidentiary hearing. Facts, which are considered relatively unimportant, precede discussion of law or policy in law-school classes. Facts in law offices, however, come when they are ready to come. Forceful attempts to elicit them by directive questions and limiting their production to a limited time-frame are likely to frustrate the client and reduce the amount of information that will become available. If decisions and plans are formulated too quickly in the office, facts that appear later, during the processes of decision and planning, may render useless all of the lawyer's clever work at collaboration and invention.

FACT GATHERING

One of the tasks for a lawyer working with a client is to get enough facts to form an accurate picture of the client's situation, facts as the client sees them and facts that the lawyer helps the client to see. The manner in which the attorney gets the facts sets the "personal climate," the tone and structure of the relationship, and is a central feature of the working agreement (most often implicit) on how things will proceed. In terms of the breadth and depth—the adequacy—of the information the attorney gathers, success depends on a number of aspects of content and process:

—the attorney's general approach, his "bedside manner";

—the client's initial impression of the attorney and of the place where they work together;

—the initial feelings the two people have for one another (and this usually includes who they remind one another of);

—the manner in which the attorney goes after information;

—the attorney's perception of the facts as the client begins to provide them;

—the client's expectations and images concerning the law;

—the attorney's understanding of the client's concerns as these are placed in their broader context (the client's story and the story of how the client sees the world); and

—theories and models used by the attorney to explain the client's behavior—both the behavior the client talks about and the behavior he engages in in the law office. (See Chapter Six.)

Analysis of these factors presents us with the essence of fact-gathering by lawyers, an essence that goes beyond and underneath facts that are, in casebook terms, relevant or irrelevant.

Lawyers by habit seek "relevant" facts. We are influenced by the model of directive interrogation in trials and depositions. Relevance here means related to legal doctrine: Lawyers want facts that are relevant to legal problems and are not concerned with facts relevant to the client's feelings. The trial lawyer forcefully guides the client's (witness's) responses with direct questions designed to elicit the facts needed for producing a legal result.

This trial-lawyer approach to fact-gathering as the primary task in interviewing is one aspect of a powerful, traditional professional model of the attorney-client relationship: The client talks and the attorney gathers the facts. When the lawyer talks it is to tell the client about the law and how the law regards the facts presented. It is this emphasis upon fact relevance and the attorney's rational, logical, analytical approach to problem-solving that focuses on legal issues and legal determinations and eschews client feelings. The detachment (what traditional lawyers call professionalism) does not provide a relationship in which a client's *emotions* are recognized as facts. The traditional model of lawyering requires that both lawyer and client keep their eyes on facts that fit legal doctrine. Other facts are not important; they are not even facts.

The most serious drawback of this approach to "facts" is that it does not allow for the expression of client and attorney feelings, feelings present in every relationship, including those between clients and attorneys. A relationship in which feelings are valued—that is, any human relationship worthy of the name—is dependent upon each person's understanding that feelings *are* facts. To understand that feelings are facts is to understand that feelings are guides to behavior; even feelings that appear to be irrational—the most "irrelevant" fact of all—are a form of communication. For example, the client may confront the attorney with an accusation that the attorney has not pursued his case vigorously or has not worked to negotiate a favorable settlement (an accusation which, if true, presents a moral problem as well as a counseling issue). A client may obstinately adhere to unreasonable demands or vehemently attack the attorney. The client may react angrily or seek to dismiss the attorney with little or no provocation. In each of these cases the client is saying something, something that probably relates to the legal work that is being done for the client.

THE KINSEY MODEL

Alfred C. Kinsey's Sexual Behavior in the Human Male (1948), an elaborate analysis of 12,000 interviews about the sex lives of American men, was a shocking book. When the book appeared, the elder author of this book was a serious Baptist boy in a small western town; he did not read Kinsey's book or know anyone who did. But there were newspaper stories about it. And when he returns (or turns) to it many years later, he finds in its second chapter a remarkable treatise on interviewing.

There is something to be learned from the methods of Kinsey and his little-known co-authors Pomeroy and Martin, who arranged to have thousands of men and (for a second book) women talk to them for hours about the most intimate, taboo, shocking, shameful corners of their private lives. The Kinsey researchers conquered a formidable set of obstacles to communication (more formidable then, by the way, than they would be now) to gather their information. Their methods and their results bear on the human activity in which one person is attempting to elicit information from another.

Interviewee as Helper. The most fundamental fact about the Kinsey style, a fact relevant for lawyers, is that Kinsey asked people to help him. He did not pay them for their information; they talked to him readily and for free. It is radical but nonetheless valid to suggest to legal counselors that they ask their clients for help—that they treat the legal interview as a process in which they *seek help* rather than give it.

Some lawyers would reject the analogy, but let us ask these lawyers: What would it cost you? What would happen if you approached legal interviewing that way? Theoretically the idea is sound. The object of an interview is information. The most important means to information is cooperation from the person who possesses information. Alfred C. Kinsey was a magnificent garnerer of information.

Kinsey's interviewing and his ability to get people to help him were premised on the regard he expressed for those he asked to help him; not only did he respect these people, he was fond of them:

Learning how to meet people of all ranks and levels, establishing rapport, sympathetically comprehending the significances of things as others view them, learning to accept their attitudes and activities without moral, social, or esthetic evaluation, being interested in people as they are and not as someone else would have them, learning to see the reasonable bases of what at first glance may appear to be most unreasonable behavior, developing a capacity to like all kinds of people and thus to win their esteem and cooperation—these are the elements to be mastered by one who would gather human statistics.

Notice that this call to humanism in behavioral science did not come from a psychologist. Kinsey was a professor of zoology. Notice, also, that "legal issues" are to law-office interviewing as "statistics" are to social research. Lawyers learn to take facts for granted—including human facts—and to "get to the issue," just as research-oriented psychologists learn to ignore the people they're talking to and to concentrate instead on statistically manipulable data.

Affection. Kinsey believed he was successful, but he admits to a sense of wonder, a feeling that no amount of theory on interviewing can quite explain his success: "We are not sure that we completely comprehend why people have been willing to talk to us." Encountering another person was, Kinsey said, a drama. That is a touching observation, from a man who was otherwise (his colleagues report) incredibly single-minded about his purposes. Kinsey attributed his success in this dramatic encounter to his own honesty. He made his purposes clear. Once he communicated his own need (a need, remember, for astounding information) and his own integrity, people wanted to help him. Many of his interviewees—especially the relatively simple and ignorant among them—required, he said, "only a gesture of honest friendship." He gives an example:

> The little gray-haired woman at the cabin door, out on the Western plain, epitomized what we have heard now from hundreds of people: "Of all things—! In all my years I have never had such a question put to me! But—if my experience will help, I'll give it to you." This, in many forms, some of them simple, some of them sophisticated as scientists and scholars like them, some of them crude, incisive, and abrupt as the underworld makes them, is the expression of the altruistic bent (however philosophers and scientists may analyze it) which has been the chief motive leading people to cooperate in this study.

Pay-off. However, Kinsey said, some pay-off for the interviewee—particularly when the subject could obtain from Kinsey information about sex in general and how the interviewee's behavior compared with the norm—increased the spirit of cooperation. The information factor should be added to consideration of how lawyers go about conducting interviews. The lawyer interviewer wants to learn and is willing to help; the client interviewee wants to explain and is seeking help. Payoff is involved in their two-way experience of being helpful: The interviewee also cooperates for altruistic pay-off, the good feeling that comes from cooperation, and he cooperates because he has trust in the competence of the interviewer-advisor.

Trust. Kinsey's techniques were quaintly conventional. He seems almost to have acted without calculation—he was, apparently, a gentle, kind man—and elevated his behavior to the level of technique only when he sat down to write about it. In building rapport, for example, he said the key factors were acceptance and trust: "It is imperative . . . that the investigator be able to convince the subject . . . that he . . . offers no objection to any type of sexual behavior in which the subject could possibly have been involved, [and] that the confidences . . . will be kept without question." Kinsey was obviously adept at convincing people that he was not judging them, and at demonstrating somehow that he could be trusted. How did he do it?

Meaning. The technique he mentions most prominently is a negative one. He said he avoided "cold objectivity." He said he could not achieve rapport of any sort with his interviewee unless he managed first to convince the interviewee that he was "desperately anxious to comprehend what this experience meant to him." It is important to notice that he did not say what the experience *was,* but what the experience *meant.* Notice that that fact would be "irrelevant" in litigation or in a law-school case book, but that Kinsey considered it fundamental to getting the information he wanted. Kinsey said this quest for meaning was necessary because the information he sought involved—as law-office information usually does—hurt, frustration, pain, unsatisfied longing, disappointment, tragedy, and even catastrophe. Presumably—one hopes—it also involved joy, victory, achievement, and happiness. The point is that these human victories and defeats are important to the client; he will not hand them over as readily as he puts coins in the subway turnstile. "The subject feels that the investigator who asks merely routine questions has no right to know about such things. . . . The interviewer who senses what these things can mean, who at least momentarily shares something of the satisfaction, pain, or bewilderment which was the subject's, who shares something of the subject's hope that things will, somehow, work out right, is more effective, though he may not be altogether neutral."

Neutrality (or objectivity, or detachment, or professionalism) is, in any case, impossible. It is a pose. Kinsey emphasized a point made throughout this book—that it is impossible to hide one's reaction to clients. "Reactions . . . are . . . readily comprehended by most people. A minute change of a facial expression, a slight tensing of a muscle, the flick of an eye, a trace of a change in one's voice, a slight inflection or change in emphasis, slight changes in one's rate of speaking, slight hesitancies . . . one's choice of words . . . or any of a dozen and one other involuntary reactions betray the interviewer's emotions and most subjects quickly understand them."

The client comes to the lawyer to find something he needs, and that something is fundamental to the interpersonal communication that makes fact-finding possible. Kinsey's point is that clarity in the lawyer's reactions has everything to do with this preliminary agenda in the interview. "If his [interviewer's] reactions add up right, then the subject is willing to tell his story. The interview has become an opportunity for him to develop his own thinking, to express his own disappointments and hopes, to bring into the open things that he has previously been afraid to admit to himself, to work out solutions to his difficulties."

Presence. However much Kinsey explains it, the impression remains that, for him, no amount of *technique* was sufficient. His success was the art of being fully and manifestly present to the interviewee. Another clue, which he only hinted at in his chapter on interviewing, was mutuality. Kinsey was trusted by his subjects and he also trusted them: "The interviewer should be as interested in the subject as he is in recording the subject's history. It is important to look the subject in the eye. . . . People understand each other when they look directly at each other."

Technical Devices. Kinsey also directed attention to a number of what he called "technical devices." This chapter will turn later to devices in interviewing, but an examination here of Kinsey's catalogue may explain how his interviewers preserved the rapport that their trust of research subjects had established.

It was important, Kinsey said, "to put the subject at ease." He did this, apparently, without calculation: "One does the sort of things a thoughtful host would do to make his guests comfortable." It was also important to assure privacy and to avoid interruptions. He recoiled with old fashioned moral condemnation from the dehumanizing interview he had once seen between a prisoner and a psychiatrist—"in a small room in which half a dozen persons were continually moving about and listening."

Kinsey looked carefully at the smallest details of how he asked questions. Several aspects of this art seem useful for legal interviewers—especially when you consider that lawyers, spurred by the image of Perry Mason bullying people on the witness stand, and trained in a Socratic classroom atmosphere (Professor Kingsfield of The Paper Chase), are inveterate question-askers.

Kinsey emphasized that the question, if used at all, should be adapted to the interviewee:

> Standardized questions do not bring standardized answers, for the same question means different things to different people. In order to have questions mean the same thing to different people, they must be modified to fit the vocabulary, the educational background, and the comprehension of each subject. It is especially important to use a vocabulary with which the subject will feel at home, and which he will understand. The college-bred interviewer needs to go to considerable pains to limit his vocabulary to the relatively few words that are employed by persons in lower educational levels. Everyday terms . . . are involved: an individual [may, in his words] never [be] ill or injured, though he may be sick or hurt. He does not wish to do a thing, though he wants to do it. He does not perceive, though he sees. He is not acquainted with a person, though he may know him.

Kinsey found, in a telling instance of this, that using the sexual vernacular when he interviewed pimps and prostitutes led to information and that failure to do so left the interviewer with almost nothing. This point involves an understanding of cultural context and vocabulary at a fairly earthy level:

> It is particularly important that the interviewer understand . . . the sexual viewpoint of the culture to which each of his subjects belong. For

instance, it is impossible to get any number of histories from prostitutes, female or male, unless they realize that the interviewer understands both the sexual situations involved in prostitution, and the social organization of a prostitute's life. A single phrase from an understanding interviewer is often sufficient to make the subject understand this, and such an interviewer wins a record where none would have been disclosed to the uneducated investigator.

With some trust in the present reader's ability to translate Kinsey's vivid experience, here is a telling example:

One starts by asking the [prostitute] how old she was when she turned her first trick (but one does not ask how old she was when she was first paid as a prostitute). She is then asked how many of the tricks return after their first contacts with her. Considerably later in the interview there is a question concerning the frequency with which she rolls her tricks (robs her customers). The [prostitute] who reports that few of the men ever return, and who subsequently says that she never robs any of the men, needs to be . . . assured that you know that it doesn't work that way. If she doesn't roll any of the men, why don't they return to her? This question is likely to bring a smile . . . and an admission that since you appear to know how these things work, she will tell you the whole story, which means that she robs every time there is any possibility of successfully doing so.

Part of this is a demeanor that does not tele-graph the answer one expects to get. Kinsey found—and several studies of legal interviewing have found—that open-ended interview questions produce the fullest answers; precise, non-leading questions produce less information; and "cross-examination" produces still less.

Kinsey warns against being evasive on tender topics. (And who should know better about tender topics?)

Euphemisms should not be used as substitutes for franker terms. In some of the previous stud-ies, many sexual terms are avoided: masturba-tion becomes "touching yourself" . . . and sexu-al intercourse becomes "relations with other persons," or "sex delinquency". . . . With such questions the subject cannot help but sense the fact that the interviewer is not sure that sex is an honorable thing, and a thing that can be frankly talked about. Evasive terms invite dis-honest answers.

Lawyers commonly notice the same evasion in interviews involving other taboo topics, such as death or suicide. Many "estate-planning" inter-viewers say, "What do you want to do if something should happen?" instead of, "What do you want to happen when you die?" Kinsey found it impera-tive to frame questions so as not to invite evasion. His style also implies more acceptance of the answer he was after. He would not ask, "Have you ever . . .?" He would ask, "When did you first . . .?" He avoided multiple questions for the same reasons.

Lies. An occasional obstacle to the trust that runs from lawyer to client (and an obstacle to getting the facts) is the lawyer's suspicion that clients lie to lawyers. When it does occur, it is often the product of distrust, of the lawyer's communicating to the client that the client is not trusted. When it does occur, the usual lawyer devices for dealing with it (bluster, threat, cross-examination) make it worse. These devices reduce the diminishing sense of trust and increase dishonesty.

Even the best efforts of the attorney to establish rapport with the client, based on trust and understanding, will not necessarily prevent client distortions and untruths. Legal techniques, such as cross-examination, apparently work in court to catch liars, but they do this at the price of stopping the flow of information; for that reason they are inappropriate in the interview setting. How then should the attorney handle a client's misrepresentations? The most direct approach is open confrontation: "I feel that you are not telling the truth, and I am going to tell you how I feel." We are not suggesting that every untruth be confronted.

It is important to notice that false information is not always caused by a lie. Andrew Watson has

found that factual distortions are more frequently
due to unconscious factors than intentional deceit
on the client's part. The problem is attributable to
the tendency of the lawyer "to presume . . . that
his client is a rational being, capable of good recall
of past events and capable of communicating objectively with little self-serving omission or interpretation of the facts." The lawyer operates at the
conscious level and bases the interview on the
ability to obtain conscious information from his
client. If Watson's thesis is correct, the attorney
hoping to be an effective interviewer in, say, a
divorce case must look beyond purely factual information. The attorney must expect the client to
distort events and omit pertinent facts. These
evasions, omissions, or distortions then become
facts in their own right. It is this kind of fact that
helps explain who the client is and what he wants
and needs; more specifically, Watson says, omitted
facts provide insight into the client.

It may be better to be the sort of lawyer who is
occasionally taken in by liars and con-artists than
to be the sort of lawyer who finds it hard to trust
her clients. That would be part of a "lesson on
lies" that Kinsey might direct to lawyers. The
other and probably more important part of a "lesson on lies" is that distrust is best brought into the
open and openly resolved, because clients will
sense its presence and may perceive it as worse
than it is. Their sense that they are distrusted
will result in their withholding facts. In any case,

as diCavour said, "The man who trusts other men will make fewer mistakes than he who distrusts them."

Morals. Kinsey did not prevent falsehood and fraud in his interviewees; he does seem to have held it to a minimum, though; his techniques for detecting and dealing with dishonesty may be useful as one of two final points on the Kinsey technique; they also require a comment on morals. First, the Kinsey technique:

If it becomes apparent that the subject's first answer is not correct or sufficient, one should ask for additional information, and re-phrase the original question in a way that will make him prove his answer or expose the falsity of his reply. In a rapid fire of additional questions, it is difficult for a dishonest subject to be consistent. With uneducated persons, and particularly with feeble-minded individuals, it is sometimes effective to pretend that one has misunderstood the negative replies and ask additional questions, just as though the original answers were affirmatives; whereupon the subject may then expose the truth by answering as though he had never given a negative reply. "Yes, I know you have never done that, but how old were you the first time that you did it?" is a question which, amazingly enough, may break down the cover-up of a feeble-minded individual. With such a technique, on the other hand, it is especially important to make sure that the subject's final admissions are not fictions which the interviewer has suggested to him.

Our reactions to Kinsey's apparatus for trapping falsehood are mixed. It is repulsive to say to anybody—"You say you've never done that; now, how often have you done it?" and it is not surprising that it only worked with people for whom Kinsey (and his generation) used the phrase "feeble-minded." That's no way to treat people. Part of the moral objection turns on the fact that the other is being treated as an object, manipulated, for a purpose which seems extraneous to him. Purpose is not the essence of the revulsion, though. It wouldn't improve the situation very much to be able to say that the manipulation is benign—"for his own good"—or for some higher purpose such as the discovery of truth. Every evil, from the most trivial to the 20th century's recurrent campaigns of genocide, is explained by relating evil to high purpose.

But there is something admirable in the interchanges Kinsey describes, something that seems to us morally opposite to manipulation. Kinsey tried, some of the time, to deal with falsehood by openly confronting it. He did that when he set aside his notes and said, "Okay, now tell me the truth." In that moment he trusted his own instinct for recognizing truth, and he trusted his interviewee enough to confront him with the truth of the interpersonal moment. The truth of the interpersonal moment was: "I don't believe you and you seem to know it." It would have been less sticky, less scary, to have stood up, said, "Thank you very much," and gone home and torn up the notes. Lawyers sometimes do that with clients and witnesses. It is easy and it is safe. But what does that behavior say? It says: "I don't trust you enough to suppose that you could ever tell me the truth. I don't trust you enough to risk having my heart in my mouth and sweat on my palms. I don't trust you enough to level with you about how I feel."

The consequences of evasive behavior are alternative; either the lie succeeds, and the lawyer has contributed to a liar's pay-off, and therefore to falsehood; or it doesn't succeed and he abandons the interviewee. The client has another of those experiences of rejection that say to him "You are a bad person." Not "You are in this instance wrong or mistaken," but "You are bad."

Another way to put this would be to ask the question: If you loved the interviewee (and love means at least that you do for him rather than do to him), what course would you follow? "Love does not rejoice in what is wrong," St. Paul says, "but love rejoices in the truth." Apply that to Kinsey's interview with the "feeble-minded" liar. If Kinsey loved that man, the best course would have been an open, trusting, loving, but clear, confrontation: "I feel that you are not telling the truth, and I am going to tell you how I feel." That is, in our opinion, a blue-ribbon response.

The worst response would be no response at all. The second-best (or second-worst) answer would be the one Kinsey used, the manipulative one. Kinsey's device is, in this instance, no way to treat people, but it is probably more humane to respond to people badly than it is to banish them from your life.

CLIENT EXPECTATIONS

There are two aspects of the client's world that the attorney often overlooks and that have an important bearing on the attorney-client relationship, matters that can be addressed in the early stages of the interview process. First are the client's conscious expectations. If these are not explored, they become a kind of "hidden agenda." Second, the client's *unconscious* motivations for seeking legal assistance affect fact-gathering; the lawyer needs to understand and address unconscious motivation.

It is essential that the lawyer determine what the client wants and expects. To what degree is the client seeking information, support, friendship, skills, aid in decision-making? What kind of role is the attorney being asked to play in providing what the client wants? Are the client's expectations and role demands (that is, what he wants the lawyer to *be*) compatible with the attorney's image of his professional role and his sense of self? In all likelihood, the client comes to the attorney with a broad range of expectations. These expectations are often based on a stereotyped image of the lawyer, what a lawyer is, what she can do, and how she works.

When client expectations are unrealistic or distorted, they may severely interfere with the attorney-client relationship. The simplest direct technique for handling client expectations is to ask the client at the first meeting but not at the beginning of it (see Chapter Four), "What do you want?" During the course of the relationship the attorney may become uncertain on the answer to this question, or may detect unrealistic expectations on the part of the client, and there will be a need to discuss this issue again. The lawyer can confront the client with distorted images, beliefs and expectations. In this manner the client, with the help of the attorney, can work through these expectations by talking about them and bringing them to conscious awareness. Everyone has unconscious motivations in seeking to establish relationships with professional people; everyone uses such relationships to satisfy psychological needs. These are least harmful, and are even useful, when we are aware of their existence.

There are times when the client's needs are so unclear that the problem (and the story) is presented in a rambling and incoherent form. A lawyer's time is money, and there may be concern that the client-centered approach encourages the client to "ramble." Certainly, demanding formal, courtroom, casebook coherence stops the flow of information. Nonetheless, too much rambling, as Gerard Egan warns, "destroys the concreteness, the focus, and the intensity of the helping experience." In other words, rambling puts the client's payoff at risk, because the theme of the client's story and the supporting facts get lost in the rambling and complex account the client gives of them. It can become impossible to deal with all of the implications of what the client is saying. When this happens, the attorney can (and should) be more directive, focusing the client's attention on discrete elements of the problem. Lawyers learn in law school how to do that; our argument is that such direction should come from the client's need for it and not from the lawyer's being the prisoner of legal doctrine.

MECHANICS

Notes. Should I take notes? Many pundits say not, but Kinsey found a way to do it (he thought) without its becoming a distraction:

In the literature on interviewing, it is customary to advise that records should not be made in the presence of a subject, but that they should be made after the subject has left at the close of an interview. This is the commonest procedure among many psychiatrists, clinical psychologists, and among social workers. It is supposed that a subject is embarrassed at seeing his statements put on paper, and that he will talk more freely if he feels that he can say some things that are not recorded. It has been said that there is a loss of rapport when the interviewer records during the interview. . . . After the first few months of this study, we began to record all of the data directly in the presence of the subject, and there has been no indication that this has been responsible for any loss of rapport or interference with the subject's free exposure of confidences. We have become convinced that any loss of rapport which comes when data are recorded directly has been consequent upon the longhand method of writing out answers while the subject sits in silence waiting for the next question. This is the thing that is destructive to rapport. By using a code for recording, it has been possible in the present study to record as rapidly as one can carry on a conversation, without loss of rapport or blockage on the subject's part.

Many modern interviewers (but surprisingly few lawyers) use a tape recorder, which, most of them say, can be explained to the client and, if explained candidly, does not become an interference. The tape serves the same function as notes; it also records inflection and mood, which notes do not. Taping also affords the interviewer a way to assess his own performance. This last point is a significant one, especially for novices in law-office practice. One student in a legal-counseling class said:

I get more out of listening to myself on the tape several times than from the comments of others. . . . I realize now, after several inter-

views, that a person can begin to develop style as
to questioning, summing up, giving the solution
or "advice." I feel that one's style is just as
much a tool of the trade as one's verbal skills.
The important thing to be kept in mind is that
the "style" and verbal skills should be a means
of establishing a personal contact between the
lawyer and his client—as two people in a counseling context, and not simply to play out a scene
where one person puts on a Lawyer mask and
cuts himself off, as a person, from the client.

Forms. It was inevitable that lawyers would
decide to save time by asking their clients to provide information on paper rather than through
interview. And there is much to be said for obtaining some information in that fashion, if only
because it frees the law-office routine for more
important interpersonal matters. The following
seems, for example, to be tiresome and unnecessary:

L: Okay, now, on that furniture: It makes a
     difference, in terms of the amount of taxes
     you'll be paying—later. We don't want to
     lump in, with the real estate, the value of
     the personal property. In other words, we'll
     show it as a total price of sixty three five,
     but we ought to put a value on personal
     property. This way you're not being taxed
     on personal property under the guise of real
     property, and also you might be avoiding

some capital gain. Okay. So—what personal property's going with it?

C: Uh. The refrigerator—

L: Okay. (Writing.)

C: And the living room furniture. There is a davenport and rocking chair and a matching chair. And—

L: Okay. (Writing.)

C: A dining set—uh—table, two leaves, and four chairs—

L: Wait, now. You're getting ahead of me here. Davenport, rocker—(Writing.)

C: And a matching chair.

L: Matching chair. Okay. (Pause, writing.) And—

C: Dining table, with two leaves and four chairs.

L: Four chairs. (Pause.) Okay.

C: And I told you the refrigerator. (Pause.) And stove.

L: And stove. Right.

C: That goes with it.

L: Yeah. Okay.

C: The stove's built in and that's part of the house.

L: Okay. Well, roughly, what value do you think we should attach to this . . .?

The most important points about using forms for facts are (1) that the device be confined to facts that are easier to write down than to speak; (2) that forms be introduced only after a working relationship is established; and (3) that the instruments demonstrate an openness and acceptance of the client. If a client receives a form to fill out even before he meets his lawyer, he draws conclusions about the lawyer, and about the law, from the form. The first conclusion he draws is that he is being categorized and treated as he is treated when he files his income tax return or visits a welfare office. That conclusion can be avoided if the forms are withheld until a working relationship is established. The forms themselves should be confined to facts that involve little or no affect, or are hard to take down in an oral interview; and the forms should be humane.

Some forms violate all three rules. Here, for example, is part of V.A. Form 21–534, "Application for Dependency and Indemnity Compensation or Death Pension by Widow or Child":

NOTE—The following information should be furnished for each period of the veteran's active service after September 7, 1939, in the Army, Navy, Air Force, Marine Corps or Coast Guard of the United States or service as a commissioned officer in the Coast and Geodetic Survey or Public Health Service.

CHILDREN: Show names of surviving unmarried children (including stepchildren, adopted, and illegitimate children) of the veteran who were (a) Under 18; (b) 18 to 22 and going to school; (c) Age 18 or disabled before 18.

* * *

I certify that the above statements are true, knowing that anyone who makes a false statement or misrepresents in connection with an application for Federal benefits is committing a crime punishable under Federal law.

Some forms ask for information that should be talked about rather than put in blank spaces (*e.g.,* illegitimate children or children disabled before age 18). Some forms ask for information that can perfectly well be put on a form, but ask for it in an inhumane way. Here is a form prepared for wills clients, and sent to them with instructions to write out the answers before they come to the law office for an initial interview:

Your name	Birth Date
Spouse	Birth Date
Former Marriages:	Who:
Any Obligations?	

Forms such as these condition people to expect the worst; they bring back feelings we had about the stubby pencils and "All right, last name, first name, middle initial," in our first days of military service. They are like filling out welfare applications, and the hundreds of bureaucratic conversations that attend the completion of forms in our everyday life. A profession ought to be able, always and everywhere, to do better than that.

The growing tendency in our bureaucracies, and even among lawyers, to use questionnaires and checklists and forms for interviewing, however useful when done humanely, is a symbol of official control of the process of gathering information. Perhaps, in a spirit of compromise, it is possible to design information forms so that appropriate information can be obtained without humiliation. This bit, from Louis M. Brown's "Periodic Check Up" form, indicates some hope:

Marital Situation

Are you now married? Yes ( ) No ( ) If yes, name of your spouse (husband/wife): ____.

* * *

Are you living with your spouse? ( ) Or are you separated? ( )

If you were previously married: Are you divorced? ( ) Or is your marriage dissolved or annulled? Yes ( ) No ( )

Are you a widow/widower? Yes ( ) No ( )

* * *

In some marriages, husband and wife have a written contract concerning their property. Do you have such a contract? Yes ( ) No ( ).

SOME CONCLUDING REFLECTIONS
ON INTERVIEWING

A personal ethic on counseling, a principle of professional service, is likely to be the most potent factor in anybody's interview style. An indication of egocentric legal counseling is the recurrent tendency to speak of clients not as persons but as problems. What does it tell you about the morals and politics of interviewing that a lawyer thinks of a new problem rather than a person when a client walks in the door? One possibility is that use of the word "problem"—and, more importantly, of that attitude toward clients—is a bid for control. Lawyers are, after all, experts in problems. Lawyers take hold of problems and tell others to get out of the way. Our experience is, though, to the contrary. We have found that the most important talent for starting an interview is the ability to let control go and stay out of the way. The client will probably not even hear what the interviewer says at the beginning; he is anxious to get started. The choice between control and staying out of the way is a moral choice: It reflects your view of what a human person is and what he can become.

The best source of learning an interview technique is your own experience. This kind of learning, like all other kinds, does not just happen. A learning lawyer listens to what she herself says and does; she talks about it with people who care about her; she develops and practices a basic, positive, acceptance of herself. She is helpful because she believes that what she says and does and cares about has value. Alfred Benjamin suggests a few more specific guideposts for evaluating interviews; these are also useful tests on whether or not mutuality in the working agreement has developed:

—Did you help the interviewee open up her perceptual field as much as possible: Was she able to look at things the way they appear to her?

—Suppose—using Benjamin's example—that the client says "I know it is wrong to steal." What is the effect of the lawyer's then asking "Why did you do it then?"

—Did you help her to explore the subject in her way, or did you lead her to where you wanted to be?

Another of our students in legal counseling made a melancholy observation about lawyering principles which says it better than psychologists or law professors can:

From my observation of attorneys representing their clients, I continue to wonder if these attorneys are really acting in their clients' behalf. By this I mean that when a client comes into your office . . . he comes . . . realizing that you possess certain tools which he does not possess, and he hopes that somehow you will be able to use those tools to his advantage. But I often wonder if we use these tools to his advantage or to our own. It strikes me that many times attorneys forget that they are representing clients. The client is someone who has given them the opportunity to improve their personal positions.

BIBLIOGRAPHY

On the art and skill of interviewing: Benjamin, The Helping Interview (1981); Gordon, Interviewing: Strategy, Techniques, and Tactics (3rd ed. 1980); Fey and Goldberg, "Legal Interviewing From a Psychological Perspective: An Attorney's Handbook," 14 Willamette Law Journal 217 (1978); Schoenfield and Schoenfield, "Interviewing and Counseling Clients in a Legal Setting," 11 Akron Law Review 313 (1977); Gilmore, The Counselor-in-Training (1973); Garrett, Interviewing: Its Principles and Methods (1970); Sullivan, Psychiatric Interview (1970); Hunt, "Problems and Processes in the Legal Interview," 50 Illinois Bar Journal 726 (1962); Wiseman, "Lawyer-Client Interviews: Some Lessons from Psychiatry," 39 Boston University Law Review 181 (1959).

On lying: Ekman, Telling Lies: Cues to Deceit in the Marketplace, Politics, and Marriage (1985); Bok, Lying: Moral Choice in Public and Private Life (Vintage, 1979); Eck, Lies and Truth (1970).

REFERENCES

Brown, Manual for Periodic Legal Checkup (1983); Brown and Shaffer, "Toward a Jurisprudence for the Law Office," 17 American Journal of Jurisprudence 125 (1972); Kinsey, Sexual Behavior in the Human Male (1948).

CHAPTER SIX

THEORIES AND MODELS IN HELPING RELATIONSHIPS

BASIC THEORIES OF COUNSELING

As we use counseling skills we learn that describing what "professional counselors" do is a way of thinking about human interactions. Lawyers learn from psychological counselors. We study *theories* of counseling because psychologists (or at least the ones we read and admire) are concerned about the process level of interaction between a "professional helper" and one who seeks help and is willing to pay for it. One of the things we learn as counselors, the lawyer kind and the therapist kind, is that counselors have limits. Some forms of personal dynamics are difficult, if not impossible, to work through in a non-therapeutic setting. There are things about ourselves and our clients that we do not understand, and over which we seem, at least on first appearance, to have little control. The more we understand the psychology of human interaction, and the counseling done in law offices, the more we find to learn from "professional counselors." Legal counselors need to know what a psychological counselor does and what such a counselor teaches that might be of

155

use in understanding our clients (and ourselves) and the work we do for clients and with them.

We have argued in Chapters One and Two that counseling is a function of how we listen to and talk with our clients. Counseling, for better or worse, is something we always do with clients. In talking and listening with clients there is a simple choice that a lawyer and every counselor makes: Can the client be seen as something other than a problem? Psychological theories of counseling can be analyzed according to the way they attempt to respond to this question. There is at least one school of counseling theory, developed by Joseph Simons and Jeanne Reidy, that refers to the ideal counselor as a friend. Some counselors prefer "companion" to "friend." They argue that people have special and idiosyncratic definitions of "friendship." Lawrence C. Porter, a counseling psychologist, defended the preference, in a personal letter to Shaffer: "For me, being a friend and being friendly are different kinds of things. My energies allow me to be friendly to a great number of people (on buses, in ticket lines, in various chance encounters), but a friend to only a very small number, because being a friend is such a complex and significant enterprise. I guess that's why *companion* seems so much easier a word for me to deal with. If I have any kind of case load as a lawyer, it will be impossible for me to deal with very many of those clients truly as friends." The choice for the counselor is significant, perhaps best described as an existential dilemma. It is no less so for the lawyer.

When counselors sort themselves out according to training and theory they tend to cluster around one of four prominent theories of counseling—the companionship theory, the non-directive theory, the interpretive theory, and the directive theory:

Companionship (see Simons and Reidy). The companionship idea is that counselor and client seek to exploit the bonds of mutual interest in a relationship of one who needs help with one who offers services in response to a need for help. It begins by inquiring into the initial attraction which brought the client to the counselor. It seeks to build the initial attraction into the basis for a professional relationship. It resists client dependence and works toward mutuality and collaboration in solving problems. It insists upon openness and candor in the counselor.

The initial obstacle to a companionship theory of counseling is the moral idea, stated as a conscious goal in professional literature, that we should be objective and detached, that we should seek only minimal involvement with the client. We imagine our clients *as* clients, not as friends or companions. We do something *for* a client, not *with* him. We lawyers are taught "independent judgment" as a professional ideal, an ideal that depends on emotional distance: Legal services are to be provided in arm's length transactions. The issue is primarily moral, and non-professional ethics for the most part argues that such "detachment" is wrong: When our relationships become too professional, they are, in Martin Buber's terms, I-It rather than I-Thou; the client is a thing, not a person. Clients then become nuisances, our interaction pained by dislike and disdain for those we serve (but serve only because we are paid to do so). The way this obstacle works is illustrated by the occasional repulsive client—who is repulsive enough to make the emotional distance that undermines companionship a logical if ultimately self-defeating choice.

The images of the lawyer as a companion, and of legal counseling as the practice of companionship, are prevalent throughout this book and are integral to our thinking about the talking and listening that lawyers do. It explains how our talking and listening as lawyers can be more consciously viewed as counseling. The companionship theory of counseling is a moral ideal as well as a behavioral theory. In practice, companionship is an amalgam of ideas and sentiments about the way professionals relate to their clients. Companionship is a style of interaction that is so natural for some counselors that they do not associate it with either theory or ideal. (Standard reference works on psychological counseling do not discuss the companionship theory as a separate school of counseling.)

Non-Directive (see Rogers, Porter). The idea of non-directive counseling is that clients contain within themselves all of the resources necessary for their choices; they need only be freed from the judgmental hang-ups that attend their lives, and the best way to help them toward competence and freedom is to demonstrate that they are not, after all, bad or stupid people. Rogerian counseling turns on "active listening" in which the counselor aims to show that she hears (and accepts) the client by restating the feelings and fears expressed by the client and by attempting to show the client that she knows how the client feels (empathy). Rogerian counselors seek to avoid client dependence and try to promote the client's growth by focusing on that part of his life and personality that is healthy and intact. The counselor rigorously avoids judgment, even supportive judgment. She concentrates on the climate of the relationship, by (a) attempting to accept client feelings, whatever they are; (b) manifesting empathy (not merely sympathy, which is intellectual, but an attempt to feel the situation as the client feels it); and (c) demonstrating congruence between her own feelings, especially those toward the client, and her actions in the counseling relationship.

The principal criticisms of non-directive counseling are that it does not avoid, but rather encourages, client dependence, because it fosters and comes to depend on a strong empathic relationship between counselor and client; and that it does not quickly enough lead to results (choices, decisions, plans of action).

Directive Styles (see Harris, Perls, James and Jongeward, Shostrom, Berne): The feature that characterizes directive schools of counseling is that the counselor is active, relatively combative, often giving orders. Albert Ellis, for instance, gave his psychological clients homework. The "Gestalt" counselors (Perls for example) believe in confronting clients with how their behavior appears to the counselor, a confrontation that goes beyond interpretation. Practitioners of "transactional analysis" relate client behavior to communications between parties in what is called a "transaction." Communications are related to parent-adult-child "ego states" that set the tone for the relationship and are the basis for failures in communications. Eric Berne, the father of TA (transactional analysis) helped us see how feelings are embedded in the frames of reference (orientation, perspective) (Berne called them ego states) that channel and structure all of the talking and listening we do with another person.

In the directive school of counseling the counselor has specific techniques and skills, often dramatic ways of intervening in relationships. These bring the underlying process level of relationships to the surface, where it can be observed and changed when it is adversely affecting the client's behavior.

Interpretive Theories (see Freud and Jung). The key in an interpretive approach to counseling is to find the underlying basis for the problem. The idea is that the client will resolve his hang-up once he understands it. The means to this resolution is a perceptive, expert person who will listen and help the client see how the hang-up works, how it got to be a hang-up. In order for the expert's presence to be taken seriously, though, this person must be seen as significant and reliable; interpretive counseling therefore encourages dependence (transference) and tends to identify resistance (to the therapy and to the therapist's interpretations) as significant.

There is debate about the value of classical, Freudian-style psychotherapy, where relationships tend to be complex and extend over long periods of time. There would be wide agreement, though, that this style of counseling is best accomplished in the practice of depth psychology by trained therapists—typically doctors of medicine. Since it involves psychological acumen it is a difficult orientation to teach and master in other professions. (See Chapter Four for an extended discussion of theories of transference and countertransference.)

* * *

We borrow, in theory and in practice, from each of the four main theories that we have presented. We have drawn deeply, as we think all counselors must, on the seminal work of Sigmund Freud and C. G. Jung, the founders of psychoanalysis and analytic psychology. We realize that both Freud and Jung are controversial figures in the psychological community, but we acknowledge our dependence on their work and their commitment to understanding the unconscious and how it makes its way into everyday life, especially into the life of professional relationships. We think it is important for lawyers to be aware of the fact that there are theories at work in law offices, as forces and as rationalizations for what is done in law office relationships.

The schools of counseling that we describe are not mutually exclusive; if they were, we would not be able to draw on each of the four theories to the extent that we do. And for the legal counselor, it is as important to see how each of the theories shares important assumptions with the others as it is to draw distinctions. An example: While we have argued for the ideal of the lawyer as companion, this way of working with clients also depends on the insights of Carl Rogers and his non-directive theory of counseling. We are more likely to see the possibilities of companionship in our professional relationship with a client that we view as a resource, a person to whom we can extend, as Rogers did to his clients, "unconditional positive regard."

An experienced counselor tends, amidst a proliferation of theories, to think of herself as eclectic. From the various psychological perspectives described in this chapter and in Chapter Five, we find the following points of significant interest to lawyers:

—The counselor is willing to ask for help, too. Alfred C. Kinsey, the researcher who first delved into the subject of contemporary Americans' sex lives, succeeded because he said to his subjects: "Would you be willing to help me?" This is often the most functional way to gather information from clients, and may be the best way to approach an understanding of their hang-ups.

—The counselor recognizes that the client has resources, talents, and insights that bear on the counseling issue and on how the relationship can best proceed.

—The counselor recognizes that, as a professional, she exercises certain "priestly" functions, not because of superiority but because she has a license to, say, prescribe drugs, argue in court, preside in church, or stand at a podium. These priestly functions imply knowledge and ability, but have little or no bearing on competence in counseling. We argue in Chapters Three and Eleven that when this "priestly" function results in wearing a professional mask counseling is significantly, and often adversely, affected.

—The counselor is honest, with himself and his client, about his biases, his need to control and dominate, his tendency to hide things or to reveal them in an obscure way, and his instincts to compete. He respects particularly the fact that part of his professionalism lies in his special awe for a limited part of human experience. (Studies show that physicians have strong anxiety about death, lawyers about aggression and order, clergymen about sin and salvation, and psychologists about emotion.)

—The counselor has a healthy respect for (and acceptance of) needs that put distance between a lawyer and her client—needs to be in charge, to compete, not to become involved in the pain and travail of another person.

—The counselor regards his relationship with his client as an adventure, as a sanctioned, privileged, awesome intrusion into the infinite value and reality of another human life.

FOUNDATION FOR A COMPANIONSHIP MODEL

We have selected four theories—Gestalt, transactional analysis, the Johari window, and psychoanalytic theory—for more extensive description. These four theories provide a framework for our counseling and teaching; we view them as foundations for the client-centered, companionship model that we present throughout this book.

Gestalt. Gestalt is a theory, a school of psychology, as well as a way of doing counseling and therapy. It is most often associated with the work of Frederick S. (Fritz) Perls, a bigger than life character, who drew on his experience (and failures) as a Freudian psychoanalyst to develop a new form of therapy (more accurately, a way of working with another person, since much of Perls's work was done in groups, not in individual psychotherapy). Gestalt work, like psychoanalysis, tends to follow well-prescribed rules. The Gestalt-oriented counselor is more directive and confrontive than most other counselors.

Gestalt follows a set of "ground rules," ways of setting a stage and interrupting modes of behavior so that learning and change can take place. The ground rules aim for enhanced awareness, at separating what a person does that is real and authentic from what he does that is phony and manipulative. Awareness comes out of confrontation, encouraged by the therapist or others in the Gestalt group, confrontation of the person with his actual behavior, and with how that behavior affects others.

Jerry Greenwald, writing about the ground rules in Gestalt therapy, suggests that "much of the work in Gestalt therapy involves increased awareness of obsolete attitudes and behavior patterns which were learned in the past and continue despite their frustrating effect on the person's well-being in the present. While he adopted these as the most effective way he could find to cope with conflicts in his past life, he may begin to see that they no longer fit present reality. As he becomes aware of these archaic responses, he may begin to experiment by taking risks in letting go of them and discovering new, more effective attitudes and behavior. The energy that had been diverted into frustrating or non-nourishing activities is then freed and available for more meaningful experiences in the here-and-now."

These general comments can be amplified by a more extended description of the Gestalt "ground rules": (i) Gestalt work is done through exercises that focus on *awareness,* and the most direct form of awareness is knowledge of one's *feelings* and an attempt to stay in the *here and now,* in contrast to explanations about feelings based on something that happened in the past, or on something that might happen in the future. (ii) Gestalt work seeks out conflicts that are out of awareness but influencing present behavior. These conflicts are explored through role playing and dialogues with those who we think are angry at us, or want to love us, or those we fear will abandon us. (iii) Gestalt work in a group requires that each person take responsibility for his own feelings, his relations with others in the group, and for his own learning (learning that being in the group makes possible). Individual and personal responsibility is a cardinal rule of Gestalt practice. The most direct way to enforce the rule of personal responsibility is to use the personal pronoun "I" when we talk about ourselves. We have been taught, in speech and in writing, to avoid "I." Gestalt work teaches each of us to say "I," to speak in the first person. (iv) To learn what our feelings mean, how we are perceived by others, and how our interactions work requires that we take risk. Gestaltists see risk as fundamental to change. Risk is inhibited by old patterns and by perceived fears. Gestalt work in a group makes possible risk-taking, which involves confrontation with fears, explicit and secret. (v) Gestalt group work focuses on the here and now and on experiential learning, usually learning from the experiences in a group. In the Gestalt perspective "intellectualizing," "psychologizing," and giving advice (gratuitous or otherwise) are discouraged.

The Gestalt rule against advice extends to any kind of talking about, lecturing, or story telling about oneself or someone else. Participants are asked to focus on their experience as of the moment. "The emphasis," Jerry Greenwald says, "is on nonintellectual awareness as opposed to thoughts and speculations." One of the ways to avoid intellectualizing and to encourage the focus on one's own feelings is to avoid questions. "Questions," Greenwald points out, "frequently ask a person to explain, defend or justify some aspect of himself or of his existence. Questions often are attempts to manipulate other people; they can usually be restated as first person statements." (vi) Participants in a Gestalt group address each other and follow a "no gossip" rule. Greenwald explains the rule this way: "To enhance feelings of contact and interaction, each person is asked to make statements directly to the other person. For example, instead of saying to the group leader about another patient: 'He makes me angry with his intellectualizing,' the person is asked to make the statements directly to the participant toward whom he feels angry; *i.e.,* 'I am angry at your intellectualizing.' " (vii) The purpose of the "ground rules" is to create an atmosphere in which each participant in the group can learn from his or her experience in the group. The rules minimize old patterned ways of interaction and make it possible to take risk and learn new modes of behavior. (See Exercises Fourteen through Eighteen, in the Appendix.)

Psychoanalytic Theory. An example of the lessons of Freudian psychology for the lawyer comes from Andrew Watson, a psychiatrist on the law faculty at the University of Michigan. Watson has explored for many years the theory that the problem that we talk about may not be the problem at all. And even when we find the courage and the will to talk about the problem, we are prone to select a "helper" for reasons that, upon examination, turn out not to be the real reasons at all: The unconscious plays a significant role not only in what we are able to say about our own lives (and the problems we confront and create for ourselves) but also affects the choice of those we will ask for help and the kind of help we will permit them to give us.

Psychoanalytic theory is a model of the mind, a frame of reference, a perspective, a map, a language of the unconscious and internal mental processes (motivations, intentions, hopes, dreams, depression, feelings). Freudian psychology is of continuing interest to lawyers because intrapsychic forces affect the way we relate to our clients, other lawyers, judges, and ourselves; they affect our professional decisions, as well as the way we live our personal lives. Watson's scholarship has explored these realities in reference to legal ethics, teaching methods, and legal education as well as counseling.

Lawyers tend to be more interested in ideas and skills that affect communication, that explain the obstacles to getting facts and the idiosyncratic ways of their clients, than the specifics of a technical theory such as Freudian psychoanalysis. But it is in the actual use of psychoanalytic theory, in the work that Freudian therapists do with patients (who are called, in psychoanalytic literature, analysands), that we learn something of value about the human psyche that can inform our counseling in the non-therapeutic setting.

The psychoanalytic method requires that a subject relate experiences, feelings, emotions, and fears to the analyst, who guides the patient or client in recognizing and understanding unconscious motivations. In this process of "working through" the unconscious material, the client obtains the insight necessary to reduce the effects of unconscious forces that underlie emotions, oftentimes producing undesirable behavior.

The psychoanalytic method also involves a specific technique for bringing forth this unconscious material. It is based on an assumption suggested by Theodore Reik, an analyst, that "men reveal themselves—all their emotional secrets—when they talk freely about themselves; not just when they talk about their secrets, but about everything concerning themselves. They give away what bothers them, disturbs and torments them, all that occupies their thoughts and arouses their emotions—even when they would be most unwilling to talk directly about these things."

In psychoanalytic terms, this technique of spontaneous and truthful utterances is called *free association*. The analyst asks the patient to free associate to words, feelings, and images in dreams, to say everything that comes to mind. The goal is to disengage the intellectual discipline that requires thoughts to be linear and rational. Freud found that the unconscious operates by a different set of rules, rules that violate the learned discipline of the intellect. Karen Horney describes free association as the "endeavor on the part of the patient to express without reserve, and in the sequence in which it emerges, everything that comes into his mind, regardless of whether it is or appears trivial, off the point, incoherent, irrational, indiscreet, tactless, embarrassing, humiliating. It includes not only fleeting and diffuse thoughts but also specific ideas and memories . . . memories of experiences at any period of life, thoughts about self and others . . . beliefs in religion, morals, politics, art, wishes and plans for the future, fantasies past and present, and, of course, dreams." As practiced in

psychoanalysis, it constitutes a process of spontaneous word and thought association that, in theory,
overcomes obstacles to self-scrutiny.

(We are not being as precisely accurate with our
terms as a psychiatrist would be. For example,
psychoanalysis, or analysis, is the home base for
counseling devices such as the interpretation of
dreams and free association. Analysis, in the
strict sense, is a prolonged process of controlled
self-discovery that is familiar to the lay world
through stories such as "The Three Faces of Eve"
and "I Never Promised You a Rose Garden." The
devices and techniques used in analysis are also
used in shorter-term and more focused treatment—
or counseling—that is probably more accurately
referred to as psychotherapy.)

The point here is not that lawyers learn to use
free association with (or on) their clients, but that
to get at the basis of a human situation sometimes
requires extraordinary measures, skills and techniques that break through the crusty, impacted,
surface areas of our lives. Freud's exploration of
the unconscious produced a wealth of information,
not only for doctors who deal with mental illness;
but also for all professionals who work with others
and have a need to understand human behavior.

We are aware that Freud's theories are now
controversial (Freud has always been controversial!), and in some instances discredited. We are
not sure that the Oedipus complex is a universal
phenomenon, as Freud and some of Freud's follow-

ers suggested. And we are confident, in the light of contemporary research, that Freud was mistaken about penis envy, and much else that he had to say about the psychology of women. But Freud is controversial because he did so much in the area of psychology that cannot easily be ignored. He created in us what Harold Bloom, the literary critic, calls "the anxiety of influence." Freud is controversial because his system of psychoanalysis grew out of empirical findings (Freud viewed himself as a scientist) and out of the art of human healing. (Freud was a notable writer, a creator of what James Hillman calls a "healing fiction," but most of all he was a physician.) Psychoanalysis remains today both a science of treatment and a theory of social science, an eloquent, literary achievement that makes Freud and Jung subjects of discussion and study in the humanities (and in law school) as well as the sciences.

Contemporary psychoanalysts and psychologists are reworking and revising Freud's theories and are using them not only for a method of treatment but also for an understanding of human motivation and human behavior for the social sciences and the humanities. (See Chapter Four for an extended discussion of Freud's theory of transference.)

There are two other psychological models—the Johari window and Eric Berne's transactional analysis—that draw heavily on Freud's insights, recasting Freudian concepts of resistance and repression, and the unconscious itself, in a different language:

The Johari Window. Joe Luft and Harry Ingham developed what has come to be known as the Johari Window, a pictorial representation (a structure) that maps what we know (or think we know) about awareness in human behavior and human interaction. The window:

	Known to Self	Unknown to Self
Known to Others	I OPEN	II BLIND
Unknown to Others	III HIDDEN	IV UNKNOWN

[B2909]

The four quadrants in this representation reflect the presence and absence of awareness (the knowledge that we have of who we are and what is happening in the relationship) in relation to others. The Johari Window applies Freud's insights in psychotherapy (resistance, repression, the ego and the unconscious, self-deception, and the difficulties of self-scrutiny) to what happens in our relations to others. The knowledge gained by physicians in treatment of neurosis is recast as knowledge for understanding personal and professional relationships in such places as law offices.

Turning to the quadrants of the Johari window: Quadrant I is *Open*, that part of our interaction of which we are fully aware, that we readily share with others, and that others know as well as we. When we say what we want, or need, to express our feelings, and are heard by another, who reflects back to us what we are saying and feeling, the interaction and communication are taking place in Quadrant I: known to self and known to others.

Many of the interactions of everyday life, and the conversations and work of the lawyer, take place in this quadrant. So long as the lawyer and the client follow the game plan, do what is expected of them, play their roles, say what they mean and do what they say, then the interaction will remain in Quadrant I. If we were perfect human beings, it is conceivable that there would be nothing but Quadrant I interactions; all of our communications would be adult-adult, I-Thou, open, mutually reinforcing, and fully understandable. No person would be able to manipulate another by withholding information: To get the information you want, all you need to do is ask for it. Dishonesty would be impossible. Gossip would lose its appeal. Secrecy would become a thing of the past. The perfection of Quadrant I is a utopian world, a world that we sometimes aspire to, that we wish for in times of misunderstanding. Lawyers would flourish in this utopian world, a point that makes us doubt whether it is a world that we would truly want. Without secrets there would be no awe and mystery. Without misunderstanding and misreadings (we misread others the way we misread texts), there would be no new understanding of the human condition. We would, in a world dominated by Quadrant I communication and interaction, have created a totally bureaucratic universe, and a leveling of the human spirit: Quadrant I might, when we think about it, be hell.

Quadrant II is comprised of behavior, feelings, motivation—all aspects of our life—that are known to others but not to self. It is that realm of interaction in which we are *Blind* and the quadrant is so labeled. Freud, as much as any contemporary or past figure in psychology and psychiatry, was an explorer of this region. The ego that helps us test (and create) a reality from our experiences, and to find a place for ourselves in the world, cuts us off from certain kinds of knowledge about ourselves. When the obstacles to self-understanding become absolute barriers, as in the case of self-destructive behavior and neurotic adaptions (ways of living that are so dysfunctional that they produce extreme unhappiness), we (those who live and must share the world with the person) become painfully aware of the pathology created by behavior to which the person is blind, but that others can see.

Quadrant II is significant in the attorney client relationship. We argue that the client is a resource, and has information, knowledge, insights and understanding that can be directed to the resolution of problems. (See Chapter Nine.) But the client is a resource in a broader sense, a resource for the lawyer; the client sees the lawyer as he cannot (will not) see himself. One of the values of the feedback that we give one another is that it tells us about feelings that are more apparent to others than to us.

Quadrant III, the *Hidden*, is that which we know ourselves and is unknown to others. The conscious elements of the shadow are found here, as are all secrets, and knowledge of negligence, incompetence, mistakes, and errors. It is Quadrant III which gives rise to manipulation, lies, secrecy, and is the ground for guilt (as Quadrant II is the ground for depression). Quadrant III is the area that produces many of the moral tensions that pull at lawyers: Confidentiality, conflict of interest, and the ideal of zealous representation arise in those settings in which what we know, but which is unknown to others, results in harm to others.

A poignant example of the Quadrant III moral tension can be found in a story told by David Hilfiker in his book Healing the Wounds: A Physician Looks at His Work. Dr. Hilfiker, at the time of the incident he describes, was practicing medicine in a rural health-care clinic in northern Minnesota, two hours by automobile from Duluth. Hilfiker had delivered Barb Daily's first baby and considered himself a friend of Barb and her husband, Russ; Barb thought she was pregnant again, and Hilfiker looked forward to sharing the joy of birth with his friends. There was no reason to think that Barb Daily's second child would present complications. Hilfiker explained: "At her appointment that afternoon, Barb seems to be in good health, with all the signs and symptoms of pregnancy: slight nausea, some soreness in her breasts, a little weight gain. But when the nurse tests Barb's urine to determine if she is pregnant, the result is negative." The test is not always accurate; Hilfiker had Barb leave a urine sample so that another test could be run. When the second test came back negative, Hilfiker was puzzled and troubled: "Perhaps she isn't pregnant. Her missed menstrual period and her other symptoms could be a result of a minor hormonal imbalance. Maybe the embryo has died within the uterus. . . . I could find out by ordering an ultrasound examination. This procedure would give me a 'picture' of the uterus and the embryo. But Barb would have to go to Duluth for the examination. The procedure is also expensive. I know the Dailys well enough to know they have a modest income. Besides, by waiting a few weeks, I should be able to find out for sure without the ultrasound: either the urine test will be positive or Barb will have a miscarriage." This information was conveyed to the patient. A month later she returned to see Hilfiker; and nothing had changed—still no menstrual period and no miscarriage. Barb was now confused and upset because she felt pregnant and both she and her husband wanted the baby.

Hilfiker's concern intensified when a third urine test was negative. Possible explanations for Barb's condition included a hormonal imbalance and even tumor, explanations which Hilfiker rules out, concluding that the most likely explanation was that Barb was carrying a dead embryo and that her body had not followed the usual course of miscarriage to get rid of the dead tissue.

Hilfiker again explained the situation to his patient: "Barb is disappointed; there are tears. She is college-educated, and she understands the scientific and technical aspects of the situation, but that doesn't alleviate the sorrow. We talk at some length and make an appointment for two weeks later." When the patient returned, with her husband, there still has been no menstrual period, no miscarriage, and there was another negative pregnancy test, the fourth. "I explain to them what has happened. The dead embryo should be removed or there could be serious complications. Infection could develop, Barb could even become sterile. The conversation is emotionally difficult for all three of us. We schedule the dilation and curettage for later in the week.

"Dilation and curettage, or D & C, is a relatively simple surgical procedure performed thousands of times each day in this country," but with Barb things did not go easily. "What should take ten or fifteen minutes stretches into a half-hour. The body parts I remove are much larger than I expected, considering when the embryo died. They are not bits of decomposing tissue. These are parts of a body that was recently alive!

"I do my best to suppress my rising panic and try to complete the procedure. Working blindly, I am unable to evacuate the uterus completely; I can feel more parts inside but cannot remove them. Finally I stop, telling myself that the uterus will expel the rest within a few days."

Hilfiker learned from the pathologist's report, confirming his worst fear, that he had aborted a living fetus, of about eleven weeks. "My meeting with Barb and Russ later in the week is one of the hardest things I have ever been through. I described in some detail what I did and what my rationale had been. Nothing can obscure the hard reality: I killed their baby."

Every doctor and lawyer makes mistakes. As Hilfiker puts it, "They happen; they hurt—ourselves and others. They demonstrate our fallibility. Shown our mistakes and forgiven them, we can grow, perhaps in some small way become better people. Mistakes, understood this way, are a process, a way we connect with one another and with our deepest selves." The process and the growth that Hilfiker envisions is stunted if we hide our mistakes from others and ourselves. Hilfiker's book is a moving chronicle of pain and honesty in professional life—of transferring experience and knowledge from Quadrant III to Quadrant I. It is, finally, a powerful moral argument for growth through truthfulness.

Quadrant IV, the *Unknown,* is that area of human interaction that is out-of-awareness for both parties in the relationship. Joe Luft, one of the creators of the Johari Window, provides the following examples of feelings and needs that are difficult to confront and that take up residence in the quadrant of the Unknown:

—feelings of inadequacy, incompetence, and impotence

—sensitivity to rejection or affection

—need to punish or to be punished

—passive-dependent feelings, especially in men and women who have high achievement aspirations

—intense feelings of loneliness and isolation

—qualities in the person that one cannot tolerate in others

—feelings of unworthiness and despair

Using the Window. The Johari Window suggests a model for analyzing the hidden agendas in lawyer and client relationships and a framework for understanding our interactions with clients. Imagine a lawyer-client relationship between A and B. The lawyer and the client may be in any one of four postures. A, for example, may be in Quadrant I in the Window:

A

This is a state of open awareness (i.e., aware of himself and open to others).

He may be not known to himself, but known to others (not aware but open; Quadrant II, the blind area, in the Window):

In this state, he is, of course, vulnerable to manipulation—because he literally does not know what he is doing. Clients manipulate lawyers, particularly when competition is in the air (see Chapter Four). Lawyers manipulate one another, perhaps more often; this Quadrant II posture is an unfortunate position in negotiation, for example.

Our lawyer might be aware of himself but not open to others:

$$\circlearrowleft\boxed{A}$$

This situation is rare; we are not as able as we sometimes think to live with a poker face. It is extremely difficult to be accurate about one's feelings unless one is able to project them on other people; this is probably what Jung meant when he talked about individuation. But the situation is at least theoretically possible, and would correspond to Quadrant III (avoided or hidden) in the Johari Window.

Finally, the lawyer may be closed both to himself and to others; this is Quadrant IV (Unknown) in the window.

$$\boxed{A}$$

If you take the simplest sort of human interaction—two people in one-on-one legal counseling—there are sixteen contexts for human interaction: Imagine the possibilities:

	A	$\boxed{A}$	$\circlearrowleft\boxed{A}$	$\boxed{A}$
B				
$\boxed{B'}$				
B|				
$\circlearrowleft\boxed{B}$				
$\boxed{B}$				

It is probably perilous to do it, but we guess (and are supported we think by Shostrom's little book *Man the Manipulator*) that many lawyers who attempt to manipulate clients are more manipulated than manipulating:

$$[A \underset{\longleftarrow}{\overrightarrow{\qquad}} B$$

And that many law-office situations are scenes in which neither participant is aware of his own feelings, so that each participant is vainly attempting to influence the other:

$$\boxed{A} \rightleftarrows \boxed{B}$$

In some situations both parties deal with one another openly:

$$A \rightleftarrows B$$

There are situations in which one party deals with the other in vain, as if he were trying to break through:

$$A \longrightarrow \boxed{B}$$

There are situations in which both parties deal with one another on a basis of mutual non-communication:

$$\boxed{A} \qquad\qquad \boxed{B}$$

There are situations in which one party is manipulated:

And there are situations in which neither party is communicating with himself or with the other:

$$\boxed{A} \qquad\qquad \boxed{B}$$

Transactional Analysis.   Transactional Analysis (TA) was developed by a psychiatrist, Eric Berne, author of several psychological treatises, including Games People Play. Berne's contribution was a road map for ordinary application of traditional Freudian teaching on the unconscious. The theory of TA was premised on the presence (during personal interaction) of a series of "ego states" or ways of being with other people, and on the observation that when one "ego state" meets another, the interaction is as likely to be dysfunctional and destructive as it is to be productive. The "ego states" are: Parent, Adult, and Child (corresponding, roughly, to stances of domination, awareness, and manipulation). Games occur on two levels—an apparent, or social, level and a psychological or ulterior level.

Berne's paradigm case was "If It Weren't For You." (His games typically had such catchy names; they came, Berne said, from patients who used his analytical system in group therapy.) "If It Weren't For You" (IWFY) is a game between (old-fashioned) husband and wife; he says, "You stay home and take care of the house." She says, "If it weren't for you, I could be out having fun." At the social level, the dialogue is between parent ("restricting husband") and child:

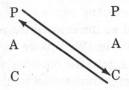

H: "Stay home."

W: "If it weren't for you. . . ."

At the psychological (ulterior) level, the game that is being played is a game of mutual terror: The husband is afraid that his wife will leave him; the wife is afraid to go out into the world and deal with other people; both are children:

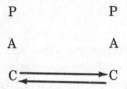

H: "You must always be here when I get home; I'm terrified of desertion."

S: "I will be if you help me avoid phobic situations."

As long as the interaction works in these ways the game can continue; thus families develop games for dealing with deviant (*e.g.*, alcoholic) members; business associates go along coping with one another in neurotic ways; and professional (*e.g.*, lawyer-client) relationships are conducted according to the model of domineering paternalism.

What stops the Bernian game and requires a re-alignment of positions and new behavior is what Berne identified as the crossed transaction. If, for example the wife in IWFY were to insist that she is going to go out into the business world and get a job, the social-level transaction would be crossed by

an adult-to-adult communication from her, one
that would stop their social game:

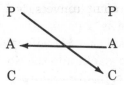

H: "Stay home."

W: "I want to get a job."

Crossed transactions stop the ulterior game, too—
sometimes in what Berne's patients identified as
"blow up." A blow up is what brings people to
professional helpers, including divorce lawyers, or
to blows, or to both.

One of our classes in legal counseling considered
a case in which the client, a young woman, was not
forthcoming about her case. The student who
worked on the case (role playing) as the lawyer
managed, though, to find out that her husband
cheated on her; and that he was brutal, financially
irresponsible, rather dashing, and more or less
indifferent. She came in asking the lawyer to do
something about the husband's current affair, and
saying she was not sure she wanted a divorce. She
was apparently vulnerable to being influenced toward divorce, but seemed to be ambivalent about
it, and she was filled with hurt and outrage and
vindictiveness. The lawyer made suggestion after
suggestion, none of which, it seemed, the client was
likely to follow. We found it useful to analyze that

interview in terms of another of Berne's games, called "Why Don't You—Yes But" (WDY). It appears to be an adult conversation:

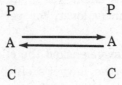

C: "Tell me what to do."

L: "This is what to do."

C: "Yes, but I can't, because. . . ."

The ulterior or psychological transaction here was child-to-parent; the client was saying, "See if you can help me, and I'm betting you can't." The game, then, looked like this (dotted lines being the psychological transaction):

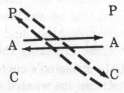

We decided this sort of game is likely to be offered by ambivalent clients and eagerly adopted by lawyers who are determined to provide advice quickly. It can be stopped by refusing to play. When we replayed the interview (same client, different "lawyers"), we saw how that might work:

—One lawyer stopped the game by non-evaluative listening; in that situation the client had no ball to hit because the pitcher wasn't throwing.

—One lawyer was more confrontive; she suggested that the client was blaming her husband, or her husband's lover, for personal inadequacies.

—A third lawyer asked the client to send her husband into the lawyer's office (and we managed quickly to set up the role-play for that). The lawyer then blustered and threatened the husband, in terms of peril to the husband's life, fortune, and sacred honor; he told the husband to shape up and he set a time for a follow-up interview with the husband.

Any of those solutions provides ammunition for further discussion; the present point about them is that they all stopped the game; they all proved that games can be stopped if the client is initiating them and avoided when the lawyer is attempting to initiate them.

A FINAL REFLECTION

The temptation of lawyers and students who have not worked at understanding counseling skills is that they don't think of a lawyer's work as counseling and they underestimate what a "lay" counselor can do. Our students sometimes argue that it is not the role of lawyers to play therapists to their clients. And we agree. Our effort is to locate and develop and improve counseling skills, because counseling is what *lawyers* do. We aim for a personal climate in the law office, one that works, one in which feelings are facts—not because we want our students to be therapists, but because feelings *are* facts. The climate in which a professional relationship grows is important; it matters. It matters to the client because it affects the way his or her case will turn out. It matters to the lawyer because the lawyer wants to be effective. It matters to the lawyer and the client because each of them wants to be treated as a person, not as a thing or an enigma. Each of them wants the opportunity to grow.

BIBLIOGRAPHY

Transactional analysis: Transactional Analysis After Eric Berne: Teachings and Practices of Three TA Schools (Barnes, ed. 1977); Current Issues in Transactional Analysis (Blakeney, ed. 1977); James, The OK Boss (Bantam 1977); Jongeward, Everybody Wins: Transactional Analysis Applied to Organizations (revised ed. 1976); Roberts, Transactional Analysis Approach to Counseling (1975); Oden, Game Free: The Meaning of Intimacy (Delta, 1975); Meininger, Success Through Transactional Analysis (1974); Steiner, Scripts People Live (1974); Berne, What Do You Say After You Say Hello? (1972); James and Jongeward, Born to Win: Transactional Analysis with Gestalt Experiments (1971); Harris, I'm OK—You're OK: A Practical Guide to Transactional

Analysis (1969); Berne, Games People Play (1964); Transactional Analysis in Psychotherapy (first Evergreen ed. 1961).

Gestalt psychology and practice: Latner, The Gestalt Therapy Book (1984); Naranjo, The Techniques of Gestalt Therapy (1980); Zinker, Creative Process in Gestalt Therapy (1977); The Handbook of Gestalt Therapy (Hatcher and Himelstein eds. 1976); Rosenblatt, Opening Doors: What Happens in Gestalt Therapy (1975); Polster and Polster, Gestalt Therapy Integrated: Contours of Theory and Practice (1973); Life Techniques in Gestalt Therapy (Fagan and Shepard, eds., Perennial Library ed. 1973); Perls, Gestalt Therapy Verbatim (1969); Eco, Hunger and Aggression: The Beginning of Gestalt Therapy (Vintage, 1969); Perls, Hefferline, and Goodman, Gestalt Therapy: Excitement and Growth in the Human Personality (1951).

The Johari Window: Luft, Of Human Interaction: The Johari Model (1969).

Rogerian counseling: Rogers, A Way of Being (1980); "The Interpersonal Relationship: The Core of Guidance," 32 Harvard Education Review 89 (1962); On Becoming A Person (1961); Client-Centered Therapy (1951); Counseling and Psychotherapy (1942); Porter, An Introduction to Therapeutic Counseling (1950).

The psychology and philosophy of C. G. Jung: Samuels, Jung and the Post-Jungians (1985); Jungian Analysis (Stein ed. 1984); Adler, Dynamics of the Self (1979); von Franz, C. G. Jung: His Myth in Our Time (1975); Singer, Boundaries of the Soul (Anchor, 1973); Hall and Nordby, A Primer of Jungian Psychology (1973); Harding, Psychic Energy: Its Source and Its Transformation (Princeton/Bollingen paperback ed. 1973); Harding, The I and the Not-I (1965); Goldbrunner, Individuation: A Study of the Depth Psychology of Carl Gustav Jung (1964).

Freudian psychoanalytic theory and practice: Rycroft, Psychoanalysis and Beyond (1985); Malcolm, Psychoanalysis: The Impossible Profession (1981); Leavy, The Psychoanalytic Dialogue (1980); Rieff, Freud: The Mind of the Moralist (1979); Moser, Years of Apprenticeship on the Couch (1977); Kardiner, My Analysis with Freud: Reminiscences (1977); Kubie, Practical and Theoretical Aspects of Psychoanalysis (revised ed. 1975); Brenner, An Elementary Textbook of Psychoanalysis (1974); Fine, The Development of Freud's Thought (1973); Friedman, Psy'cho-a-nal'-y-sis: Uses and Abuses (1968), and The Depths of the Soul: A Christian Approach to Psychoanalysis (Image Books, 1967); Brill, Basic Principles of Psychoanalysis (Washington Square Press ed. 1960).

Our understanding of Freud is undergoing a slow shift, in particular our "reading" of Freud, and the "text" that he produced. See e.g. Bettelheim, Freud and Man's Soul (1983); "Guest Editorial: On the Question of Revision of the Standard Edition of Freud's Writing," 66 International Journal of

Psycho-Analysis 1 (1985) (commenting on the questions now raised about the Strachey Standard Edition of Freud's works, published between 1955 and 1967); Ornstein, "Freud's Conception is Different from Strachey's," 33 Journal of the American Psychoanalytic Association 379 (1985) (arguing that the Strachey translation of Freud portrays Freud's psychoanalysis as more rigid, structural, and even "scientific" than a more literal translation would support. Ornstein argues that "Freud's fluid ways of understanding are tentative and his irony is charming." But, he says, "Freud's steady scientific skepticism is often missing in Strachey's Edition." The Strachey translation takes as fixed what Freud viewed as provisional and tentative; it converts into "structure" what Freud had portrayed as fluid and subject to varying descriptions and interpretations. Id. at 410).

French intellectuals, notably Jacques Lacan, have "rediscovered" Freud. One commentator notes that "Lacan has articulated a radical discourse based upon his reading of the primary Freudian texts. What appears more radical than his own polemics is Lacan's observation that what was most original and most important in Freud has remained ignored and denied ever since its discovery. Lacan's appeal to psychoanalysts is to return to Freud, reread his works, and rediscover what has been left out in current interpretations of psychoanalytic theory." Stewart, "The Linguistic Unconscious of Jacques Lacan," 45 American Journal of Psychoanalysis 348, at 348 (1985). See Catherine Clement, The Lives and Legends of Jacques Lacan (1983); Roustang, Psychoanalysis Never Lets Go (1983); Lacan, The Language of the Self: The Function of Language in Psychoanalysis (1968).

Freud is also the center of lively interest in feminist writings. See Chodorow, The Reproduction of Mothering: Psychoanalysis and the Sociology of Gender (1978); Mitchell, Psychoanalysis and Feminism: Freud, Reich, Laing and Women (Vintage, 1975).

REFERENCES

Berne, Transactional Analysis in Psychotherapy (1961), and What Do You Say After You Say Hello? (1972); Buber, I and Thou (Kaufman trans. 1972); Freud, Dora: Analysis of a Case of Hysteria (Collier ed. 1963); Greenwald, "The Ground Rules in Gestalt Therapy," in The Handbook of Gestalt Therapy (Hatcher and Himelstein eds. 1976); Harris, I'm Okay, You're Okay (1969); Hilfiker, Healing the Wounds: A Physician Looks at His Work (1985); Horney, Self-Analysis (1942); James and Jongeward, Born to Win (1971); Jung, The Psychology of the Transference in the Practice of Psychotherapy, in 16 Collected Works (Bollingen, 2nd ed. 1966), and Analytical Psychology (1968); Kinsey, Sexual Behavior in the Human Male (see Chapter Four); Luft, Of Human Interaction (1969); Perls, Gestalt Therapy Verbatim (1969); Porter,

An Introduction to Therapeutic Counseling (1950); Reik, The Inner Experience of a Psychoanalyst (1949); Rogers, Client-Centered Therapy (1951), On Becoming a Person (1961), and A Way of Being (1980); Shostrom, Man the Manipulator (1967); Simons and Reidy, the Human Art of Counseling (1972); Watson, "The Quest for Professional Competence: Psychological Aspects of Legal Education," 37 University of Cincinnati Law Review 93 (1968); Watson, Psychiatry for Lawyers (1968).

CHAPTER SEVEN

SKILLS AND INTERVENTIONS

PHASES IN LEGAL COUNSELING

We propose, in discussing skills, that we consider that our work with clients in the law office—that is, counseling in the broad sense—usually proceeds through and around four logically distinct phases:

The first is fact gathering (Chapter Five). It is analogous to evidentiary hearings in administrative law, or trials in courts, or legislative investigations. The skills involved in gathering facts from clients are interviewing skills. Facts are here, as elsewhere in the law, the basis for further professional work.

The second, third and fourth stages are means to the achievement of a result. These stages can be identified as (2) choice, (3) decision, and (4) solution. Each stage is associated with the questions a client puts: In the *choice* stage the question is: What do I want to do? In the *decision* stage the questions are: How am I (are we) to do it? What legal devices can you use for me, or we use together? And in the *solution* stage the question is: Has my appeal to lawyers and the law got me what I wanted (or needed)? These different aspects of counseling are presented as stages (which suggest a chronological sequence); each is often identified with a distinct (and explicit) closure that signals a movement to the next stage. It would be overly simplistic to suggest that all counseling relationships follow this progression. Each of the stages is normally an identifiable element or aspect of a counseling relationship. In reality, the stages are reached in varying orders.

The first kind of result that normally issues from a process of helping the client make her own way is the tough choice: This is what I want to do. Choice as we are using it (and as non-legal counselors use it) is the direction clients determine to take as a result of counseling in the narrow sense (as the word is used by non-legal counselors). Counseling in this sense is the process of helping a client make up his mind.

The second kind of result issues from a process of working with the client toward a decision. Decisions in law offices are analogous to decisions in courts or legislatures. They are in an essential sense "legal." They are precise; they can be implemented. They are similar to legislative decisions following legislative choices: The legislature may make a choice for the state. For instance, legislatures decided in the 1960s to pursue policies of racial equality. Some of them then, more precisely, made decisions to implement their choices through fair employment practices commissions. Some legislatures chose racial equality and then came to a decision against enforcement of equal rights. They contented themselves with admonitions. Law office decisions are, in a similar way, answers to the client's second question—How am I (are we) to do what I (we) have (already) chosen to do? They follow choice.

Take the distinction between choice and decision one step further: To carry out the legislative decision in favor of an F.E.P.C., a legislative lawyer must plan and draft a complex, comprehensive statute and resolve in it the expectations of legislators and the needs of people in minority groups. This is the third kind of result. In looking at law office practice, we are calling this operation problem solving, and its result a solution.

Some examples:

—A client decides that she wants to terminate her marriage. She and her lawyer working together decide that the way to do that is to seek a separation rather than a divorce. And her lawyer, now initiating a fairly technical aspect of his work, figures out a solution to the problems of how, when, and where to file; how to seek child custody; what position to take on support; and what sort of strategy to pursue with the husband's lawyer. (We don't suggest that the client is not involved in problem solving. The difference is more narrow expertise, more initiation, than is involved in arriving at choices or making decisions.)

—The lawyer and client make the decision to merge the client's twenty corporations and reincorporate them; the client decides that he wants the new corporation to be publicly owned; and the lawyer arrives at a solution to the problems of timing, tax saving, which state to incorporate in, stock restrictions, and the form and content of prospectuses and "blue sky" statements. Note that solution could come before decision here, or even before choice. Note, too, that fact gathering and interviewing may not occur exclusively at the beginning of the process. Lawyer and client usually need to return to the facts throughout the process.

—The client decides she wants to sue the trucking company whose truck she collided with, rather than accept a token settlement; she and her lawyer decide that the way to carry this out is through a suit of a certain scope; and the lawyer arrives at a series of solutions on forum, strategy, motions, trial time, and evidence. (Query: How should we classify her determination not to include the driver of the truck as co-defendant?)

The lawyer's function differs from one stage to another and between interviewing and the three second-tier operations that produce closure or result.

Interviewing skills are involved at the fact-gathering stage. Those were explored in Chapter Five. Counseling skills (in the narrow sense of "counseling") are involved in helping the client choose what he wants to do. These are, broadly, to provide information and a climate of freedom in which choice can be made. Some counselors speak of these skills as a matter of "opening up options." The skills include such things as alert reaction, accurate reflection, congruence, acceptance, understanding, empathy, and the most delicate side of the ability to listen.

The skills that lead to decision about how to do what the client chooses are interaction skills, skills involving cooperation, coordination, explanation, foresight, and a sense of consequence. John Dewey talked about socially-conscious judges following a "logic of consequences." Much the same quality is involved in working toward collaborative law office decisions.

The skills that result in a solution involve more lawyer initiation, more substantive knowledge, and, most of all, a high level of creativity. The analogy to courts is again compelling. The great creative judges—Cardozo in the McPherson case, John Marshall in the cases that established the independence of the federal judiciary—set an important example for law office problem solvers.

These operations are not as discrete as the stages of a trial or the parts of a will. It is best to think of them as functional more than chronological: A client says he wants to disinherit his errant son. His lawyer proceeds to a series of suggestions on life insurance beneficiaries, the text of the disinheriting will, and what to do about grandchildren; and then the client suddenly demonstrates that he has not really chosen what he said he wanted to do. The lawyer may then need to set his collaborative or creative skills aside and get back to helping the client decide what he wants to do. They may even have to return to fact gathering. The process of problem solving (in drafting a will or planning a securities registration) may turn up key areas for collaboration, or even for tough choices, which require the lawyer to put his pencil down and close his book and think more carefully about his relationship to this unique client with his unique concerns.

These four functions are not chronologically discrete but they are valid categories and the skills appropriate to them are legitimately distinct. Lawyers who approach clients as problems and not people are not likely to notice the categories, but there is a difference between solving problems and facilitating choices. Lawyers who press for implementing decisions where the issue is tough choices may find neither decision nor choice but, maybe, a client who decides to go to another lawyer.

Richard Wallen proposed for industrial psychologists a diagram for organizational development consultation. We adapt it a bit to indicate how functions may be broken down somewhat further. This scheme starts after fact gathering and after essential client choices have been made:

Adaptation of
Wallen Chart to the
Law Office

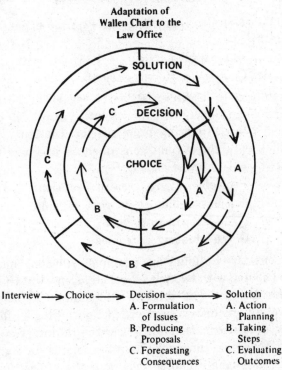

Interview →	Choice →	Decision →	Solution
		A. Formulation of Issues	A. Action Planning
		B. Producing Proposals	B. Taking Steps
		C. Forecasting Consequences	C. Evaluating Outcomes

[B2942]

The chart serves three useful purposes. First, its circles and arrows suggest that the process is dynamic; it does not stop for recess. Second, the points of choice suggested by the lines and arrows indicate that collaboration may result in further collaboration, that problem solving may require a return to collaboration (or even a return to tough choice). This adds the important dimension of testing decision and solution. Finally, Wallen breaks down collaborative decision making into further steps, so that our outline can be expanded a bit:

I.   Interviewing (facts)

II. Counseling (tough choices)

III. Consulting (collaborative decisions)
   A.   formulation of issues
   B.   producing proposals for decision
   C.   forecasting consequences and testing proposals

IV. Problem solving (creative solution)
   A.   action-planning
   B.   taking action steps
   C.   evaluating outcomes

Consider the following example: A young married couple with two pre-school children want their wills drawn. The process of dealing with them involves one or two hours of fact gathering. Most lawyers perform this function with oral interviews. We have also considered written devices for some fact gathering (Chapter Five), but the almost universal custom is to do this kind of work in person, with questions and answers and yellow pads. Fact gathering results in a significant amount of information on assets, family relationships, and biographical data (ages, state of health, employment, etc.).

The clients must then choose what they want to do. If the wife dies first, does the family wealth pass to the husband outright or is it necessary to establish a system of property management for him? (We assume her share of it is to pass to him, but that too may be a tough choice.) For example, if both parents die when one or more children are minors, is management necessary? Are the ordinary assumptions about succession applicable ("all to mama and if she's dead to the kids," as the country lawyers put it)? The lawyer's professional function in helping the clients decide what to do also turns up some other, more specific areas of client choice, areas that have to do with feelings about death, about property, and about loved ones. These show up, for example, when questions are asked about disposition when parents and children are all dead and distribution must be made outside the immediate family. All of this process relates to tough choices; the skills involved are counseling skills. The objective is a personal and psychological climate in which each of the clients experiences enough freedom to make the choices clearly and with confidence in each partner's ability to choose.

As the choices are made, collaborative decisions become necessary. If, for example, property-management is chosen for minor children (or for the widow or widower), what form is it to take? There is an enormous difference between guardianship (conservatorship) for a child and trust management. There is a difference between a trust administered by a bank and a trust administered by a relative. This decision making process is more collaborative than the counseling process is. It involves (1) formulation of issues, (2) producing

proposals for decision, and (3) forecasting consequences and testing proposals; for examples:

1. The issue, given a decision to establish a
trust for children, is whether the shares of adult
children should be held in the trust until all
children are of age. The lawyer usually poses
this issue. ("Of age" in trust planning is a
decided-upon age, not necessarily the age of majority dictated by statute.)

2. Proposals for collaborative decision (coming from both the lawyer and the clients) include
holding all trust funds in one trust until the
youngest child reaches majority; making distribution to each child as he reaches majority; and
making distribution as each child either reaches
majority or finishes college. Here is where it is
significant that the definition of "majority" is a
decision and may be a choice. The lawyer here
functions as one who poses alternatives that oft-
en seem subtle to laymen but are blatant when
played out in human lives. This family lawyer
might, for example, suggest that the first alternative can be varied a little by giving the trustee
authority to distribute principal to adult children if their educational or family needs require
funds and if the minor children are adequately
provided for.

3. The proposals are tested hypothetically. If
rigid-shares distributions are made, and one minor child has serious medical needs or proves to
be a child prodigy at the violin, will trust funds

be adequate? (Perhaps the trustee can function as a parent would.) The lawyer, because he has less attachment to the people and property involved in the client's choices and decisions, is a valuable bridge to reality, a valuable barometer for the logic of consequences.

Finally, as these collaborative decisions are made, the lawyer initiates the process of problem solving. The trust for children, for example, is chosen and its main outlines decided. The clients decide that the wife's brother should be trustee. It is now necessary to solve the problems of trustee authority, beneficiary ability to assign assets, problems of accounting and bonding, and fiduciary powers over property and people. These issues are relatively technical but they involve serious consequences. They make significant differences in human lives; the drafter of a trust is important for these human lives. A lawyer who respects his clients involves them in solving these problems, even though he will probably find that he must initiate solutions with more direction than was true when decision making was in process, and certainly with more direction than was involved when the clients were making tough choices. Using Wallen's outline:

—Action-planning points to two documents, an inter-vivos, contingent, life insurance trust and two "pour-over" wills, one for each spouse, along with appropriate changes of ownership of assets, and changes in insurance beneficiary designations.

—Action steps are taken; the documents are drafted; the wife's brother is consulted about his trusteeship; documents are drafted with clarity and with explanation and the clients are asked to read them and to think about what they will mean to them and to their family.

—Outcomes are evaluated. The plan is tested against feelings. The clients adjust and change and re-think.

It may be apparent to you that a given result may be a choice about what one wants, a decision about how to do what one wants, or a solution, depending on how the lawyer looks upon client involvement and upon his own control of the situation. Solutions involve lots of lawyer control; collaborative decisions involve less control, more partnership; and tough choices involve client control. The lawyer is, in most cases, in a position to affect, even determine, outcomes. She is also in a position to define the process by which outcomes are reached.

The primary distinction in lawyer-counselor functions that we make here is between hard choices (What do I want to do?) and collaborative decisions (How are we to do it?). Hard-choice counseling is a process in which the counselor helps the client make his own way. As "counseling" is used, in this narrow, restrictive sense, its objective is help as the client determines what she wants. The skill involved is, most of all, to provide a climate of freedom in which hard choices can be made. This skill includes the difficult ability to listen to feelings as well as to words.

When the issue is hard choice, the client does not need an expert as much as she needs a friend or companion. If the client is hung up he or she needs companionship and safety and room to move—these more than "guidance." In choice cases, clients usually also need some simple information, but it should be obvious in cases like these that no amount of information, no aggregation of facts or rules, will give the relief needed. (See Exercise Ten, in the Appendix.)

THE MOVEMENT FROM CHOICE TO DECISION

Decision-making differs from counseling on hard choices in terms of the relative contribution of the parties. In choice counseling, the client asks "What am I to do?" The lawyer helps him find his way. The client seeks to make up his mind and to emerge from the process with dignity. The appropriate counselor behavior, when the issue is hard choice, is reflective and, perhaps, supportive; the counselor works best on hard choices when he thinks of himself as a companion (or friend) more than a contributor.

In decision-making, the lawyer's role is, we think, more appropriately active. The lawyer can suggest options, provide information (about law and about other things), identify moral concerns, predict consequences, and suggest the interests of persons who are not in the room but who will be affected by the decision. The client is also active; the agenda involves his deepest interests and the interests of people he cares about. Most intangible information about consequences and impact are in his possession, not the lawyer's. A counselor who respects his client contributes to the decision but does not dominate it. He aims for collaboration. In this respect, decision-making is not like problem solving; problem solving assumes both a client choice and a lawyer-client decision. It involves narrower expertise in implementing decisions, and greater lawyer control of the process.

Another way to chart these distinctions is in terms of interests:

—When the client is being interviewed, the counselor's interest is a curious interest—like Joe Friday saying, "Give me the facts, Ma'am," or, better, like Alfred Kinsey saying, "Would you help me?"

—When the client is making a hard choice, the interest is personal, often deeply personal. The counselor's interest is to understand, to sympathize, and to accept the client's feelings, whatever they are.

—When the client and lawyer are arriving at a decision, the interest is closer to the task, a mixture of psychological interest in the client and professional concern for resolving issues and predicting their impact and influence beyond the law office.

—When the issue is problem-solving, the interest is craftsmanship. It is an interest in doing a lawyer-like job of drafting, negotiation, litigation, explanation, or protection.

It is probably a useful exercise to pause once in a while when dealing with a client and ask yourself where your interest is at that moment: In the client as a person? In the task? In some agenda of your own? And where is the client's interest? These examinations of interest may help in deciding whether the lawyer-client relationship at the moment is an interviewing relationship, a counseling relationship, a decision-making relationship, or a problem-solving relationship.

36

SKILLS

There are discrete and "practical" techniques for legal counseling. Some of these are more appropriate for one stage than for another. We propose now to talk about three of these skills: active listening; an awareness of non-verbal communication; and the effective use of questions.

Active Listening. Calvin Shrag, the existentialist philosopher, suggests that our everyday lives in coffee shops, living rooms, and cocktail parties prepare us poorly for the business of hearing what clients say. "Talk," he says, "is a degenerate form of communication which merely expresses the accepted, average, everyday interpretations of the public.   No real content is communicated, and nothing is genuinely understood.   All attention is focused on the talking itself, which always uses the conventional cliches."   The point is related, in Shrag's thought, to a moral imperative he borrows from Kierkegaard: "The majority of men are subjective towards themselves and objective toward all others, terribly objective sometimes—but the real task is in fact to be objective towards oneself and subjective toward all others."

This is useful philosophy, but reducing it to a skill or a technique is not simple.   As Schrag implied, to be active may be not to listen.   But as Annette Garrett said, "One who frequently interrupts to say what he would have done . . . is not a good listener [but] . . . neither is he who sits like a bump on a log.   Absence of response may easily seem . . . to reflect absence of interest." She goes on to say that:

> Even when our primary interest in a given interview is to obtain the answers to a set of questions, we can profit much from letting the client talk rather freely at first. . . .   [This] tends to counteract any preconceived ideas about him which the interviewer may have allowed himself to entertain.   It gives the interviewer the immense advantage of being able to see the situation and the client's problem from the client's point of view.

Active listening is a way to avoid both interruption and being a bump on a log.   Active listening is more than listening for facts. Fact gathering is only one aspect of listening to a client. The kind of active listening we have in mind is that of listening to the *situation.* It is a listening that involves the other senses, as in "seeing" through the surface level, watching for clues and signs about what is really being said. Listening is not so much a matter of being quiet and passive, letting another speak, as it is an active engagement with the person as he speaks. Active listening is *imaginative* listening. An active listener is able to hear what is being said and is able to place himself in the world that he hears (and imagines) being described. Counselors began some time ago to refer to this as *empathy:* An active listener is empathic; he feels what the client is feeling, *and* he is able to communicate that he feels what the client is feeling.

Active listening is, then, in the deepest sense, listening to what is really being said. Each of us can remember saying more than we said in words—saying more than would have been reflected in a transcript. We usually depend on those who hear us to realize what we are saying—*all* that we are saying—and to supply what is not in our words. Active listening is this listening for meaning and for feeling, as well as for words. It is a skill, a technique, and often an art. (See Exercises Eight and Nine, in the Appendix.)

One way we see the meaning in the words and the feeling behind them is to listen to the story that the client is telling. (See Chapter Two.) Clients tell stories with words, stories that have plots. The plot in a client's story is often complex, twisted, sometimes perverse, but it is a plot. The meaning of a story is embodied in the plot, as well as in the words and the facts from which the plot appears. Listening to the story, and to the plot in the client's story, is one way to engage in active listening.

The client's story is integral to what the client is saying and essential to the fact gathering that every lawyer does in talking and listening to a client (see Chapter Five). A story shapes and defines expectations and experiences of the client and is the best clue to "seeing" what the client wants and needs, as well as what he or she asks you to do. When a client is saying one thing and meaning another, there is some element or aspect of his story that he does not himself fully understand. (None of us is fully aware, all of the time, of the whole story he is telling or that can be observed in watching his behavior.)

Another way to practice active listening is paying attention to the relationship. Finding out what the client needs (which goes deeper than asking what she wants), what she means, and something of her story is not so much a matter of science or of psychology, as of the lawyer's determination to establish a particular kind of relationship with the client. Professional relationship is broadened and made a part of practice by a set of skills:

—knowing that communication takes place by means other than words (listening between the lines);

—willingness to hear the story;

—looking for metaphors and images that capture the client's sense of self and world;

—being aware of unrealistic expectations and fears (in yourself as well as your client);

—making an assessment of the emotional involvement of the client in an idea, another person, a business, an object, an injury; and your own emotional involvements which support and conflict with the client's involvements;

—realizing that some relationships are neurotic (and pathological) and that these ways of relating to others and the world around us are debilitating, depressing, and anxiety provoking.

Questions. Questions serve lots of purposes, the least of which is to learn facts. Watch two television lawyers in action in the courtroom (or out of it) and see if you can make some generalizations about (1) the purpose of the questions they ask and (2) what that tells you about how a person (who writes television scripts) sees the legal profession. Television-lawyer questions are close to a completely wrong technique for interviewing, counseling, and collaborative decision making. As Garrett said, the purpose of counseling is "to understand and be of assistance." Even in fact gathering the interviewee is where he is in order to convey information, and he is only infrequently reluctant to convey it. If Kinsey can bring others to talk (see Chapter Five), surely we lawyers whom they seek out can.

Anthony Trollope's character Lucy Morris was a good listener. Here's what Trollope said about her: "She would always be saying a word or two [not a *question* or two], just to help you—the best word that could be spoken, and then again she would be hanging on your lips. There are listeners who show by their mode of listening that they listen as a duty—not because they are interested. Lucy Morris was not such a one. She would take up your subject, whatever it was, and make it her own." Here are some specific suggestions for lawyers who want to become Lucy Morrises:

—Manner and tone are most likely to convey a desire to help if the lawyer is aware of her own feelings and has clearly decided to be helpful, a companion, and perhaps a friend. It is almost impossible to over-emphasize the value of self-awareness as a first step in attempting to become aware of and useful to other people. The world would be a better place, and so would law offices, if more lawyers spent more time at understanding themselves. The principal dogmas for legal counseling—to repeat—are: (a) Counseling is a people skill, not a black-letter skill. (b) The best way to learn about people is, as Socrates said, to know myself. (c) The second best place to learn about people—and a good place to learn about myself—is you.

—Discovery of something the client is not quite aware of is most likely to be accepted if the discovery is explained with empathy rather than with one-upmanship. Questions ("Isn't it true that . . . ? ") are almost always a poor way to express discovery. Requests for help ("Let me see if I understand") are almost always a good way.

—Probing for no apparent reason usually makes the client defensive and may cause him to avoid telling you the things you need to know; "a good general rule," Garrett says, "is to question for only one of two purposes, to obtain specifically needed information, and to direct the client's conversation from fruitless to fruitful channels."

—Expression of the interviewer's dilemma is likely to be more successful than interrogation. If I don't understand what the client has said, I am less threatening when I focus on my reception ("I don't understand") than when I focus on his inability to be articulate ("What do you mean?"). Questions tend to focus on the client's shortcomings; they also imply that the interviewer is superior.

—Open-ended questions work better than "cross-examination" questions; good questions go after information and not after a score ("yes" or "no" is a score); "even if questions that imply an answer do not result in false answers, they tend to give the impression that the questioner is lacking in fundamental understanding of the situation," Garrett says. Extensive research demonstrates that cross-examination, which may be a good way to catch hostile liars in court, is the world's worst way to gather information.

—Let the client set the pace; if the interview goes too slowly for the client, he will become bored, and boredom, according to psychological theory, is often a manifestation of anger (anger at the lawyer in this case); if the pace moves too fast for the client, he is likely to experience his own confusion as a rejection by the interviewer, which it usually is. The school-photograph interview, in Chapter Four, contains an example of misplaced pace setting.

Alfred Benjamin suggests that the average interviewer uses questions too readily and without considering alternative ways to gather information. "His questions seem to keep him afloat; take them away from him and he will sink." Questions, he says, confuse and interrupt the client; they are often impossible to answer; often the actor doesn't even want an answer, and he doesn't listen when he gets an answer. "However," Benjamin says, "my greatest objection to the use of questions . . . lies deeper":

> If we begin . . . by asking questions and getting answers, asking more questions and getting more answers, we are setting up a pattern

from which neither we nor surely the [client] will be able to extricate himself. By offering him no alternative we shall be teaching him that in this situation it is up to us to ask the questions and up to him to answer them. What is worse, having already become accustomed to this pattern from previous experience, he may readily adapt himself to it. . . . [H]e will perceive himself as an object, an object who answers when asked and otherwise keeps his mouth closed—and undoubtedly his mind and heart as well. By initiating the question-answer pattern we are telling the interviewee as plainly as if we put it into words that we are the authority, the boss, and that only we know what is important and relevant for him.

[The] unstated assumption . . . [is] that the interviewee submits to this humiliating treatment only because he expects you to come up with a solution to his problem or because he feels that this is the only way you have of helping him. As for you, the [lawyer], you have asked your questions and gotten your answers; now show your tricks. If you do not have the solution up your sleeve, if you cannot help after the long third degree, what right had you to ask? What are you good for?

In other words, questions, in addition to all of their other shortcomings, encourage inappropriate dependence.

Benjamin raises a difficult issue for lawyers—and seems to set an almost impossible standard. He recognizes, though, that we sometimes have to ask questions. Ultimately, he says, we must learn to discipline ourselves with a few protective standards:

1. We should be aware of the fact that we are asking questions.

2. We should challenge the questions we are about to ask.

3. We should examine carefully the various sorts of questions available to us and the types of questions we personally tend to use.

4. We should consider alternatives to the asking of questions.

5. We should become sensitive to the questions the client is asking, whether he is asking them outright or not.

Benjamin's pet peeve is the "why" question: The word "why," he says, "connotes disapproval, displeasure. Thus when used by the [lawyer], it communicates that the [client] has done 'wrong' or behaved 'badly.' Even when that is not the meaning intended . . . that is how the word will be understood. The effect . . . will probably be negative, for he will . . . have grown up in an environment in which 'why' implied blame and condemnation." The result, in Garrett's opinion: "Whenever the interviewee hears the word 'why' he feels the need to defend himself, to withdraw and avoid the situation, or to attack." Benjamin gives examples of the "why" questions we have all grown up with and learned to use—"Why did you get the floor muddy?" "Why did you break the dish?" "Why did you take my bike?" "Why did you do that?" "Why don't you listen?"

Listening to What Is Not Said: Non-Verbal Communication. Miguel de Unamuno, through his character St. Immanuel the Good, says, "We should concern ourselves less with what people are trying to tell us than with what they tell us without trying." One way to begin to improve the difficult skill of listening non-verbally, of observing the way the client is presenting himself, is to characterize broadly. Does he act as though he were visiting a doctor? Is he treating me the way he probably treats business colleagues? Does he seem to be wary, as if he were talking to someone he does not trust? Another way to approach this skill is to look for specific clues. Garrett emphasizes the more obvious non-verbal clues—tenseness, rigid posture, clenched hands, facial expressions, as well as the things one can observe (dress, physical condition, gait) that talk about the client's life. We suggest that an understanding of non-verbal behavior and communication involves both approaches, both broad characterization and training in observation.

Some of the research on "body language" carries encouragement for psychological amateurs, who may with good reason wonder if they must study psychology in order to practice law. (The answer may be yes, but probably not because of psychology's information on non-verbal behavior.) The research suggests that accurate non-verbal communication comes across more or less in wholes, not in parts. We receive non-verbal signals most accurately when we receive them in broad, non-verbal impressions of our own. Some examples were suggested above: What is my client's physical attitude toward me? Does he act as if he were here to see an undertaker? A principal in school? His father? His friend? This research suggests that the best way to get good non-verbal communication going is to be aware of one's own non-verbal attitudes and watch for the ways these attitudes are carrying messages for us. What am I saying, for instance, when I put the client on one side of the desk and myself on the other, with all of the apparatus of lawyering and mastery on my side and bare desk or at best an ashtray on his side? What am I saying when I keep my hands writing and my notes in front of me and my eyes down most of the time? What would I say (and what would I feel) if I moved around to the other side of the desk? Or took off my coat? Or threw the yellow pad away? What would happen if I interviewed my client at some place other than my office? (Review Chapter Five, on Kinsey's interviewing practices; and see Exercise Eleven, in the Appendix.)

THINGS TO LOOK FOR (AND DO) IN LEGAL COUNSELING

Interview answers tend to fall into patterns which tell more than their content. The *process* in the interview and the *context* of what the client says are sources of information:

Open and Closing Sentences. First words may tell most about the client's agenda in the interview; and last words may tell most about the way he feels about his relationship with the lawyer.

Shifts in Conversation. These are probably defensive; they occur in client statements and in the lawyer's behavior. (That is, one wants to listen for them from the client and also to listen for them from oneself.) An example is the shift that occurs when the client has touched on something he doesn't want to talk about any more (in which case, assuming the topic is relevant, it may be best to make the observation to him); shifts may also indicate an association. Lawyers use shifts to avoid pain, even when pursuit of the topic is both germane to the discovery of facts and is something the client is willing to do (a point abundantly clear in studies of will interviews such as those reproduced in Shaffer's Death, Property, and Lawyers). There is some kind of evil convention which perpetuates shifts of this sort; it is illustrated in this exchange between Ann Landers and one of her readers:

"My mother . . . talks of nothing but sickness and death. Her favorite topic is friends who have cancer. She goes into great detail about how they are suffering. If there was surgery, she knows all about it.

"Grandma is only 52 and in good health but she takes pills for menopause as well as tranquilizers and aspirin. She invites the children to watch her take her medicine and makes a big production of it.

"I have told Mother that morbid talk is unhealthy for children. She pays no attention. It's the same story every time we go over there. What should be done about this?"

Troubled.

"Dear T:

"Whenever Grandma starts to talk about illness or death, change the subject to something cheerful and happy. If she returns to the gloom-and-doom recitals, cut in and say, 'Your sad stories spoil our visit, Mother. . . .'

"In other words, get control of the conversation and don't let go."

That is great advice for everybody but Mother; it ignores her needs and feelings. Lawyers should be more sensitive to that fact than Troubled and Ann were.

Themes, recurrent references. A man's references to his wife, in an interview about the purchase of real estate, may tell the interviewer that

the state of the client's marriage is a central concern in matters of investment. "Talking in circles" may tell the interviewer that, for some reason, the client may not want to get down to the
business at hand. Examples occur frequently in
will interviews possibly because people don't like to
talk about death, or because lawyers think they
don't. Maybe it's true that the client does not
want to talk about his death or his wife becoming a
widow or his children becoming orphans; maybe
he wants the lawyer to lead him into those subjects.

Inconsistencies and gaps. Contradiction may indicate that the client is experiencing troublesome
feelings about the subject being discussed—guilt,
maybe, or confusion, or ambivalence. What is left
out or expressed inconsistently is probably what is
most important to the client. Garrett says: "A
woman may discuss in great detail certain difficulties she has been having with the children but say
nothing about her husband. The significance of
such gaps or inconsistencies often becomes clearer
through their cumulative force. One such occurrence may suggest a barely possible interpretation.
But if ten others confirm this hypothesis, it is no
longer a mere possibility."

Association of ideas. Part of noticing how clients go from one subject to another is a matter of
gathering information; and part of it is a matter of
avoiding interference. The interference part of
idea association is a matter of the lawyer's being

aware of *his own* associations; "when the client mentions . . . lying, divorce, a grandmother, there may be started in the [lawyer] a stream of association which has little to do with the client's feelings about these things," Garrett says.

Concealed meaning. A boy who says he doesn't like baseball may be saying that he is suffering from a lack of friends (Garrett's example); a businessman who protests that he only "wants to do the right thing" in litigation may feel guilty because he wants to do the wrong thing. Or—the commonest of all commercial examples—as Abe Martin (and Artemus Ward) said, "Whenever anybody says to me 'It's not the money, it's the principle of the thing,' it's the money." (See Exercises Three and Fourteen, in the Appendix.)

FEEDBACK

Modern psychology borrowed from electrical engineering the term "feedback" to describe conversation that is reflective, person-centered, and, often, a bit hard to take. "Feedback," in literature on counseling, usually describes the hard truth; it depends on honesty, even when honesty hurts. We avoid feedback because we avoid hurt. They (feedback and hurt) are essential, or at any rate inevitable, in the stages of the lawyer-client relationship that we have called choice and decision. It sometimes comes up in interviewing (as, for example, when the client is wandering off the subject or seems seriously unrealistic or is not seeing facts that are apparent to the lawyer).

A good law office climate for personal growth and tough choices needs a lawyer who will level with the client about what the client is doing, what the client's style is, and what the immediate interpersonal environment is really like, and do this without adding to the client's feeling that he is stupid or bad or both. "In almost every phase of our lives—at home, at school, at work—we find ourselves under the rewards and punishments of external judgments," Carl Rogers says. " 'That's good'; 'that's naughty'. . . . Such judgments are a part of our lives from infancy to old age."

The counseling literature suggests these skills for effective feedback:

1. *Feedback Should Describe, Not Evaluate.* The client should be free to use it or not use it, as the client sees fit. If one pursued that idea in law practice she might decide finally that the traditional ideal of lawyer independence is overblown, or at least misapplied. A moving and personal argument for the possibility was made by Professor Stephen Wexler when he was a young poverty lawyer:

The dominant attitude in law school is that the client is a troublesome pain-in-the-neck. Occasionally, the law student hears hints that he should present his clients with the legal alternatives, among which the client should choose. Many lawyers are now aware that people should control their lawyer, and are beginning to present alternatives from which their clients can choose. But the control which poor people should exercise over their lawyer is much greater than that of merely selecting among his proposals. . . . [B]ecause they know what is helpful to them and possible for them, they can and must structure their own alternatives and make their own choices.

Mr. Wexler's insight will shock many lawyers. Most of us, accustomed as we are to being guru, shaman, and Delphic Oracle to our clients, will not be able to accept it. But it could be part of a humanistic working relationship with our clients, and lawyers need humanism as much as anybody else. Even poverty lawyers.

2. *Feedback Is Specific.* "John, you're trying to dominate me" may be a true observation, but it is less likely to be acted upon than "John, just now when you and I were discussing that lease, I had the feeling you were not listening to me. I had the feeling, just then, that you wanted me to agree with you, regardless of what I thought."

3. *Feedback Takes into Account Needs of Lawyers As Well As Needs of Clients.* A lawyer acts, in the nature of things, from a position of enormous interpersonal power. And pushing people around gets to be fun; it can be used for pure recreation. We all know an occasional sadistic lawyer who uses his influence over clients, and junior colleagues, and clerks in public offices, for entertain-

ment. Paradoxically, though, a person cannot move toward action with sensitivity for others until he recognizes and accepts the demands of his own needs.

4. *Feedback Is Directed Toward Behavior the Client Can Change.* It won't do any client anything but injury to tell him that he is inept, stupid, or evil. What is usually involved when a "helping person" takes that tack, of course, is misdirected aggression in the helper. Compare the classic model of a so-called Socratic law teacher, who abuses law students, perhaps because he lacks enough status or enough opportunity to abuse his professional peers as much as he wants. Another side of destructive feedback is that it is usually a misperception. The client who is perceived as impotent because he is old or inept may simply be coming across that way. He may, out of some need of his own, be trying to appear old and inept; that may be his manipulative device ("poor little me"). If that is so, and the lawyer's perception is accurate, it may do the client a world of good to have the benefit of the perception. The challenge is to give it to him without appearing judgmental. (See numbers "1" and "2".)

5. *Feedback Is Best When Solicited.* Not all law office situations imply a desire in the client for honest reaction—but many do—and the best feedback comes to him who wants it and says so. Another and more helpful way to put the point is that the most useful reaction is in terms of a

question the client asks. It often takes courage to answer questions such as "Do you think I'm being selfish?" or "Does it seem to you that I'm fooling myself about the matter?" or "Do I seem to you to be vindictive?" The trick is to have the courage to deal with that sort of question honestly (we rarely do), to deal with it in a way which leaves the client free to act, and to help him without making him dependent on his counselor.

6. *Feedback Is Well-Timed.* The time to answer interpersonal questions (such as those above) is when they are asked. That's when the counselor's reaction is most honest. Delay encourages evasion at one extreme and judgmental evaluation at the other.

7. *Feedback Is Checked.* An honest reaction, based on an immediate perception, may for all its candor be wrong. One way to find out, to keep personal channels of communication intact, and to guard against evaluative feedback, is to ask if the perception seems right to the client: "Yes, I have a feeling that you are being vindictive. Does it seem that way to you, too?"

* * *

Carl Rogers puts a stern list of questions to himself when he sets out to enter the world of another person, when he arrogates to himself the role of helper. The questions are, inevitably, probing and personal. But counseling is a personal enterprise. Here are some of Rogers's questions:

Can I be some way that will be perceived as trustworthy, as dependable and consistent?

Can I be expressive enough as a person that what I am will be perceived unambiguously?

Can I let myself experience warmth, caring, interest, and respect for my client?

Can I be strong enough to be separate, and am I strong enough to allow him to be separate—to be who he is?

Can I see things as he sees them, and accept him as he is?

Can I be sensitive enough and accepting enough that my behavior will somehow free him from the burden of external evaluation?

Can I meet him as one in a process of becoming, so that I need not be bound either by his past or by my past?

Feedback is a difficult skill (it is also an art) for most lawyers. The goal of good feedback to a client is to show him the consequences of his style and the subtleties of what he is doing in the lawyer-client relationship, and in the human relationships that are involved in his (the client's) tough choices. The idea is to help him gear his behavior for effective movement toward his goals and needs. The trick is to help him without judging him. And it is hard for lawyers to be non-evaluative—because lawyers are moralistic people. Our moral perceptions are what brought us to law school; moralistic temperaments are attracted to

the study of law. Law school—with its dark laby-
rinths of fault, malice, harm, breach of promise,
good faith, and dogs who know the difference between being tripped over and being kicked—rein-
forces our tendencies to pass judgment. Those
tendencies do more harm than good in law office
practice. (See Exercises Seven and Eighteen, in
the Appendix.)

INTERVENTIONS

At the everyday and most visible level, interventions consist of observations to the client, legal
advice, answering questions about law, or pointing
out options. Here are 12 illustrative types of intervention in decision-making:

Discrepancy. This intervention calls attention to
a contradiction in action or in attitudes. It is
useful in systems (corporations, business groups)
for keeping the organization on the course it has
chosen. It is a matter of reminding the client of
the client's hard choices. Discrepancy is also useful in keeping an individual client's decisions in
line with his choices.

Example: Wilma Brown chose in her will to
leave her property in trust for her husband. She
chose to do this in such a way that her husband
would have maximum access to the funds, with
professional management. The present question is
whether Mr. Brown is to enjoy a power to reach up
to $25,000 per calendar year from the principal of
the trust fund (a common provision, suggested by

tax considerations). Mrs. Brown says, "No, I think not."

Example: Acme Corporation was advised by you that it had only minimum compliance duties under federal law on equal employment opportunity, but its officers, in counseling sessions with you, decided to integrate fully its manufacturing plants—to go, that is, beyond what the law requires. The issue now is whether to also integrate employee bowling teams. The plant manager says, "Do we have to do that?"

Psychological Theory. A theoretical intervention occurs when the counselor draws on theory to throw into relief the connection between underlying assumption and present behavior. In addition, theory sometimes can be useful in predicting the consequences likely to follow from embarking on any specialized course of action.

Example: Ralph Walker insists that his lawyer in a divorce action (a) seek custody of the children and (b) seek to deny to his wife visitation rights or the temporary custody of the children for vacations. But he does not appear to believe that his wife is a bad influence on his children. He appears to believe that she will care for them well.

Example: Mr. Knox, a rigid patriarchal figure in his family, wants his will to distribute his property among his three adult children. However, his youngest son married against his father's wishes and is in an occupation of which his father disapproves. Mr. Knox wants his son's "share" of the estate placed in a tight "spendthrift" trust and parcelled out to him over his entire life, with a prohibition on distribution to or for the benefit of his son's wife. The probable size of the trust is so small that half of current income each year will be taken in trustee fees.

Procedure and Consequences. The client may not understand the cause-and-effect relationship in what he proposes to do; he may benefit from an intervention that puts events in sequence and relates them logically. This is an insight at which lawyers are expert.

Example: Mr. Baxter is terrified of criminal prosecution for making false statements in his federal income-tax return. These statements amount to a failure to disclose $5,000 in income on which the tax would be $1,150. He has not been contacted by the Internal Revenue Service. (Note here the difference between a procedural intervention and acceptance of Mr. Baxter's feelings, however illogical they are.)

Example: Roger and Sharon Luke have three children, ages one, five, and seven. The Lukes are in your office to make their wills and have decided on a contingent trust for the children if both parents die before all of the children are reared. They wish to have all their assets—$44,000 in physical assets and $100,000 in life insurance—held for the college education of the children.

Relationship. Relationship interventions focus the attention of clients on issues that arise between people as they work together. (We have referred to these aspects of the relationship as process-oriented.) They are needed to understand and reduce or eliminate interpersonal fictions. The lawyer here seeks to focus attention on personal feelings, especially on negative tensions that hinder coordinated effort. She acts from a belief that emotions can be examined and resolved. Everyone has been in a meeting—of directors, or business associates, or spouses—in which bickering and disagreement over apparent issues seem to obscure something else; what is being said and talked about (the agenda on the table) is not what is really at stake. Maybe there is a hidden agenda being worked out—rivalry, struggle over leadership, or resentment over events outside the room. The best evidence from behavioral science is that these struggles will prevent productive consensus, negotiation, and bargaining. The evidence also indicates that a third-party consultant's best move (and the lawyer's best move) may be to point out what she sees and senses. This is a matter of focus on the process, rather than on the content, of what is being done. This intervention does not guess at causes, or pass judgment, or attempt to read minds; it reports what the counselor sees. (See this chapter on "feedback" skills.)

Example: In a discussion of the terms of a loan agreement, among business associates in the borrowing organization, not even the most minor matters can be settled. What would happen if the lawyer said: "We seem to be bogged down here, unable to move. I can't understand the bickering—say, when Henry complained about the wording of the repossession clause and George said, sort of heatedly I thought, 'I don't split infinitives.' I don't know what's going on here, but it is keeping us from getting the job done. I think we ought to talk about it."

Example: Susan March is the president of Medical Products, Inc., a small incorporated manufacturer of cotton balls. There are 12 investors in the company; six of them are on the board of directors and three of the remaining six are executive-level employees. Susan has been approached by George Passant, an agent for an undisclosed company that wants to acquire Medical Products. Susan wants to talk to you about the possible acquisition. She has not mentioned her visit with Passant to any of her business colleagues.

Experimentation. Experimentation permits testing and comparing two or more courses of action before a final decision is taken, particularly when the way to proceed has become bound by tradition or custom. This intervention says in effect that a person or organization should be open to new ideas without assurance in advance that the ideas are safe.

Example: A number of large, prosperous law firms were built on a willingness to take labor cases in the 1930s and 1940s as the National Labor Relations Act took hold, even though those cases teemed with the unfamiliar—governmental control of employment relationships, employee elections, "trials" before administrative agencies, etc.

Example: Smigel says of Wall Street lawyers (quoting Beryl Harold Levy): "They helped make possible the growth of corporations 'by both counsel and by invention of new forms of credit, financing and control.' The holding company was one such device. The collapsible corporation . . . another. In fact, Levy finds, 'Our contemporary, credit-industrial economy of abundance could not have been fashioned without the brilliant imagination of the daring corporation lawyers of the 19th Century who forged one device after another to lead the way, pressing far beyond existing law.'" The credit here is well placed, no doubt, but one wonders whether these devices were developed without active contribution from business people, bankers, and investors.

Example: Arthur Getliffe wants to make a will which gives his house to his wife. His house is the only asset of significance he owns, but, if transferred by will, will be subject to the probate process and possibly to inheritance taxes. Does Mr. Getliffe have any options?

Dilemma. A dilemma intervention seeks to identify a point at which choices are being made unwittingly or implicitly; it often helps the client re-examine her assumptions and search for alternatives other than those under consideration.

Example: Frank Giapetto has been coming in for legal help for years. The history of his small, sole-proprietor doll shop is the history of the growth of the corporate state. He has had problems with zoning regulations, fire codes, retail licensing, sales tax, income tax, city tax assessments on sidewalks, federal and state excise taxes, electrical code requirements, adequate sewer venting, garbage collection, and weeds growing in the alley. You are able to deal with these problems as they come along—for a fee—but the price of Mr. Giapetto's dolls is already twice that of comparable, mass-produced competitors' products, and he is losing money. The issue is whether he should mortgage his shop to pay current property taxes.

Example: Sharon and Roger Luke in making their wills say that they want to talk to you about whether they should make their minor children contingent beneficiaries of Mr. Luke's life insurance or make Mrs. Luke's parents the beneficiaries, since her parents will care for the children if both Roger and Sharon die in the near future.

Example: Beth Simon's husband left town last week, without telling her. She is running out of money and the house payment is due. She says she came in to talk to you about a divorce, but in a previous session last week, when you first talked to her, she said she does not want her marriage dissolved.

Perspective. Individuals and organizations lose their sense of direction; when that happens, it is difficult to reestablish a course of action that moves the client away from momentary problem-solving toward larger issues. A perspective intervention permits present actions to be evaluated by providing a background of broader historical orientation.

Example: A common source of strain between students and teachers is that the history of one group is very short and the history of the other is generational. This is not a matter of "generation-gap" or of tradition. It is an instance of the fact that a person interprets the world from his own experience. "The past is not dead," Faulkner's lawyer, Gavin Stevens, said. "It's not even past."

Example: One of our legal counseling students said, "For me, awareness of the fact that most lawyers see themselves as dealing with problems, and not with clients or people, came this past summer while I was clerking for a plaintiffs' personal-injury firm. Initially, it came as a surprise to me that a law firm rejoiced in the gravity of their client's injuries when liability against the defendant was clear. This was especially true when pain and suffering was involved. The same sort of thing must be true of other kinds of practice. I wonder if business or corporate clients can visualize themselves as human beings being counseled on corporate matters or whether they feel like part of the cog in the corporate machine."

Structure. The structure within which clients function—familial, organizational, even personal—

may need to be examined. The client's habits may prevent communication, decision-making, and the application of effort from being as effective as it might be if habits were changed. It may be necessary to confront the client and the framework (perspective) that he brings to the law-office.

Example: "Most human institutions," William James said, "by the purely technical and professional manner in which they come to be administered, end by becoming obstacles to the very purposes which their founders had in view."

Example: The managing partner in your law firm cannot understand why decisions on secretarial personnel are uniformly ill-advised. He believes lawyers who solve other people's problems should be able to solve their own. Personnel decisions in the firm are made by a committee of three lawyers; the managing partner, who is chairman, always calls these committee meetings for 5:30 p.m. on Friday, because the office is quiet at that time.

Example: An expert on job enrichment reduced tardiness, absenteeism, and other dissatisfaction among loan officers in a branch bank after the expert noticed that the entrance to the officers' area was opposite the desk of the vice-president in charge of loans. The result was that customers came first to the vice-president and then were assigned to loan officers. The expert moved the door to the other end of the officers' area and put an opaque partition between the vice president and the loan officers. After that, customers came directly to the loan officers and no one consulted the vice president except in problem cases. (See diagrams in Chapter Eight.)

Example: Another legal counseling student asked, "What is it about our profession, or one's needs, that forces a non-lawyer who is talking about lawyers to embellish the facts when he presents a situation? What is wrong with the good old folksy telling it like it is? Is it because people are suspicious of lawyers, or possibly that they feel they are in an inferior position?"

Culture. A cultural intervention examines traditions, precedents and established practices. Challenging culture is difficult, because culture permeates actions, is salient in them. But the intervention most needed may be one that will bring culture into the area of deliberate decision-making.

Example: Miguel de Unamuno's character Antonia (in Abel Sanchez) "did not need to be shown anything, for she was a woman who had been born to live in the sweetness of custom."

Example: Atticus Finch, the lawyer-hero in Harper Lee's To Kill a Mockingbird, practices law in Maycomb, Alabama. Lee tells the reader that Atticus is "Maycomb County born and bred" and we learn in the story that she tells about Atticus and his children the possibilities and pathologies of being a part of rural southern, small-town culture. When Gregory Peck came later to portray Atticus, in the movie version of the story, he said he understood Atticus because he (Peck) grew up in a small town in California. He was partly wrong.

Example: In Faulkner's "Intruder in the Dust," a small-town, white, Mississippi lawyer successfully defends an old, rural, black man who is accused of murder. The defense is difficult and time-consuming. The lawyer, Gavin Stevens, spent weeks doing little else. At the end of the book, the old man comes to the lawyer's office and asks, "How much do I owe you?" Stevens says, "Three dollars." The client pays him in full.

Example: A legal counseling student says, "I spoke with a successful New York attorney about our legal counseling class. He was rather surprised that there was such a thing, and when he asked me what we were doing, I was almost at a loss for words. He seemed to think we were indulging in an academic exercise, that it had no practical value. His practice is primarily concerned with trial courts and he told me that his concern was with getting settlements, not with holding the client's hand. I wonder how many other lawyers have the same attitude. Perhaps I'm being a bit too judgmental, but, as a pure gut reaction, 'getting settlements' or 'just getting settlements' turns me off. I want to be a good lawyer. But I don't know what a good lawyer is. In the final analysis, I have to practice law by my own rules. For example, if I feel uncomfortable in counseling a woman who wants a divorce, I have to admit this to myself and it's my duty to advise my client of my uneasiness and then my client must decide whether or not she wants to obtain a new lawyer, or stick it out with me."

Logic. Every system has a logic, and individuals do what they do according to a logic. Some behavioral observers distinguish between a logic inherent in the activity (*e.g.*, the logic of business is profit; the logic of marriage is mutual support, or the rearing of children, or both) and an operating logic (*e.g.*, the logic of a particular business decision may be public responsibility or the preservation of tradition; the logic of a client's behavior in his marriage may be punishment or escape). An intervention that identifies the logic at work may help open up client options. This is often another instance of attending to process as much as content (see Chapter Four).

Example: Mrs. Baldwin says she has a lover and no longer cares for her husband. She asks, "Do you think I should divorce him?" You tell her what is involved in a divorce but she persists: "Do you think I should divorce him?"

Example: Mr. Van Cleve, one of several legatees under the will of his late and wealthy father, notes that his father disinherited one daughter, Mr. Van Cleve's sister Agatha. Some members of the family feel that the fair thing to do is to pool a fund and give Agatha a share. Others feel that the right thing to do is to follow the wishes of the testator.

Solution-Seeking. Some decisions may be bogged down simply because they are being deliberated too much. It may be appropriate for the counselor to crystalize a decision which seems to him apparent but not yet expressed and to move from decision-making to problem-solving.

Example: Roger Harris represents a young man, Bennett Wilson, who has risen quickly within the ranks of one of the aggressive savings and loan associations. Harris is charged in a criminal indictment with violations of the state banking and securities laws. One of the difficult decisions in preparation for trial is whether Wilson will take the stand and testify.

Morals. Decisions may be impaired because of a conflict of morals—a conflict among clients, between a client and some absent person, or between the client and her lawyer. Describing the moral issues would then be an appropriate intervention. (See Chapter Ten, and Exercise Seven, in the Appendix).

BIBLIOGRAPHY

On non-verbal behavior: Hall, The Silent Language (1973); Merrbian, Silent Messages (1971); Hall, The Hidden Dimension (1966).

For excellent, comprehensive, descriptive surveys of counseling skills, with useful examples of the skills in use, see Egan, The Skilled Helper: A Model for Systematic Helping and Interpersonal Relating (1982); and Johnson, Reaching Out: Interpersonal Effectiveness and Self-Actualization (2nd ed. 1981).

REFERENCES

Benjamin, The Helping Interview (1969); Dewey, "Logical Method and Law," 10 Cornell Law Quarterly 17 (1924); Garrett, Interviewing (1942); Rogers, Client-Centered Therapy (1951); Schein, Process Orientation (1969) (includes Wallen article); Shaffer, Death, Property, and Lawyers (1970); Smigel, The Wall Street Lawyer: Professional Organization Man? (1964); Wexler, "Practicing Law for Poor People," 79 Yale Law Journal 1049 (1970).

CHAPTER EIGHT

THE PRESENCE OF THE PLACE

PLACE

The physical situation is usually of the lawyer's choosing. Traditionally, it has been an atmosphere of tacit intimidation. The lawyer's chair is larger. She is barricaded behind an imposing desk. The light is in the client's eyes, not the lawyer's. If the physical setting is changed, so that—for example— the lawyer and client sit as equals at a table, or in a living-room atmosphere, it is the lawyer who chooses the change. It is the lawyer who decides on the alignment of physical objects in the room; the distance between her and her client; and how vocally and visually available the two people are to one another. It is the lawyer who decides whether the lines of communication (speech and non-verbal communication) are open or closed, formal or informal, loud or soft, vulgar or elegant.

An alternative to lawyer domination of the physical situation would be to meet in the client's office, or in neutral territory, such as a hotel suite or a bank conference room. But even there the lawyer is usually the person who decides whether to meet on other turf. To honor equality in the matter, she would have to negotiate with the client whether there was to be a change of setting and if so where the new setting was to be. This sort of negotiation on physical setting is common in the literature of romantic love ("my place or yours?") and of diplomacy (seating arrangements at summit meetings and the shape of the table in peace talks); it is not common in American professional practice.

Nonetheless, domination is reduced and communication is usually improved when lawyer and client meet in the client's place. Alfred Kinsey (see Chapter Five) illustrated this in his procedure for interviewing children:

> For younger children, especially for those under . . . eight years of age, an interview becomes a social session involving participation in the child's ordinary activities. . . . The technique is one in which the interviewer looks at dolls, at toys of other sorts, joins in games, builds picture puzzles, romps and does acrobatics with the vigorous small boy, tells stories, draws pictures, gets the child to draw pictures, shares candies and cookies, and withal makes himself an agreeable guest.

The technique here is dazzling. The use of it—to get sex information from kids—may bother you a bit. But put that aside if you can and consider technique; technique here is deeper and broader than it appears to be. Children under eight do not easily adapt to a passive sit-there-do-what-you're-told interview setting. Because the child would not enter Kinsey's world, Kinsey was forced to enter the child's world. He was forced to do what

modern teachers of counselors stress as essential
for the atmosphere of trust that is important to
lawyers (who are paid by the hour) and was essential to Kinsey (and to the rest of us who arrogate to
ourselves the role of helpers). Kinsey's device for
children was an instance of Carl Rogers's maxim
that the counselor say to his client, "I will enter
your world as fully as I am able."

But the technique goes beyond even Rogers. Rogers after all has the client come to him; he deals
with the client on his turf, not the client's. The
client comes when she is told, leaves when she is
told, sits where the counselor indicates, and reacts
on cue. Not so one of Kinsey's children. Kinsey
shared the child's place with him. He shared the
child's physical environment, the child's chronology, his agenda for the use of time, his activity, and
his vocabulary. It would be radical for a client-
centered psychotherapist to so completely come
down from his professional dais. It would be even
more radical for a lawyer to do it—but we lawyers
may be closer to world-sharing than psychotherapists are. Here is a quizzical example:

The National Client Counseling Competition had
as its theme one year consultations with clients for
business planning. The interview problems involved business people seeing a lawyer for legal
help. Some of the problems were of the "should I
incorporate?" genre; others involved movement into new, regulated areas of business activity; some
involved buy-sell agreements and insurance fund-

ing for them. In each case the dynamics of the client's business life turned on *the presence of a place*—his office or plant, his relationship there with associates and employees, what he did there with his time, where and when he hoped and where and when he was tempted to despair.

But in no case—not once—did these law-student interviewers say to the client (what seemed the most obvious, logical human thing to say): "Let's meet at your place." The time, the place, the chronology and pattern of activity, the interpersonal environment of these interviews were all the lawyers'. The place that was present was the wrong place, at the wrong time. When judges in the competition talked to practicing lawyers about this observation, the practitioners agreed that leaving the law office would have been a good idea. Many of them indicated that they did so routinely in similar situations. The image of a businessperson's lawyer, involved in a routine, workaday client need, leaving the book-lined walls and meeting the client in the client's world, is a lot like the image of Alfred C. Kinsey, bouncing a ball with a child while he learned about the child's life, in the child's room, at the child's pace, using the child's words.

Some more detailed aspects of the presence of place:

—*Formality.* Research indicates that tables or desks between people serve as barriers (or, in a more neutral phrase, creators of distance); they tend to produce more formal behavior.

—*Posture and body language.* Studies show that strangers or casually acquainted people deal with one another less openly when they are, as the Newfoundlanders say, "side by each." That is, each presents a bodily profile to the other and turns his head when he wants to interact face to face. When people sit fully facing one another ("eye-balling") the atmosphere is more confrontive, more risky, but also probably more productive. People choose to sit facing one another because they want to confront one another, or at least because the more dominant of them wants to confront the less dominant. The confrontation can be tuned down, though, by increasing the distance between chairs or by putting a desk or table—a low coffee table—between them.

—*Distance.* Given some minimum distance (some respect for the "critical space" of the other person), research indicates that distortion in communication varies directly with the amount of distance between the communicators. Distance also tends to indicate animosity or issues between two people, as it indicates issues of membership when one of several people sits apart from the rest of a group.

—*Importance of status.* If status and feelings of superiority or inferiority are on the minds of the lawyer and his client (or of the lawyer), more attention is likely to be paid to increasing or decreasing tacit and physical dominance. If the lawyer is conscious of the fact that his client is of another race, for example, or of a significantly different economic, age, or social group, he is more likely to take care that the furniture, and his posture, and other environmental aspects of the interview are consciously arranged to say what he wants to say. Arthur Train's lawyer, Mr. Tutt, had one client chair from which he sawed an inch off the front legs. This chair was not for all clients.

—*Two-way communication.* There is always an issue in the air on whether intended or unconscious signals are received and understood by the client. What was meant to be equalization may be received as condescending or patronizing. What was meant to be a gesture of homage may be received as manipulation.

TIME

The temporal setting is, at one boundary, an appointment time, and, at the other, a deadline and expectations for the future. Lawyers usually—but not always—control both ends. A common modification is to leave it up to a lawyer's secretary to negotiate an appointment time; if the secretary really negotiates, one end of the temporal setting is then arrived at with equality. Having one's secretary set appointments can, depending on the way the secretary acts (or is told to act), say to the client either that the lawyer cares about the client's time or that the lawyer is far too busy to bother with the issue of the client's time.

The deadline issue is the question of when the meeting is to end. This can be announced or negotiated in advance, in which case the intimidation at work will be largely a function of the openness with which the lawyer considers the client's convenience. It can also be kept hidden, so that the lawyer establishes his dominance by being the one who can say, at any moment, "Time's up." Variants include alarm clocks and prearranged telephone or intercom announcements that it is time for the next client, or for lunch, or for an appearance in court. All of these devices may have a legitimate purpose in terms of the lawyer's leading an orderly life. That is their content. They also serve as scores in a competitive game, or as opportunities to demonstrate to the client that he, as a person, is important. That is their process.

Deadlines, even where agreed upon, have a number of effects on the meeting. If the deadline is perceived as distant, for instance, the research indicates that the lawyer and client will be likely to relax and may even neglect the business at hand. If it is perceived as a threat, the deadline will increase anxiety, which may in turn cause the client (and, less often, the lawyer) to make hasty concessions, give simplified information, or agree to interpretations that are not accurate. A somewhat more subtle aspect of the temporal issue is future relationship. The impact of temporal one-upmanship will be different depending on (1) whether the client's business with the lawyer is a one-shot affair; (2) whether the client is an established client; (3)

whether she is someone the lawyer would like to work for again; or (4) whether the meeting is part of a series of meetings. People act differently when they know they must depend on one another in the future. The research indicates that one-shot relationships encourage the parties to exploit one another and are more likely to foster a fear of exploitation. These facts show up in institutional habits in law firms: Law firms will often let clients who are regarded as having slight significance, or who are coming to the office only once, wait for long periods of time; but let a junior associate ignore important, established business clients in the waiting room (or on the telephone) and "the Firm" will take notice, in one way or another.

DEPENDENCE

The "presence of the place" may engender dependence and powerlessness in the client. There are advantages and disadvantages in dealing with powerless clients. One disadvantage is that powerless people tend to become lethargic; they tend to participate less; their resources for the solution of problems and for creative decision-making tend to be cut off. Consider these physical factors in terms of ecology, purpose, arrangement of people, and territoriality:

Ecology. One of Ann Landers' correspondents said she was afraid that her concern for order would make her children neurotic. "I was raised in a house where the rule was, 'a place for everything and everything in its place.' Mother taught us that when your surroundings are cluttered your mind is cluttered. I know this is true because I am at my calmest and happiest when my home, closets, and shelves are in perfect order. In other words, my emotional condition is directly connected to the condition of my home."

This mother was concerned about the effect of order on others, a sensitivity not always manifest in discussions of law-office ecology. Some ecological factors are obvious and affect everyone in the same way. The pollution by noise—clamor, racket from machines—and clutter are obvious examples. So are ventilation, light, temperature and humidity. Our environment contributes to illness, fatigue, boredom, and dissatisfaction. The client will have adverse reactions to an unpleasant place. She may quit and leave, or she may quit and stay, which is worse. Ecology has effects on behavior which may not be conscious. Here is the way a welfare client experienced the welfare office:

You have to sit there for hours waiting, waiting, while the welfare "workers" drink coffee and talk and laugh together—and pointedly ignore you. The waiting room there was very warm in the winter, but I noticed that the people who came in never took off their coats. Some of them were young men who had always supported themselves but now just couldn't find work. They were so humiliated by necessity that they sat there clutching their coats to

them, as if they were protection against the cold,
unfeeling system. Anyway, the experience
. . . made us a lot more radical than we had
ever dreamed we could be.

Another and more subtle example involved work
by an organizational development consultant for a
bank. The consultant was called in because the
turnover and absentee rate among junior loan officers disturbed the bank's management. He made
only one change in the bank's system for treating
juniors, an entirely physical (non-verbal) change
that solved the bank's problem. When he came to
the bank, the four juniors and the senior officer in
charge of them were arranged this way:

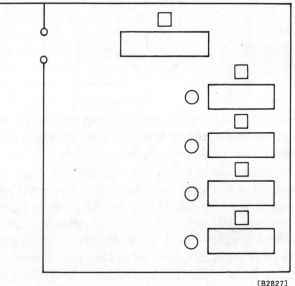

[B2827]

When he left the bank, a partition had been erect-
ed and the gate in the barrier between the open
area in the bank and the interview area had been
changed, like this:

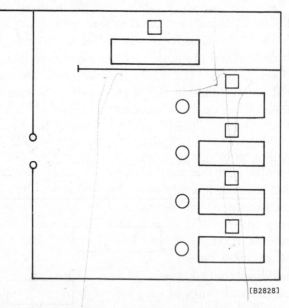

[B2828]

Before the change, no one had established a rule
that customers report first to the senior officer, for
assignment to junior officers. But that is what
customers did. After the change, no one announced a different rule, but the customers then
went directly to junior officers, as junior officers
were evidently available. The physical change—
without a word—changed the political structure in
the bank from a supervised system to a system in
which officer and client contacted one another

without supervisory direction. It resulted in less absenteeism and less turnover.

Purpose. Steele notes that the presence or sense of physical environment (what we have called place) serves four purposes in the lives of those who work (and live) in a particular place. The first of these is instrumental; certain directions are, he says, "received from the physical environment." The branch-bank case illustrates that point, as does the fact that some places are more relaxing than others because they are quiet, or cordial (well lighted, say, or arranged so that the tools needed for work are easily available). Instrumental purposes may also be political: "Nothing can tell more quickly about the impersonality of an organization than seeing an area where there is very little individual influence on the space (decorations, markings, personal items, or private sense of personal space)." He mentions a new office building that featured glass interior walls and movable curtains, so that people in the office could have "a large degree of choice . . . about whether they wanted an open view or a close, private sense of personal space, and that this could be changed as they felt appropriate." But, he says, there developed a norm in the organization. The new norm said, "Anyone with nothing to hide will leave his drapes open." That norm destroyed the flexibility and the democracy of the architect's idea. The organization was stern and hierarchical, so determined to be impersonal that this relatively subtle effort toward personal independence would not work there.

A second purpose of place is symbolic. Because of a fraternal tradition, lawyers are more subtle about rank within firms than business people are. But each lawyer's place symbolizes status. In most firms, senior lawyers have the offices at the corners of the building. These are the larger offices, and they have multiple windows, including windows on two sides. The least senior have offices with no windows at all, although this symbolic demotion is sometimes muted by making the interior offices larger than the offices on the outside of the building. This is a bit like the Bob Newhart sketch in which he finds his office chair moved to a telephone booth, and says, "They're trying to tell me something," or like the fact that physicians' offices have signs that tell patients (1) not to smoke, and (2) to pay their fees before leaving. Much of the symbolism of the place is subtle to the senses and blatant to the psyche. Distance is an example. It makes a difference in interviewing whether the client and lawyer sit across the room from one another, across the desk from one another, or so close to one another that they occasionally touch.

A third purpose of place is pleasure. Frank Lloyd Wright's architecture attempted to give people in a building the feeling that the natural environment outside the building was accessible to them. Considerations of pleasure cause lawyers to buy comfortable chairs for themselves and, maybe, for their clients. Disregard of pleasure causes an office to feel stifling or oppressive; for instance, a law-office waiting room proclaims intellectual one-upmanship when there is nothing in it the client wants to read.

A fourth purpose of physical climate is the growth away from dependence of the people who inhabit the place (Steele):

An environment may . . . be a force . . . for learning about self, for stimulation to experi-mentation, and the like. It may also be neutral or negative, that is, stagnating rather than growth-producing. A space that demands that a person be aware of who he is and how he is using the space can be a positive force for growth. One that requires no consciousness to use it, such as a totally comfortable suburban house with all decisions made and no choices required, is likely to be a force toward non-growth, since the user is not called upon to think about why he prefers one thing over another, what this says about him as a person, or to deal with changes which open new ways of doing things.

Such considerations seem to speak more to the lawyer than to the client, because it is the lawyer who plans the way her office is to be. The lawyer's decisions indicate whether she wants to grow to-ward her client, to be open to her client, and the extent to which she considers her client as a person.

It is possible to imagine a law office in which the *client* is invited to think about "how he is using the space," is "called upon to think about why he prefers one thing over another" (Steele). Suppose every piece of furniture in the room had wheels and the client was invited to arrange the furniture before he sat. Suppose the working space in the room was a plain table with identical chairs around it, and the client was asked to choose his chair.

We have heard of lawyers who use such possibilities as fact-gathering devices: One of these lawyers meets her new clients in a conference room with a rectangular table and identical chairs, one of which is placed at the "head" of the table. This lawyer comes to the room after a secretary has shown the client or clients in and invited him, or them, to take their places. This lawyer says she learns a lot about the unaccompanied client when the client takes the chair at the head of the table. If there is more than one client, she learns a lot about their relationship(s) by the way they put themselves around the table.

Arrangement of People. There are differences in feelings created by the way people are located in rooms. The objective here is to open a lawyer-reader's awareness to the effects of seating arrangements and distances among people and to suggest that he broaden his knowledge with his own experience and experimentation. Here are a few pointers:

—People who know one another well feel emotionally closer when they are seated "side by each," but people who are not well acquainted feel less close in that arrangement and closer (and perhaps more anxious) when seated face to face. Research indicates that groups of five people communicate better among themselves when seated in a circle, but that this arrangement tends to discourage the recognition of a leader for the group.

—People inject emotional distance into situations if circumstances place them too close together. We ignore other people in a crowded elevator, for instance. Or, for a more apposite instance, invasion of the "critical space" around a person causes him to feel anxious and to reduce communication. A lawyer who sits too close to his client may find that the client scoots back emotionally, even when the client does not scoot back physically. Experiments with groups for conversation indicate that five and one-half feet is the preferred distance between people, whether they are talking across from one another or side by side; less than that appears to risk invasion of personal space. However, most furniture in living rooms is spaced ten or eleven feet apart.

—Reactions to physical closeness vary according to the personalities of clients. "Introverts," for example, prefer more distance than "extroverts" do and, if they don't get distance, are likely to become anxious. People who feel anxious want to increase distance; people who feel comfortable (because they have been praised or feel they are accepted) want to get closer. Two women operate more comfortably within critical distances than two men do.

—The way people place themselves may express issues of leadership. People who want to be leaders, and people with high social status, tend to take the end places at rectangular tables. In one experiment, jurors who occupied the end place at a table in the jury room tended, because of this, or because their place encouraged them, to talk more than people who sat at the sides of the table. Another experiment compared the effect on pairs of leaders by first putting them at the opposite ends of a table and then placing one on the side and one at an end. Breaking up the pairs in this fashion tended to diminish the leadership of each member of the pair.

—A person tends to talk more freely—in most business circumstances—to someone who is opposite him than to someone who is beside him. However, if the person opposite exercises more control of the situation than is comfortable, the tendency is to direct conversation toward a third person at one's side. This finding shows up in taped sessions between two law students or lawyers and one client (as in the A.B.A. client-counseling competition).

Territoriality. Territory resembles critical distance, or personal space, but is not the same concept. A lawyer is likely to regard all of his own office, and, probably, all of his firm's premises, as his territory, when the person he is dealing with is a client. And his client will likely honor the claim. But the lawyer's critical distance, his personal space, is unlikely to be greater than a circle around his body about ten feet in diameter. The client, who will not claim territory in the law office, will retain—and may expand—his own claim for personal space.

Several significant issues of law-office territoriality have been discussed in this chapter. Two points might bear cross-reference: (1) The obvious fact that a lawyer's office is his place, that it, and his claims on it, say things about his personality to clients and, if he listens, to himself. A client's reaction to the lawyer's place may be as significant in their relationship as the client's reaction to the lawyer's person. (2) A person tends to act differently when he is in his own place than when he is in another's place; this difference tends to become greater if the place of the other is also a status-heavy place (as a lawyer's office is to most people), and as the personality of the client varies toward the unusually shy or more than normally upset. (See Exercise Eleven, in the Appendix.)

BIBLIOGRAPHY

On the "felt experience" of space: Tuan, Space and Place: The Perspective of Experience (1977).

On personal space in the law office context: Fey and Goldberg, "Legal Interviewing from a Psychological Perspective: An Attorney's Handbook," 14 Willamette Law Journal 217, 221–224 (1978).

REFERENCES

Rogers, Client-Centered Therapy (1951); Steele, "Physical Settings and Organizational Development," in Hornstein, Bunker, Burke, Gindes, and Lewicki, Social Intervention (1971).

CHAPTER NINE

SHARING AUTHORITY: COLLABORATIVE DECISION MAKING

THE CLIENT AS RESOURCE

The everyday law-school image of a lawyer is of a person who is sharp, objective, takes charge, and wins arguments. The ideal of a counselor, as counseling psychology puts it, is of someone who is accepting, understanding, and congruent. The two ideals are not entirely compatible. Lawyers suffer difficulty in reconciling them. Maybe, as a result, we function poorly in relationships with clients. Let's consider the clash more specifically by comparing lawyers and counselors:

lawyers are:	*counselors are:*
Conscious of facts (keep their eyes on the ball)	Perceptive (conscious of human facts)
Conscious of relevance (only the key facts, please)	Empathic (feel what the client feels) and congruent (aware of their own feelings)
Comprehensive (leave no stone unturned; are prepared)	Careful listeners (try not to miss what's in the room)

lawyers are:	*counselors are:*
Foresightful (are aware of the consequences; plan ahead)	Resilient (recover quickly, stay in the room)
Verbally sophisticated (can say what they think)	Open (are accurate in expressing what they feel)
Orally aggressive (win arguments) and	Reflective (understand what is said) and
Thorough (get the job done)	Accepting, caring (try not to learn how to face a problem so much as how to face a face)

Clients and nonlegal counselors are often skeptical about lawyers and even about the law. The law seems formal, insensitive, rigid, and inhuman. Lawyers are often manipulative and overbearing. Lawyers who have a broader perspective on their craft sense the reality of these feelings. But the description also suggests the possibility that clients who feel that way about the law and lawyers are using the law and lawyers as screens for their personal projections. A client has a tendency not to see himself in anything as demanding as the law and in anyone as competent and self-assured as the average lawyer. The lawyer's world overwhelms him; and so he is docile when he comes to a law office. But his docility may be a psychological evasion. It may be a way for him not to see the unbending, aggressive, orderly, and insecure parts of himself. It is easier to see unappealing qualities in other people, in systems, or in law itself.

There is, then, confusion and tension on both sides of the lawyer-client relationship (as there is in any significant human relationship): The lawyer, who is in fact and in aspiration both lawyer and counselor— who is a counselor at law; and the client, who seeks, wants, and yet suspects the order and oral aggression that is in our popular picture of lawyers. The great masters of 20th century psychology would, we think, see this situation not so much as a meeting of tension and discourse but as a meeting of resources.

The analytical psychology of C. G. Jung, for example, is a helpful way to understand the idea that *clients are resources.* Jung diverts attention from our modern penchant for focusing on roles rather than on people. (The client role is to be docile and receptive, the lawyer role is to be informative, helpful, and—traditionally—authoritative.) Jung shows that the client has it within himself to be informative, helpful, and authoritative; and the lawyer has it within himself to be docile and receptive. If the conduct of the actors in a law office does not transgress the boundaries of role it is because the actors choose to confine themselves to their roles. The evidence—and it mounts (see Rosenthal)—is that this choice produces poor working relationships and poor results for clients and, we think, for lawyers as well.

Respect for the client as a resource has first to take account of the fact that clients may have personal resistances to parts of—aspects of—themselves, as well as to lawyers. They may resist their own skills. They may, particularly, resist the abilities and tendencies they see, not in themselves, but in lawyers. And lawyers may resist some of the values

and ideals they have put aside during the course of
their professional training and in their efforts to
become effective lawyers. There is a psychological
reality in these resistances: The client in me is
afraid of the lawyer in me, and vice versa. The
lawyer is afraid to let himself be soft; the "client" is
afraid to let himself be hard and demonstrate that
he knows or tries to know what he wants. We cut
off our own effectiveness and the effectiveness of one
another. Finally, together, we may close out the
effectiveness in what we each can do when we act
together: We act together to avoid the strength that
comes from our working together.

Jung's theory of psychic function is that each of us
operates on two spectrums. The first of these is a
vertical spectrum from thinking (the function that
tells us what things are) to feeling (the function that
tells us what things are worth). The horizontal
spectrum is from sensation (the function that receives stimuli from the outside world—sights, sounds,
smells, etc.) to intuition (the function that, as Jung
put it, lets us see around corners):

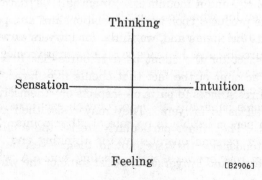

Thinking

Sensation————————————Intuition

Feeling

[B29906]

A person habitually operates more toward one end of each spectrum than the other, but she can learn to be comfortable with the opposite (remote) function. She can learn to feel (*i.e.*, evaluate) more than is habitual for her; and she can learn to listen to her intuition more than to words. Respect for these different functions within oneself, and for the large measure of choice each of us has, on each spectrum, is a necessary first step toward respect for them in another person—a client, say.

The object, as we derive it from Jungian psychology, is to respect the client as a professional resource—to discover and to make use of the client's talents and abilities; but we suspect that we lawyers will not call honestly for help from clients until lawyers begin to be honest about what they are doing with their own competencies for understanding and intuition. And clients will not begin to respect the qualities a lawyer can bring to them until they begin to have respect for the rational, orderly, and manipulative side of themselves. In the absence of understanding there is a diminished respect for what the client can figure out for himself. But it begins with a diminished respect in the lawyer for what the lawyer can do.

In Jung's view of things, the client is a valuable resource because he tends to operate in psychological areas which the lawyer, out of training and habit, has learned to overlook in his own life. A person operates habitually at some point on each axis, and each person is able to operate at other points. The lawyer persona operates at the thinking end; the client role operates at the feeling end. A whole person empowered with an awareness of his own psychic freedom can operate flexibly on each scale. When we see our own strengths, especially those strengths we do not habitually use, we are able to respect and to gain from somebody else whose habitual function is elsewhere on the scale. The heart of the idea is that there is a lawyer and a client in each of us:

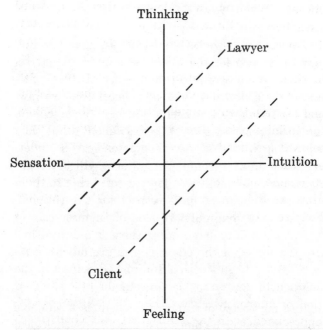

The horizontal axis is a sensation-intuition axis. Using sensation is a matter, as we are told in law school, of keeping your eye on the ball. Lawyers are supposed to be good at it. We are supposed to be sharp—not to miss things that are there to be seen. Intuition is a softer and, for some, more mysterious function. The lawyer persona (and lawyer role) is usually described as operating on sensation, but there is a person within (one might call this an inner client) who operates intuitively; there is probably a part of the lawyer's self that has been denied as the lawyer has learned to be a lawyer. When a lawyer learns to locate and respect her own intuition, she will learn to respect intuition in others—including clients. (The giants of 20th century psychology teach, and demonstrate in their autobiographical writing, that your *first* resource in learning about people is *you*. Clients and lawyers then complement one another, just as the infinite possibilities within a person—a counselor at law, for instance—complement one another, teach interpersonal and inter-professional respect, and make it possible for lawyers to learn and grow as they serve their clients. (See Exercise Fourteen, in the Appendix.)

SHARING AUTHORITY

Much of counseling is description and exploration of alternatives, how they can be viewed and appreciated, with the realization that choices can be made and clients are competent to make them. The counseled person is in some sense "hung up," cannot decide what to do or cannot get others to do what they should be doing. The lawyer is seen as one who can help resolve the hang-up by some combination of information, freedom, and action. The client, in other words, seeks to move from hang-up to choice, and the counselor is seen as one who can provide information and freedom for that movement. Counseling skill is a proper balance of information and freedom; it is the resolution of hang-up with information and freedom. Lawyers may shy away from counseling and feel more comfortable with taking over (doing something, being in charge, solving problems). Taking over is not counseling; it is often a refusal to be a counselor. Physicians, for example, are often criticized for providing too little information; lawyers are criticized for providing too much and too little information, but almost certainly for allowing the client too little freedom. The one fault is to leave the client in a state of ignorance; the other is to lecture to the client and leave him no room to make a choice that is his own.

One helpful distinction here is the distinction between tough personal choices and collaborative decisions. A client sometimes needs to decide what he wants. Sometimes he knows what he wants but needs to decide what to do. The difference is that a choice about *what one wants* calls for freedom (acceptance, concern, support), and a decision about *what to do* calls more for information, and for an active and collaborative style in the counselor. The counselor has more openings for providing information, and even for giving his own opinions, when the issue is what to do. He has

more openings for providing understanding, acceptance, and care, when the issue is what the client
wants. (See Exercise Eight, in the Appendix).

"Freedom" means leaving the client room to
move. Many counselors smother their clients with
advice, information, legal knowledge, and personal
theories about how the world works. All counseling requires freedom; counseling when the client
cannot decide what he wants requires a great deal
of freedom. One way to look at freedom is in
terms of counselor behavior, on a spectrum from
telling people what they want to developing options for them (which involves organization of information), to the provision of a nonjudgmental,
accepting climate (which often involves no information at all).

Client freedom is an attractive aspiration (who
can be opposed to freedom?) but it is a troublesome
principle. It is troublesome, first of all, because
counselors argue about it a lot. There are good
lawyers—that is, persons of both character and
skill—who say, "A good lawyer takes charge and is
in control. I would not have a client who didn't do
what I told him to do," and there are physicians
who take that view of their patients. It is troublesome, secondly, because the serious practice of freedom, of client self-determination, is in fact rare,
regardless of stated or implicit professional ideals.
There seem to be four reasons:

1. *Counselors Often Fail to Provide Enough Information for Decision.* This is a common com-

plaint against physicians. The most common source of formal grievances against lawyers comes from the client's feeling that he doesn't know what his lawyer is doing, which is at least partly a failure to provide information. This failure seems to proceed from a domineering parental attitude in the counselor. He or she has taken a paternal or maternal role in the relationship; and Papa (or Mama) knows best. Anthony Trollope writes of two such lawyers in one of his novels (The Eustace Diamonds): "The outside world was a world of pretty, laughing, ignorant children; and lawyers were the parents, guardians, pastors, and masters by whom the children should be protected from the evils incident to their childishness." A climate of acceptance and congruence in counseling relationships is rare: Douglas Rosenthal found that clients of lawyers are not allowed to participate in decisions on their automobile accident cases, even though clients who do participate receive more money in legal judgment; a Missouri Bar Survey found that lawyers believe their clients want domineering parental relationships but that clients prefer friendly, open lawyers.

2. *The Counseling Relationship Tends to Domination by the Counselor.* Empirical support for this statement seems abundant. Even psychological counseling relationships invariably involve rivalry and one-upmanship. Classical psychotherapeutic theory (Freud, Jung, Eric Berne) locates the source of professional paternalism in the parent-

child relationship and in the transference of parental and filial feelings to the counselor. (See Chapter Four.) This theory would have it that there is a pervasive tendency in counselors to make judgments and give orders, and a pervasive tendency in clients to depend on their counselors for judgment and direction. The vigor with which counselors, clients, and scholars defend parental counseling is some evidence of the accuracy and depth of this traditional psychological insight.

3. *Professional Disciplines Encourage Dependence.* Every professional has something to sell. Surgeons are likely to want clients to decide upon surgery. Trial lawyers are likely to advise clients, "Sue the bastards." Genetic counselors are inclined to advise amniocentesis. Lawyers who know a lot about taxes believe that saving taxes is important. One is inclined, always, to lead with her strength, and, in these cases, part of the strength is knowledge and a set of habits that the client does not possess. Part of this—the habitual part—is a set of official professional positions on what clients should do. Witness the ebb and flow in pediatrics on whether children should keep their tonsils; or the fact that it became much easier for real estate brokers to lend their skill to the racial desegregation of housing when their professional organizations (and the law) gave official disapproval to segregation. In a sense, particularly in the more esoteric professions, "science" (the Latin

word for knowledge) is used as a buffer against the professional's ability to respond to his client.

For all of these reasons, and others, professionals tend to stack the deck against client self-determination. In fact, they do it unconsciously. Clients come to professionals; professionals do not come to clients. The time and place of consultation is set by the professional, and he keeps the time clock. The space is his and is arranged to suit his tastes. Notice, for example, professional offices: The professional's chair is not only larger and behind a desk, with space on his side of the desk for legs, but it also swivels and tips back and has more padding. The light falls across his shoulders and into the client's eyes; all conveniences are in his hands. The professional sets the norm for proper dress, appropriate posture, access to refreshment, and level of seclusion. He decides as well how conversation is to be conducted (narrative, question-answer, cross-examination, or awkward silence). (See Chapter Eight.)

4. *The Tendency to Moralize.* Lawyers tend to be moralistic; that is one reason we find it hard to be accepting. There are even respectable professional voices which say we should be the consciences of our clients, that we should pronounce moral judgment on what they want and on how they seek what they want. The main argument against this pervasive moral evaluation of the client is that it denies the client's humanity and forecloses the possibility that both client and law-

yer may be able to learn from each other and grow together in a new adventure. As Carl Rogers says:

The major barrier to mutual interpersonal communication is our very natural tendency to judge, to evaluate, to approve or disapprove the statement of the other person. . . .

The stronger our feelings the more likely it is that there will be no mutual element in the communication. There will be just two ideas, two feelings, two judgments, missing each other in psychological space. I'm sure you recognize this from your own experience. When you have not been emotionally involved yourself, and have listened to a heated discussion, you often go away thinking, "Well, they actually weren't talking about the same thing." And they were not. Each was making a judgment, an evaluation, from his own frame of reference. There was really nothing which could be called communication in any genuine sense. This tendency to react to any emotionally meaningful statement by forming an evaluation of it from our own point of view, is, I repeat, the major barrier to interpersonal communication. . . .

Real communication occurs, and this evaluative tendency is avoided, when we listen with understanding. What does this mean? It means to see the expressed idea and attitude from the other person's point of view, to sense how it feels to him, to achieve his frame of reference in regard to the thing he is talking about.

From the client's perspective evaluative communication seems to plug into all of those hidden feelings of guilt and worthlessness that each of us learned to feel in childhood. There is a part of us which says, in Thomas Harris's phrase, "I'm not okay." And that part of a client may be what a good lawyer can help overcome, so that freedom, growth, choice, and real communication are possible. What may be happening in evaluative counseling is an experience that revives feelings of guilt, worthlessness, and stupidity, and confirms them—what E. H. Porter calls a "proving experience":

> By proving experience is meant an experience which tends to confirm the impression set in the psychological atmosphere. To illustrate the concept we might think of a five-year-old boy who says to his mother, "I'll help you clear the table, Mother. I'll carry out the dishes." Should the mother doubt his adequacy and competency and express her feelings, we might expect her to reply, "No! Well, OK. But do be careful and don't drop them." If at this point Johnny stumbles on that skate he left by the stove and the dishes do fall and break, it is much harder to deny that his mother wasn't right in her feelings. Such an experience tends to prove the implications of her attitudes as to his inadequacy and incompetency.

Good counseling assumes and depends on respect for client self-determination. Freedom is a necessary condition for the decisions and choices that are the result of counseling. This means, at a minimum, that the lawyer is open to the conscience of the client, and respects it, and that the lawyer claims respect for his own conscience. But there is much more to client self-determination and a lawyer's moral concern than that. Counseling requires more than respect for the client's point of view. It requires, and depends on, the client as a resource—more valuable than the lawyer in many situations—for the resolution of the difficulty that is brought to the lawyer. Our argument on self-determination goes beyond traditional professional and ethical norms. We suggest—we argue—that the client is a valuable resource for legal decision as well as non-legal decision.

Counseling, generally and in all of its vocational manifestations, involves both implicit and explicit morals. One traditional norm among American lawyers is that the client's interests come first. Another, less obvious, is that choices and decisions are for the client to make—at least in the final analysis. This client-decision norm is expressly stated in the Code of Professional Responsibility and in the proposed Model Rules of Professional Conduct for lawyers; it is implicit in the conduct of physicians, salespersons, and, usually, school counselors and pastors. It is essential (definitional) in counseling.

The ideal and the legal profession's guidelines for professional conduct are stated in the Code of

Professional Responsibility, Ethical Consideration
7–8:

> A lawyer should exert his best efforts to insure
> that decisions of his client are made only after
> the client has been informed of relevant consid-
> erations. A lawyer ought to initiate this deci-
> sion-making process if the client does not do so.
> Advice of a lawyer to his client need not be
> confined to purely legal considerations. A law-
> yer should advise his client of the possible effect
> of each legal alternative. A lawyer should bring
> to bear upon this decision-making process the
> fullness of his experience as well as his objective
> viewpoint. In assisting his client to reach a
> proper decision, it is often desirable for a lawyer
> to point out those factors which may lead to a
> decision that is morally just as well as legally
> permissible. He may emphasize the possibility
> of harsh consequences that might result from
> assertion of legally permissible positions. *In the*
> *final analysis, however, the lawyer should always*
> *remember that the decision whether to forego*
> *legally available objectives or methods because of*
> *non-legal factors is ultimately for the client and*
> *not for himself.* In the event that the client in a
> non-adjudicatory matter insists upon a course of
> conduct that is contrary to the judgment and
> advice of the lawyer but not prohibited by the
> Disciplinary Rules, the lawyer may withdraw
> from the employment. (Emphasis added.)

The Code states the general principle in the clearest possible manner.   Client self-determination is, however, a complex subject.   These codified professional norms in fact represent *conflicting* ideals. Client self-determination is set against a duty in lawyers to supply information available from their experience, from their learning, and from their "objective" observation; this includes moral considerations and consideration of what John Dewey called "the logic of consequences."   The Code places upon lawyers a duty to initiate this kind of conversation—that is, to insist upon it, regardless, apparently, of how docile or uncommunicative the client is.   Finally, the Code notices (albeit timidly) that lawyers also have consciences.   It affirms a freedom to withdraw from employment if the client seems to the lawyer to be wrong.

COLLABORATION

Many lawyers are instinctively skillful at collaboration with clients.   And many are not.   The result of our being poor collaborators is a decision that does not promote our clients' ability to be themselves.   There is evidence for the generalization in the "estate planning" practice—the prevalence of spendthrift clauses in trust instruments, for example.   There cannot be so many clients who think of their loved ones as dim-witted.   Another example is the staggering amount of sexism in wills and trusts—dehumanizing disabilities on widows, assumptions that daughters (but not sons) need trustee protection, biased distinctions between sons-in-law and daughters-in-law.

Another set of examples clusters around draftsmanship that facilitates commercial transactions at the expense of the people the instrument is supposed to serve—testamentary distributions of tangible personal properly outright to minor beneficiaries, for instance, so that the trustee need not be bothered with storing and selling it; protection of third persons who deal with the trustee, at the expense of the beneficiaries; provisions that relieve trustees from a duty of loyalty, or a duty to account, or a duty to observe investment guidelines, or a duty to post surety bonds. One can argue about the abstract merits of dispositions of this sort. They are sometimes appropriate and sometimes not. The present issue is this: How often do these significant provisions proceed from the client's own needs and interests, his ability to contribute to a decision? And how often do they proceed from routine and inappropriate domination by the lawyer?

The best argument for collaboration in decisions is the lawyer who lives a people-centered life. Here is one glimpse, a literary one: C. P. Snow's novel, Time of Hope, is about the professional preparation for the Bar of the lawyer who is central in Snow's Strangers and Brothers series. Young Eliot has read for the Bar, passed his examinations (and passed them well), eaten the requisite number of dinners at his inn, and he is well into his internship with a senior barrister. The scene involves a difficult trial for libel in which young Eliot has his first big chance. He has been engaged to represent one of the parties. He is on display before the solicitors who can make or break him, because it is through solicitors that a barrister receives his cases. It is a crucial moment in a lawyer's career.

Snow's point is subtle. Eliot does a good job—wins the case—and probably makes a fair mark with the discriminating solicitors. But in one tense instant in the trial he becomes convinced that he should not be a trial lawyer; the consequences are that he becomes a salaried corporate lawyer and then a law professor. The moment of truth occurs during a witness examination, when Eliot asks a question that does not bear on the case. It is a question that might have turned out badly for him. Because of that question Eliot decides that he was, in that instant, more interested in the facts of the person in front of him than he was in the facts of the case. He was more interested in the human connection, the nascent bit of personal relationship he had with the witness.

Eliot decides he is not cut out to be a trial lawyer because he is more interested in people than he is in courtroom competition. He forsakes analysis for one perilous moment and tends to prefer—sees himself preferring—the interpersonal search that is involved in understanding another human being.

Moments of insight, of self-awareness, such as that experienced by Lewis Eliot, are integral to counseling. We find an interpersonal approach to lawyering much more hopeful, much more inspiring somehow, than the win-lose approach that many lawyers, some law students, and most lay persons associate with our ancient, proud, contentious profession.

This literary insight applies both to hard-choice counseling and to collaborative decision-making. The disagreement about what constitutes the best law-office practice, can be analyzed in terms of what a counselor—any counselor—is supposed to be able to contribute to his counselee. When the agenda is choice the counselor is there to help his counselee move. The client is stymied, frustrated, maybe confused, usually uninformed. For some reason he cannot act. The counselor is there to deal with that freeze in human activity. What the client usually needs is a new perspective on his options.

When the agenda is decision-making, the collaborative principle is that there are human, economic, and social advantages in involving people rather than mastering them. The enlistment of the client, in a serious and purposeful way in his own cause, and in collaborative strategy, is the topic of this chapter, which will: (a) pursue the initial issue of collaborative pay-off; then (b) consider specific strategies in collaboration (interventions); and finally (c) discuss the issue of conflict.

COLLABORATIVE PAY–OFF

The fact persists that many lawyers (and those apparently the most vocal) see themselves as telling their clients what to do. Their successors in law schools see themselves as having to learn how to tell people what to do. The assumption that a lawyer has to be wise and domineering is perhaps the source of the querulous terror with which a young lawyer contemplates her professional life with clients. The domineering image tempts her to dread one of the greatest of her life's adventures. That is the experience of companionship with another person, of walking in his shoes, and living in his world.

This would be a hard case to make if one were arguing against the economic realities of the practice of law; law professors tend to do that, and, because they do, they are ignored even when their urging is consonant with a comfortable material life. But research on this point establishes that the domineering model of lawyering, the model suggested here as least human, harms the client:

Douglas Rosenthal conducted a well-organized survey of lawyers and clients involved in automobile accident litigation in Manhattan. He assembled data from records, from interviews with clients and lawyers, and from judgments made by a panel of expert trial lawyers. He then asked of his data a series of questions about lawyering. These questions considered appropriate client behavior in

the relationship; the quality of professional service, and methods for judging quality; processes of
decision in the law office; accessibility to lay understanding of law and fact; professional ideals
and practices of the lawyers who worked in the
cases; and measures of professional competence.

Rosenthal derived two models for and from his
data. One model, which he classified as "traditional," assumes that the client is best advised to be
docile and dependent on the lawyer. The alternative model ("participatory") assumes that the relationship is collaborative, and that the client should
be an active partner. It is the latter model which
follows the moral aspirations of professional relationships that we argue for. Rosenthal went beyond aspiration; he classified the cases he studied
within one or the other of these models, put the
cases to a panel of trial lawyers for evaluation, and
compared the panel's figure with the monetary
recovery (settlement) in each case. He could then
determine which model produced the larger
amount of money in settlement. He found that
the participatory model was more lucrative for the
client; clients who collaborated—were invited to
collaborate—got more money.

It might be useful to look at more detailed aspects of the two models. Rosenthal enumerated
these:

In the traditional model, clients are expected to
be passive; in the participatory model, they are
expected to be active. The traditional model as-

sumes that legal problems generally have only one best solution and that lawyers are more likely to be competent in arriving at it than lay persons are; it assumes that professional competence is a difficult thing to judge, and only lawyers can judge it well. It assumes that professional service by lawyers is usually competent, that it is readily available to persons of modest wealth, and that ethical standards are high and consistently enforced. Fees, according to this model, should be set by the lawyer, and second lawyer opinions are not usually advisable.

In the participatory model, the quality of professional service is expected to vary; second lawyer opinions are thought to be valuable; legal problems are complex, open to many solutions, and open as well to a layman's common sense and first hand knowledge. The participatory model assumes that lawyers are not often able to be disinterested, that fees should be negotiated, that laymen can judge the quality of professional services, that the middle class in America is not able to get good legal service, and that ethical standards are unclear and, even when clear, not consistently observed and enforced. These details in each model were compared against what lawyer and client in each of Rosenthal's cases said to him about his or her experience; that comparison made it possible for Rosenthal to place each case in the "traditional" or "participatory" column. Most of the cases he studied fell into the "traditional" column; it was those cases in which clients felt oppressed, and in those cases they also recovered less money.

The choice of model is usually but not necessarily the lawyer's choice. Clients want, often, to let the lawyer lead the way. A lawyer can insist on a collaborative relationship with his clients, and can even terminate the relationship if clients refuse to deal with him on adult terms. But the choice of traditional or parental model is almost always, in some sense, a shared choice; clients may prefer a parental (filial) relationship, and may resist their lawyer's attempt to make them responsible for themselves. (There may be here a subtle question about how domineering a lawyer can be in refusing to be domineering.)

There is good authority—professional and empirical—for the point that it is better to be a companion than a domineering parent in our relationships with clients. The client benefits, materially and psychologically. We argue that the lawyer benefits as well. The final pay-off is both social and personal: Collaborative decisions are less likely than lawyer dominated ones to lead to litigation. The father of preventive-law jurisprudence, Louis M. Brown, says:

> In preventive law, the lawyer's purpose is to guide his client so as to minimize risks, and maximize rights. Insofar as law applies, it can be said that often the purpose, and effect, is to avoid possible dispute. Where such a result is

successful the forum is the law office rather than the courtroom. The legal matter never reaches the courtroom. This observation is important because it means that the final determination of legal consequences takes place in the law office. Legal decisions are finalized by client and lawyer. In this context, the decisional process of the law office is as significant for a particular client as would be the decision of a court for a litigant.

The decision in the law office is assented to, worked out, by at least two people; but, like "justice" writ large, it depends for its validity on a sense of "rightness" that comes from beyond the law office. A litigated decision must be "just"— that is, it must satisfy most of the people most of the time. A law-office decision must satisfy the people who are to live with its consequences. A negative way to express that is that law-office decisions should avoid litigation; a positive way to express it is that law-office decisions should rest on the implicit consent of those whose lives the decisions affect.

Non-legal counseling, by contrast, can afford to pay less attention to consequences and consensus. It aims at information and at the facilitation of choice by the client, as legal counseling does. But legal counseling is different because it is always done in the shadow of external, even institutional validation. A lawyer and client who decide that the client should seek every advantage possible in the Internal Revenue Code are making a decision with accounting consequences, risk consequences, and social consequences analogous to the consequences of the same sort of decision being made in the Tax Court. One consequence of this difference is that the legal counselor has to make up his mind; non-legal counselors often do not have to make up their minds; they often don't even want to. Non-legal counseling often need not go beyond the client's hard choices.

BIBLIOGRAPHY

On client self-determination see Maute, "Allocation of Decision-Making Authority Under the Model Rules of Professional Conduct," 17 University of California, Davis Law Review 1049 (1984); Spiegel, "The New Model Rules of Professional Conduct: Lawyer-Client Decision Making and the Role of Rules in Structuring the Lawyer-Client Dialogue," 1980 American Bar Foundation Resource Journal 1003; Cihlar, "Client Self-Determination: Intervention or Interference?" 14 Saint Louis Law Journal 604 (1970); Mazor, "Power and Responsibility in the Attorney-Client Relation," 20 Stanford Law Review 1120 (1968).

REFERENCES

Brown, Manual for Preventive Law (1950), and Lawyering Through Life (1986); Brown and Dauer, Planning by Lawyers (1978); Dewey, "Logical Method and Law," 10 Cornell Law Quarterly 17 (1924); Harris, I'm Okay, You're Okay (1969);

Jung, Analytical Psychology (1968); Psychological Types, in 6 Collected Works (Bollingen, 1971); Porter, An Introduction to Therapeutic Counseling (1950); Rogers, Client-Centered Therapy (1951); Rosenthal, Lawyers and Client: Who's in Charge (1974); Snow, Trollope: His Life and Art (1975).

CHAPTER TEN

MORAL ISSUES IN THE IDEA OF SHARED AUTHORITY

MORAL OPENNESS IN THE LAW OFFICE

It strains belief to assume that the lawyer always respects the moral impulses of her client. One's explicit or implicit view of human nature may make respect for conscience very difficult. Even if the disposition of Trollope's lawyer, Mr. Camperdown, to treat his clients as children is avoided, it is sometimes hard to respect clients' moral judgment. Our argument is that a my-conscience-or-yours standoff is less likely when the client's desires have been elicited and cared about and the lawyer's conscience is brought into the open and cared about. What we propose is a moral conversation. We propose that the lawyer's moral view of her client's behavior be expressed. Such an expression is, we think, required by the principle of openness in dealing with the client.

When the counseling climate is not open, lawyer conscience becomes a source of subtle (or not so subtle) pressure on the client-pressure amplified by client dependence. In such circumstances, the client's freedom to act is circumscribed as much as it is when the decision is made and imposed by the lawyer, and even more than it will be if the lawyer asserts her position and then refuses to act unless the client adopts her position. The cure for *ulterior* moral influence seems partly to be the lawyer's understanding of her own moral impulses, and partly humility enough in the lawyer to admit to herself that her impulses may be wrong and can be educated. It is possible for moral impulses to be wrong. It is possible to learn how an impulse is systematically wrong and to learn how to change it. Much of our moral life is intuitive, no doubt, but conscience is an intellectual as well as intuitive faculty. It is the product of reason *and* imagination. It needs information and guidance, and the client is a source of moral information and of moral guidance. Much of a lawyer's influence and advice is moral, and moral influence and advice is, as Karl Barth put it, conditional: "He who takes the risk of counseling must be prepared to be counseled in turn. . . . Such mutual counseling . . . implies that he refrain from too much and [from] becoming thereby a lawgiver."

The purpose here is to look at law-office decisions in terms of the proclaimed value in our profession for client self-determination. The principal influence threatening that ideal, in a law-office decision, is the influence of the lawyer, and, most particularly, relatively inaccessible but stubborn lawyer behavior that proceeds from undisclosed moral impulse. All of our examples have assumed that the lawyer listens to and understands his moral impulses and deals with them consciously (even orally), and that he respects the moral impulses he observes in his client.

In fact, though, moral impulses are subtle. They are often difficult to understand, and they are, in our "pluralistic universe," even more difficult to articulate. This is another instance—and this book teems with them—where effective legal counseling requires a resolute effort to achieve self-awareness.

MORAL FEELING AND MORAL JUDGMENT

Moral leadership in law offices usually comes, at least at first, from lawyers. David Riesman, a lawyer who became a social scientist, gave insight into his choice of career when he noticed this moral leadership. Lawyers are testing grounds, he said, for the client's disposition to distrust government, or business, or whatever it is the client seeks protection from when he sees a lawyer. It is probably not possible for the lawyer to turn off the client's moral sensitivity, but it is possible to render it inaccessible to the business of the office. And one way to do that is to treat conscience as irrelevant. The result is not a choice for neutrality; it is a choice that is anti-moral. It is not possible not to choose, as Sartre would say; if law-office decisions are made without reference to moral feelings, they are made without regard to moral issues and moral outcomes. But morals operate whether the people in the law office invoke them or not. They are part of what people say and do, in the law office as well as everywhere else: To choose to ignore morals is to choose against morals.

Holmes' bad-man theory of law is the melancholy social principle that a citizen will do anything he can get away with. Legal decision is tested against the implicit empirical judgment that people are no damned good, that it is never the principle of the thing and always the money. The theory has usefulness, much appeal, and great peril, in education about and practice in the courts. In litigation—or so the Holmesian might insist—there is no room for shades of feeling, or for the fragile seedlings of conscience. Good and evil exist—crude and obvious and clear. We state the possibility that the bad-man theory may flourish in litigation, not to agree with it, but to argue that it has pernicious effects when it is brought into the law office. Most legal decisions are made in law offices, not in courts; the law-office climate is intimate and interpersonal; it is a place where sensitivity is possible, a place for the good person theory of law.

There is, of course, the possibility that the client may choose something horrible. There is also the possibility that the client may choose horrible methods for doing what he wants to do, even if what he wants to do is not horrible. But the moral issue for the lawyer (an issue about what the lawyer does or is) arises only because the client has the freedom that makes possible immoral choices and decisions. There is a strain of reasoning in professional ethics that says the way to avoid the horrible in professional behavior is to make sure we are not corrupted by our clients, and the way to avoid being corrupted by our clients is to make sure they do only what we tell them to do; if that line of reasoning prevails the only visible moral issue is whether the lawyer has made a good choice.

Take an example of interest to students of modern American legal ethics: Our client, a wealthy, middle-aged widower, wants to disinherit his elder daughter and give all of his (as we lawyers call it) "estate" to his younger daughter. We lawyers wonder why. (Notice that our wondering why is one moral act, and that our asking why is another.) The reason he gives us is that the elder daughter voted for the wrong candidate in the last presidential election. The client wants our expert help in doing something we think is wrong-headed and perhaps immoral. Some lawyers react by saying they would refuse to help this client. We react by saying that the situation needs preliminary analysis:

1. *Interests.* We really don't know yet what the client wants, what, as the ethics codes usually put it, his *interests* are. We haven't talked with him enough, for one thing, and, for another, the notion of "interests" imposes an order on the human

spirit—an order that doesn't describe the way people are. As Warren Lehman puts it:

> Everything we want to achieve we want ulti-
> mately because of the connection we suppose it
> to have to a desired feeling. Therefore, what we
> want is not the things we say we want, but the
> feelings we suppose they will produce. The list a
> client brings to a lawyer's office is not a ranking
> of desired states, but only of what the client
> supposes may produce them. Our judgment on
> issues of that sort is especially likely to be bad at
> the crucial time we go to a lawyer. We say we
> want justice when we want love. We say we
> were treated illegally when we hurt. We insist
> upon our rights when we have been snubbed or
> cut. We want money when we feel impotent.
> We are likely to act most sure of ourselves when
> most desperately we want a simple, human re-
> sponse. If this is true, the lawyer presenting
> himself as an uncritical [instrument] is not a
> satisfaction but a disappointment. The lawyer is
> in the deeper sense not then doing what the
> client wants. It may well be that in a given
> situation a lawyer can do no more than accept a
> particular client's statement of his desires. But
> that is not because he ought to be his client's tool
> or because he must be.

2–a. *The Law.* We could use the law, and our
skill in it, to deny our client any choice at all. We
could say: The law won't let you do that (perhaps
using, in this case, the curious body of case law

that speaks of "unnatural wills"). In this or somewhat more subtle ways we could coerce or manipulate our client into doing *the right thing*. ("Why
don't you give this some thought and we'll schedule
an appointment next month to decide what to do.")
"About half the practice of a decent lawyer," Elihu
Root said, "consists in telling would-be clients that
they are damned fools and should stop." The
troublesome principle of client self-determination
would say that our client should be free to make
the right choice, and that he is not free to be right
unless he is free to be wrong. A deeper moral
notion would say that the client's being good (instead of right) is what is important, and for that—
for becoming a better person—he needs a friend,
not a judge.

2–b. *The Client's Morals.* We could immediately make a moral objection to the client's desire to
disinherit his elder daughter. (That is another
way to read Root's principle.) We could refuse to
lend our assistance to him. Or we could immediately take an instrumental view of our craft and
say we will draft whatever he wants. These positions, as radically different as they first appear,
are on one count the same: They both amount to
saying that the client's morals are irrelevant. We
argue that the client's morals are relevant and
should be sought after and listened to and considered. (Lehman makes the somewhat more subtle
argument that until we come to understand the
client's morals we won't *know* what he wants.)

This means that our client may have a moral influence on *us*. Such a possibility is a risk and also an opportunity. We might even end up agreeing with the client that the moral thing to do is to disinherit the elder daughter.

3. *Moral Conversation.* These two positions—that the client has to be free to be wrong, and that we are interested in hearing from him on the moral question, and even in being persuaded by it—mean that what we now have to talk about is a conversation: a conversation between lawyer and client in which the moral feelings, arguments, and principles *of both of us* are sought, learned about, listened to, and accepted as resources. It is still possible, of course, that the direction the client takes after this conversation will be one we will not take (or vice versa). (These issues are argued more elaborately in Dr. Jay Katz's persuasive book, The Silent World of Doctor and Patient, 1985; and, in reference to Jewish and Christian religious ethics, in Shaffer's On Being a Christian and a Lawyer, 1981; and Faith and the Professions, 1987).

Consider the client who "wants" to disinherit one of his daughters from the bad-man point of view. The dynamic is to find the boundary beyond which the bad man may not pass, and then to work from the boundary into the territory of "legitimate" decision—*i.e.,* decision that will be implemented by the courts, and that is not likely to get the client (bad man) into trouble, or to fail at what the client (bad man) wants. The bad man, in this example, seeks to disinherit a daughter. It is one of hundreds of moments in legal education, and in the practice of law, when clarity beckons teachers and lawyers to work on ethical discernment. The issue in the law office is not whether the law will allow it, but whether a good lawyer and a good person should do it. This is as much an issue for the client, as a person alone, as it is for the lawyer, and therefore it is an issue for them together.

The essential law-office bad-man lesson here is that a will-making client can, with routine assistance from his lawyer, disinherit a member of his family. The temptation—and, often, the reality—for a law teacher is to use a hypothetical planning problem that will invite students to speculate on the legal engineering necessary, and then to scoff at the timid voice of those who suggest that the case invokes something more than lawyer craftsmanship.

The counseling lessons in all of this—if students, or lawyer and client, talk it through—are: (1) Lawyers can do almost anything the client wants done. (2) The only moral limits on the lawyer's efforts are the limits of the law. (3) "The limits of the law" are set by legislatures and judges, not by conscience. "The limits of the law" are whatever, to return to Holmes, the bad man simply cannot, as a matter of minimum public order, be permitted to get away with. That reasoning about the law office, and about morals in the law office, according to the bad-man theory of law is common in legal education. And, we think, it is wrong.

The will-client example shows how powerful morals are: In the law office moral instinct and moral feeling are powerful, pervasive, determinative forces, much of the time—far oftener, we think, than they are in courtrooms. (See Exercise 12, in the Appendix.) Moral sensitivity is doubtless felt in the law school classroom, but it is not often spoken. Lawyers may act their parts from a bad-man script; if so, it will likely be a script they have seen acted out in the drama of the law school classroom. But morals have borne on the decision, in the law office, as they bear on the various activities and conversations that go on in law-school classrooms. Moral influence has been decisive in the result, for the client and for the student. If we don't know that, we don't know what is going on.

Education for the law office, when education uses a bad-man theory of moral judgment, is bad education, not only because it is anti-moral but also because it is untruthful; it does not represent what happens. There is no escape from the fact that what a lawyer does for a client is still action by the lawyer. Our adversary tradition—which is, to begin with, less a part of the law office than most students and some lawyers would imagine— has encouraged lawyers to suppose that the crucial moral decision is the client's and that it is private. It is not a fit subject for conversation in the law office. In other words, lawyers have tended to work on the unstated assumption that advocacy (and, by extension, everything a lawyer does) is immune from conscience. The lawyer who acts professionally, for someone else, ceases in this view to act as a person; he is not morally responsible for what he does as a lawyer, and (maybe even worse) he does not care about the conscience of his client.

A teacher encounters this view when he raises a moral consideration and is told by astonished students that lawyers should do whatever the client wants and the law permits. But newspaper reports, common sense, and even lawyer ethical codes suggest that conscience submerged in partisanship and zealous pursuit of limited goals is conscience denied. It is no more admirable in the law office than it was in the White House, no more defensible among lawyers than in business or medicine. Our Code of Professional Responsibility is a morally modest document, but even it says that "a lawyer should bring to bear upon this decision-making process the fullness of his experience as well as his objective viewpoint," including "those factors which may lead to a decision that is morally just as well as legally permissible." An American lawyer's codal duty is clear: to keep sound morals in the picture; to seek and to respect his client as a moral resource; finally to withdraw from either adversary or law-office relationships, rather than to violate conscience.

The principle is that we choose, and are responsible for, whatever moral judgment the client makes or fails to make. It is not possible not to choose. Professional norms that assume that lawyers lack consciences of their own are bad professional norms, partly because they are untruthful and partly because they are wrong in ordinary moral principle. Professional norms that cause lawyers to define client interests selfishly (without really asking) are equally unrealistic and are squarely wrong, both in ordinary moral principle and because they are contemptuous of clients.

PROBLEMS

The struggle with client self-determination extends both to cases involving legal conduct that seems immoral and to cases involving moral conduct that seems illegal. Examples cover (1) cases where the lawyer's moral influence is invoked even beyond the informational level contemplated by the Code; (2) where the client proposes conduct that seems moral to the client but not to the lawyer; (3) cases where the conduct is illegal but is seen by the client as moral; and (4) cases where the conduct seems contrary to the public interest.

Lawyer's Moral Influence Invoked. This example, from Brown's and Shaffer's essay on law-office jurisprudence, occurred in the early 1960s—before modern federal (or state) civil-rights legislation: "We had a corporate client with large industrial plants in the Deep South. Our client was a fourth-tier contractor with the federal government, which meant then that it had some, but very slight, duties to racially integrate its work force. Our client had discussed this with my senior in the firm, who asked me to research the client's duties under a presidential executive order on equal employment opportunity.

"I drafted a memorandum outlining the client's minimal duties. My senior, with memo in hand, telephoned the secretary of the corporation; he explained my memo ('the law'). The secretary—who was himself a lawyer—said he understood this advice but still wondered what the corporation should do. My senior in the firm then said we had reviewed the situation, and that our advice was to integrate fully in all plants. This advice had all the jurisprudential clarity and economy of Brown v. Board of Education. This law-office decision went beyond the letter of the law, as most law-office decisions, from income taxes to the corrupt practices act, do. Lawyer-client decision-making is not, after all, a form of technical journalism. I have often wondered why my senior gave the advice he did:

"He may have been putting his own social opinions into the decision-making process.

"He may have believed that the law was in a process which would soon reach this client with full-integration requirements; that is, he may have been simply predictive. (In which case he was right.)

"He may, in addition, have assessed the economic and human costs of compliance (which were great in this case) and have decided that early compliance was cheapest.

"He may, finally, have assessed the moral implications of full integration, minimal integration, and no integration, in terms of his own and the client's moral posture. This last is my preferred speculation; it involves consideration of a wide array of factors—the consciences of the executives we were advising (the decision-makers); corporate image; the welfare of the workers (white and black); the social posture in the South and the nation at that time; and, most important, his own perception of the moral openness of the people he was advising. Any of these factors implies a recognition of the fact that the corporation was inevitably a moral leader in the community."

The client in this example took the lawyer's advice; all plants were fully integrated, about a decade before "the law" began to require integration of them. The lawyer's behavior here seems, by the way, to have gone beyond advice on what the law required, but to have been fully within two phrases in E.C. 7–8: "a decision that is morally just as well as legally permissible" and the "possibility of harsh consequences that might result from assertion of legally permissible positions." Its defect is its failure to respect what the Code calls a "decision-making process." There was a right decision here, but the process seems to have been poor.

The moral decision, for all that appeared, came solely from the lawyer. The client may have done the right thing, but its officers were deprived of counseling and conversation—the important human satisfaction and growth in virtue that comes from considering alternatives and making a praiseworthy choice.

The lawyer also took upon himself moral, as well as legal, responsibility for the client's behavior. That could have turned out to be professionally and emotionally troubling; it seems to have demonstrated too little regard for the conscience of the client. (An aspect of this case that calls for more detailed discussion is the corporate lawyer's role as the conscience of the corporate enterprise. There, too, the ideal and frequently the practice is a moral conversation between lawyers and corporate managers.) (See Exercise Twelve, in the Appendix.)

Client Conduct That Seems Immoral to the Lawyer. Frank Cihlar gives this example, which we edit slightly: "Mr. D., a lawyer, received a call from one of his clients who told him that he had decided to commit suicide. Mr. D.'s response to this information was not one of hysteria or of immediate activity designed to get his caller into the protective embrace of some life-sustaining authority. He simply indicated that he hoped his caller would not choose to take his life since Mr. D. regarded him as a friend whom he liked very much and would regret not having around. Mr. D. did not urge his caller not to take his life nor did he endeavor to reach him in person. Instead, he merely expressed his concern over the potential loss but stressed the fact that he thought the decision was ultimately his caller's. With this, Mr. D. concluded the conversation and returned to sleep." Mr. D. said later that he felt his client "had sufficient command of his faculties so as to permit him to make up his own mind in the matter." He said he would regard killing himself as immoral, but that he felt it inappropriate to intervene in his client's decision on the matter.

The example is probably more dramatic than the present point requires, but it suggests a host of less dramatic cases where clients make choices that seem wrong but that a lawyer who believes in client self-determination may feel bound to respect. Many of these choices involve more overt activity by the lawyer (drafting of instruments, negotiation, and even litigation), but the suicide example is not one of passive professional conduct; Mr. D. cannot honestly claim that he was "not involved" in the matter. The fact that the caller was a client—let alone a friend—means that Mr. D. was involved. In addition, Mr. D. refrained from calling "some life-sustaining authority" and refrained as well from any attempt to interfere physically with the client. (See Exercise Twelve, in the Appendix.)

Client Conduct That Is Illegal But Seems Moral. Examples include civil disobedience in civil-rights controversies and refusal to serve in the armed forces during some national military adventure such as the Vietnam War. Those of us who had such cases in the 1960s—and there are many of us—usually found ways to avoid direct confrontation with the authorities that impose professional discipline. These were not typically cases of professional misconduct. We were able, for example, to restrict what we said about flight to avoid military service to relatively wooden advice on what the law said (*e.g.*, analysis of the provisions of the several extradition treaties between the United States and Canada, without stating the opinion that the client should go to Canada). We gave advice on what level of physical destruction of draft cards would constitute a felony under the Selective Service laws, and careful analyses of the law of criminal trespass as it pertained to demonstrators. In moral effect, many of us admired what our clients did; we even supported them as far as our consciences would allow. (Some lawyers, of course, felt that the conduct of clients in such situations was wrong. They were in the category considered in the next example.)

Client Conduct Seems Not to Serve the Public Interest. Abe Krash gives an example that clearly involved the public interest and, for many lawyers, would have involved moral judgment as well:

For many years, the outside General Counsel for the New York Times was an old and distinguished New York law firm. In 1971, the editors of The Times informed their General Counsel that they had obtained possession of secret documents involving America's involvement in Viet Nam—the Pentagon Papers—and the editors asked counsel for an opinion as to whether the materials could be published. Counsel reportedly advised The Times that if they published the documents before they were declassified there was a risk of criminal prosecution. The law firm [also] reportedly advised the editors not to publish on the grounds, among others, that it would be contrary to the 'public interest' to do so. The Times editors determined to publish notwithstanding this advice. When the Department of Justice notified The Times that it would seek a preliminary injunction to restrain further publication, the law firm informed The Times that the firm would not represent the newspaper.

Mr. Krash, himself a partner in a large law firm in Washington, D.C., said he did not disapprove of the lawyers' conduct in this case, but gave the example "to demonstrate how extraordinarily difficult it is in any given situation to know where the public interest lies." Dean Roger C. Cramton sounded a vague murmur of dissent to that (and other lawyers would be more vehement in dissent): "The radical critique . . . does not accept the assumption that ultimate values can be determined by the conflict of private interests. The radicals have discovered truths . . . that do not depend upon the votes of the political process of the advocacy and rationality of the legal process.

While the value choices that are asserted are subjective, it is also true that the preferences of the
rest of us for a procedural definition of ultimate
values is also ultimately subjective." In other
words, there is discontent with client self-determination when the issue involves public interest, and
voices of discontent can be heard. The idea of
"public interest" could assume the role of limiting
client self-determination, as the conscience of the
lawyer limits client self-determination in other
matters. Lawyers do argue, as we think they
should, on whether to decline to act for clients who
make choices that are seen as contrary to public
interest.

ANALYZING MORAL INFLUENCE

How does a lawyer go about considering moral
feelings in the law office? One way is to do what
some professors do in law school—to open discussion to expressions of moral impulse, to hear everybody out, and then to close discussion with solemn
expressions of respect for all moral opinions. That
is just barely better than nothing. It implies that
moral processes are immune to analysis and evaluation; it is a way to deny that morals matter. A
second way to learn law-office moral processes is to
analyze them as we analyze our morals among
friends or in reference to family, community, and
religious heritage. This is thinking about morals;
it is analytical. It invites some sort of analytical
framework for the moral influences at work in law-

office decisions. Here is such an analytical framework:

MORAL FORCES IN THE LAW OFFICE

Circle A	Circle B	Circle C
(left circle)	(center circle)	(right circle)
Client Morals	Our Morals	Lawyer Morals

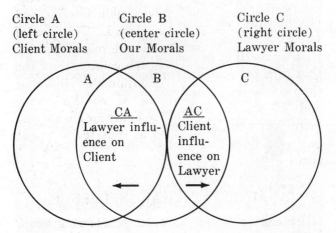

[B2907]

The lines of influence—because of the dependence clients have on lawyers—tend to be more
toward the left ("CA") than toward the right
("AC") (arrows). The circles are, of course, movable; each could move away from the center and
leave a larger area for discussion and mutual resolution on moral questions; our guess about the way
law practice is described in legal education is that
the area of consensus ("B") is the smallest of the
four areas represented here. (This figure oversim-
plifies things, of course. It apparently overlooks
third-party and social influences; it suggests lawyer and client are lonely individuals, and of course
they are not.)

The areas of private (or internalized) moral judgment ("A" and "C") dominate, in the law-school
description of what lawyers do, which is a result of
the view that moral judgment is not an appropriate subject for law-office conversations. This polite
taboo means that areas of moral choice are either
radically individual ("A" and "C") or within the
push and pull of personal forces ("AC" and "CA")
that turn on emotional influence (process) rather
than on discussion and negotiation (content). "A"
and "C" are, therefore, take-it-or-leave-it areas of
moral judgment, which means that "CA" and "AC"
become playing fields for deception and manipulation.

A gentle example—often, probably, not a moral
example at all—is the universal experience of "estate planning" on advice about gifts to avoid death
taxes. Almost any client with significant wealth
can reduce shrinkage in his "estate" by giving his
property away during life; many lawyers spend a
great deal of time explaining this, to clients who
nod and admire; but few clients follow the advice.
They decide to hold on to what they own, despite
the cost and in disregard of legal advice. The
lawyer's explanation of differential tax rates somehow fails to get to the issue, which is then an-
swered in the take-it-or-leave-it area of client decision ("A").

The distressed center circle ("B") is the area of
negotiation and compromise, the area that will
yield to open communication, collaboration, and

analysis; and the area in which lawyer and client are moral resources for one another. Its possibilities assume that people are able to talk about their moral judgments; able to ask for and give help when making up their minds about the right thing to do; and willing to subject what they have decided to processes of analysis and evaluation. An example: A lawyer told one of the authors (Shaffer) about an elderly widow who had one living child and two grandchildren; the grandchildren were the children of a dead child. The elderly widow told her lawyer that she wanted her estate divided into three parts and given one part to each descendant. The lawyer said he told her she shouldn't do that. What she should do, he said, was give half to the child and one-fourth each to the grandchildren. That, he said, was the proper way.

I (Shaffer) told the lawyer that I was appalled at the way he imposed his idea of propriety (and at its source, which is apparently the 17th century English Statute of Distributions). I asked him if he always did things like that, and he said that he did—always. Then I asked him what he did when the client insisted that she meant what she said. I gather from his answer that this sort of arrogance from clients, about their lives, their property, and the people they love, doesn't occur very often in his office; but, he said, when it does, he does what the client wants. Eric Berne would have called that a game; he might have called it "what should I do,

Daddy?" In his analysis, the rare client stops the game by saying, "This is what we are going to do together." What would happen then, in terms of the schematic figure we have been using, would be to move the issue from "CA" to "B."

"AC" in the figure is the area in which clients influence lawyers. The influence is sometimes naked power, as much take-it-or-leave-it as client judgment in area "A" is (except that in "AC" the client's judgment is being used to influence the lawyer's judgment); in these cases, the lawyer's moral decision is often Sartrean—he decides by doing nothing; he pretends not to choose; he tries to hide his moral responsibility in the adversary ethic. If the lawyer resists and defies, it will often be at considerable expense to himself. A much discussed example is the lawyer who refuses to go along with his client's violations of the laws on disclosures in securities registrations. He may end up defying both the client and other lawyers in the law firm—in which case his employment is on the line. He may feel compelled or even be required— as the Securities Exchange Commission is beginning to insist—to report his client to law enforcement officials.

The power of a client over a lawyer in moral areas ("AC") may be benign and subtle. Clients may decide "to do the right thing," even when lawyers see no necessity either for its being done or for its being right. In this "AC" area, the client may simply announce his judgment; he may not

offer it for negotiation. From the standpoint of
conscience, this may be an easy judgment for the
lawyer to implement, especially when the client's
moral instinct is better than the lawyer's, but
lawyers have been known to resist the influence,
"for the client's own good." If resistance is open
and discursive and negotiated, the dialogue is
moved from "CA" to "B."

In many law offices "CA" (lawyer influence over
client's moral choices) is much larger than "AC"
(client influence over lawyer's moral choices); that
is, we think, typical. The reason for imbalance is
the professional relationship; some of it is what
psychology calls transference (see Chapter Four),
some of it is lawyers taking advantage of a social
role that gives them power over others. A "lay
person" habitually yields much of his independence to the professionals he employs. If it is a
desirable thing to move decisions from this area of
moral influence to an area of moral discussion and
analysis (from "CA" to "B"), the lawyer will have
to employ strategies of (1) open communication
(about his own feelings, since those are the principal forces at work in the pressure from right to left
in the figure); (2) acceptance of client feelings, an
understanding that "feelings are facts" and that
the client's feelings matter to the lawyer; (3) a
demonstration that the professional (lawyer here)
understands how the client feels (counselors call it
empathy); and (4) a willingness to collaborate on
moral choices, a conviction that moral choices are

as often what we do together as what we draw out of a dark night of the soul; moral decisions can be discussed and negotiated, and even compromised. They can be analyzed and dealt with—to use Thomas More's phrase—"in the tangle of the mind."

The first step in negotiating moral choices is acceptance of the client's feelings about them. Strategies that operate toward openness about moral judgments in the law office also include skills for evaluating morals, skills lawyers learn in law school, where the principal announced objective is to learn how to evaluate legal decisions. But morals are not the same as legal decisions. It is probably a mistake, for example, to act always as if moral feelings can be confronted with and overruled by logic. This exaltation of the rational faculty—often a good thing, of course—assumes that non-rational sources of behavior are inferior. It is expressed in a number of ways in a culture such as ours:

—A moral feeling is irrelevant. It is impolite to talk about it ("I don't discuss religion or politics"). The values that come from moral feelings are, if worthy of human beings at all, intensely personal things which one talks about as little as (or less than) her sex life.

—Moral feelings are inevitable. Nothing can be done about them. They are the result of the prejudices of one's parents, or stern schooling at the hands of nuns or fundamentalist teachers in the primary grades.

—Moral feelings are a matter of conscious choice. This is the opposite of the-way-I-was-brought-up theory. Or, rather, it is the disgust with which a champion of logic regards the-way-I-was-brought-up excuse. The champion regards the assertion of conscience as a cover for obstinancy. Both approaches are invalid; one denies that morals are a matter of feeling; the other denies that morals are subject to reason.

—Moral feelings are the fault of society. This is a variant on the-way-I-was-brought-up excuse, but the variation is significant. The fault-of-society theory assumes that "they" (the government, the schools, the "power structure") are responsible for shoddy moral judgments. It also assumes that morals are a product of manipulation; morals can be changed by social engineers, and will be, once the right engineers get their hands on the television cameras and are elected to run the government.

These perceptions and theories about moral feelings and moral concerns, and others one might identify, have two things in common: They reject the moral feeling which is at issue, and they imply that a whole person (and the good professional) is not subject to impulses or instincts, or whatever, that tell him what he should do. The answer to both of these implications is that we experience moral concerns, worry about doing the right thing, are plagued with moral doubt—all of which can and should be a part of our professional lives.

* * *

Lawyer theories about client self-determination occupy a spectrum that is broader than the cool, rational dialogue contemplated by the Code. At one extreme, for example, there is often a species of interpersonal demand on the lawyer that is usually—and, no doubt, properly—excluded from client choice. In Frank Cihlar's example, "such limitations may take the shape of a decision to avoid becoming . . . friend or lover." At the other extreme, most lawyers insist, more vehemently than the Code, that a lawyer need not lend her talents to client objectives she regards as immoral. This latter limitation has taken on atypical insistence since "Watergate" and an increase in public doubt about the moral decency of lawyers. Many today resist the principle that a lawyer's duty is to represent her client's interests to the limit of the law, without regard to moral and social implications.

* * *

It is possible to identify four hypothetical principles, from all of this, for dealing with the moral impulses of clients: (1) Moral feelings are facts. Denial of them and ignoring them are poor counseling. (2) Moral feelings are in a significant way the evidence of the client's morality—a significant indication, that is, of the way he holds himself together, is able to forgive himself, defends himself against the shrew's disapproval he hears from within and without.   (3) Moral feelings cannot be submerged in logic or overcome by logic but they are accessible to the mind.   They can be examined and evaluated by reason, even though one will occasionally look at his moral choices, and at logic, and end up saying, as William James did, "so much the worse for logic."   (4) All three principles are as valid for the lawyer as for the client.   She cannot fail to be a poorer lawyer if she supposes that her profession requires her to deny her own conscience, or to suppose that conscience is a sort of calculus.

An attitude found in legal education and in some law offices, and one we urge our reader to outgrow, is that moral choice is irrelevant, in the law and to the client.   As a matter of fact, law is mostly moral choice.   And once we get beyond the bad-man view of clients (and litigants), fostered by the adversarial view of justice, law and client decision-making are rendered accessible to moral dialogue, in the law office and elsewhere.

If nothing else, the never ending revelation of shabby practices in government, in the professions, and business should cause us to be skeptical of legal educators who tell their students to put moral instincts aside when they come to law school. Karl Llewellyn told his beginning law students: "The hardest job of the first year is to top off your common sense, to knock your ethics into temporary anesthesia.   Your view of social policy, your sense of justice—to knock these out of you along with woozy thinking."   He aimed at a temporary bracketing of morals; he wanted legal analysis freed from morals. But law and law office work freed from moral judgment is not worthy of the tradition American lawyers claim or the place they occupy in the lives of their clients.

BIBLIOGRAPHY

We argue that lawyering is a moral conversation, the practice of a moral art. The lawyer counselor constantly confronts and struggles with moral issues. See, Shaffer, Faith and the Professions (1987), and American Legal Ethics: Text, Readings, and Discussion Topics (1985); The Good Lawyer: Lawyers' Roles and Lawyers' Ethics (Luban, ed. 1983); Redmount, "Client Counseling and the Regulation of Professional Conduct," 26 Saint Louis University Law Journal 829 (1982); Shaffer, On Being a Christian and a Lawyer (1981); Richards, "Moral Theory, The Developmental Psychology of Ethical Autonomy and Professionalism," 31 Journal of Legal Education 359 (1981); Noonan, "Other People's Morals: The Lawyer's Conscience," 48 Tennessee Law Review 227 (1981); Kelso and Kelso, "Conflict, Emotion, and Legal Ethics," 10 Pacific Law Journal 69 (1979); Greenebaum, "Attorneys' Problems in Making Ethical Decisions," 52 Indiana Law Journal 627 (1977); Watson, "Lawyers and Professionalism: A Further Psychiatric Perspective on Legal Education," 8 Michigan Journal of Legal Reform 248 (1975).

An alternative perspective, grounded in traditional professional concerns, is presented in Curtis,
"The Ethics of Advocacy," 4 Stanford Law Review
4 (1951), and It's Your Law (1954); Fried, "The
Lawyer as Friend: The Moral Foundations of the
Lawyer-Client Relation," 85 Yale Law Journal
1060 (1976). For a response to Fried, see Dauer
and Leff, Correspondence: The Lawyer as Friend,
86 Yale Law Journal 573 (1977).

REFERENCES

Barth, The Epistle to the Romans (6th ed. 1968);
Berne, Games People Play (1967); Brown and Shaf-
fer, "Toward a Jurisprudence for the Law Office,"
17 American Journal of Jurisprudence 125 (1972);
Cihlar, "Client Self-Determination: Intervention or
Interference," 14 Saint Louis University Law Jour-
nal 604 (1970); Centennial Issue, 55 Chicago Bar
Record (1973) (Krash and Cramton); Lehman, "The
Pursuit of a Client's Interest," 77 Michigan Law
Review 1078 (1979); Llewellyn, The Bramble Bush:
On Law and Its Study (1951); Riesman, "Some
Observations on Law and Psychology," 19 Univer-
sity of Chicago Law Review 30 (1951).

CHAPTER ELEVEN

UNDERSTANDING OURSELVES

A LAWYER'S DISCOVERY

The sub-plot in John D. MacDonald's mystery story The Last One Left is about a lawyer who learns to be a human being. Early in the novel the lawyer's wife leaves him because of his pursuit of the ideals our profession tends most prominently to exalt: "You are a very civilized man, dear. You are polite. You are considerate. You are thoughtful. But you demand of yourself an absolute clarity, total performance, complete dedication. There is something almost inhuman about it, really. What is lacking, I think, is the tolerance to accept—the inadequacies of things . . . . You have this terrible impatience with carelessness and muddy thinking and laziness. You drive yourself so hard. It isn't money hunger. You just seem to want to go around neatening up the world."

"Life itself is the basic magic, the real miracle," his wife says. "You are trying to impose your sense of order and fitness on the randomness of people and the illogic of fate. You want to refute the basic textures, the crazy mixture of life." The lawyer, Sam, resists this advice and accepts the separation. He tells himself that his wife has ignored "the essential stuff of survival. Did she want softness, apathy, amiable sloth?" Then one day he notices that he is driving his car at nearly 100 miles an hour while he thinks about what his wife said.

Sam wonders aloud, among friends, where his inhuman expectations had come from—from himself or from "the man I have been imitating all my life." And then Sam notices that his friends look shocked, and he says: "The lawyer has flipped, huh? Ever notice how uneasy people get if you try to say some of the weird things that happen inside your head? I used to hold everything back. That's part of the incantation." And then he says, "I'm going to tell people what I think. It's going to raise hell with my law practice. But it's the only way I can think of to stop being completely alone in the world."

Sam's conversion may be expressed in the way he talks and the people he talks to, which is the way Sam says he plans to express it. It is likely also to be expressed in greater self-awareness. Sam presents an issue for other lawyers, an issue on which it may be useful to consider whether lawyers differ from other people in their needs and what devices are available for a more self-conscious life in the practice of law.

ROLE AND IDENTITY

Sam's problem is indicative of a significant obstacle to the model of counseling we outline here— the conflict between a lawyer's sense of role (what he sees when he closes his eyes and says, "I am a lawyer") and identity (what he sees when he closes his eyes and says, "I am a person"). Here are some examples of it, and of its sources:

Conflict of interest, although often denied or obscured by professional aspiration, is a constant presence in professional relationships. A trial lawyer who specializes in plaintiffs' personal-injury cases, for example, although called to zeal for his client by Canon Seven of the Code of Professional Responsibility ("A lawyer should represent a client zealously within the bounds of the law") and by Rule 1.3 of the Model Rules of Professional Conduct, is as a matter of fact pulled by his relationship with persons "on the other side." He has many cases, virtually all of which he will compromise and settle; his livelihood depends in fact and in amount on the outcome of these compromises. The persons with whom he negotiates tend to be the same from case to case. He knows them better than he knows his client.

A busy lawyer is, for another example, often torn between his life with his family, or his personal fulfillment, and his devotion to his clients. The telephone is a ubiquitous and tyrannical symbol of that conflict. Lawyers who aspire to the development of their skills as counselors are brought into conflict with hourly rates, the expectations of partners, office overhead, and the hundreds of routines and traditions that give rise to the lawyering ethos and ethic.

Still another example. The image of the lawyer as counselor, companion, and friend conflicts with the financial rewards that lawyers (and we realize that there are exceptions) seek for their services. Douglas Rosenthal, in his empirical survey of personal injury lawyers, confirms the presence of a substantial conflict. Rosenthal points out that "The single source of pressure upon the lawyer most likely to affect adversely the client's interest, and which can most easily be documented, is the strain of prolonged litigation and the economics of case preparation. Simply put, a quick settlement is often in the lawyer's financial interest, while waiting the insurer out is often in the client's financial interest."

Aspirations conflict with the images and stories that students confront in legal education. The portraits that adorn law-school walls—of Cardozo, Holmes, Lord Coke, and Thomas More—are significant symbolic figures to most law students and to many lawyers. They are not vapid; they are often not as remote as common cynicism about the legal profession supposes. But students are confronted, within days of beginning their professional lives in school, with other images—images of the police-court lawyer who allows the morals of the marketplace to erode his ideals; images of the senior partner who expects his associates in the practice to produce money—big money—for the firm and therefore for him. Both sets of images are real and influential.

The lawyer's sense of herself as a person is broader and deeper than her sense of herself as a lawyer. Members of a discussion group of students in one of our legal counseling courses remarked to one another that they did not like law students. The class, and that discussion group, spent several hours working on this discovery, resolving the "problem" by establishing the fact that the people these students disliked did not exist. One way we did that was to establish our own diversity. Each was less law student than other things. The class had artists, musicians, parents, spouses, a gourmet or two, skiers, Jews, Christians, atheists, and a physician. In working this "problem" through in these terms we perhaps convinced one another that there were no law students left to dislike. Or, maybe, we discovered that what we disliked was a projection—a part of ourselves we had first cast out, then noticed elsewhere, then despised. Perhaps we managed to reintegrate the law student part of us by deciding to like it after all. And perhaps what we first exorcised and then reintegrated was the role which threatened our identity. At least what we had done was to put role and identity—lawyerhood and personhood—at odds, and to consider them, and the conflict between them, in a clearer reality.

The traditional model of the lawyer running the show exacerbates the conflict. The image lurking behind most of this role-identity conflict is an image of the lawyer as a dominating authority figure—someone who has to know, to do, to tell and to be cautious and responsible. It is an ironic image when one approaches the Code and the Model Rules as expressing a professional consensus among American lawyers. Our ethical aspirations insist that the law is something the lawyer uses to help the client. The determination of what to do with the law is for the client, although the lawyer does not give up his own conscience in the process.

Models, traditional and otherwise, are vague. It is surprising but true that many law students come to law school without knowing well even one lawyer. And many young lawyers enter the practice without knowing well any lawyers other than their law-school teachers. Judges are not models because most of us do not think of ourselves as judges. Professors are not adequate models, although they are inevitable models. Professors often do not practice law; they are not perceived as having experienced or anticipated the role-identity conflict discussed here (although most of them have experienced it, and some have resolved it by escape). Women provide a particularly poignant instance of the vague-models phenomenon; few of the pictures on the law-school wall are pictures of women. Few of the professors are women.

These instances of conflict combine with a traditional bias for academic discourse in law schools; the result is stress, unmet needs, frustrations, and anxious anticipations. One result of this is a sense in students that they are being manipulated by teachers. ("I don't know what is happening to me, but they do, and they are making it happen.") The common condemnation of the Socratic method in legal education is usually less disapproval of a style of teaching than disapproval of manipulation.

RESPONDING TO THE ROLE-IDENTITY PROBLEM

A student avoids the role-identity conflict by shouting it down. It is there he develops, perhaps, the occupational disease of lawyer cynicism. He hides the conflict in values that the profession presents to him:

—Teachers of legal counseling see this in student interviews, when the "lawyer" adopts a "whatever you want" demeanor, and seems to have no conscience of his own.

—Lawyers in the "silk stocking" practice deny these moral conflicts by refusing to deal with the human problems that present conflict in an unattractive setting (criminal defense, divorce, personal bankruptcy). When moral conflict arises in the vaguer and sometimes more subtle contexts in which they do practice, they cloud it behind the motives and ambitions of their clients.

—Students regard conscience as a private matter and insist that stated rules of professional conduct are inadequate and even hypocritical, that tough moral choices are a matter of conscience. Conscience, they say, is none of the

profession's business. It is not proper for law
schools to require study of it, or evaluation of it.

Other defenses involve denial ("Hell no, I'm not
worried"), or avoidance. We manage to avoid the
disagreeable parts of reality that we cannot admit.
More dangerous is the denial of those feelings that
are inconvenient and difficult to express in our
everyday professional life.

Professionals, doctors and lawyers in particular,
are susceptible to identity formations that cut
themselves off from others, even as they enter so-
called helping professions. Richard Sennett has
observed that this process of cutting-off oneself is a
way for those in authority, as are lawyers, to exert
"a peculiar kind of strength—a power to cut themselves off from the world around them, to make
themselves distant, and perhaps lonely, by defining
themselves in a rigid way. This fixed self-definition gives them a strong weapon against the
outside world. They prevent a pliant traffic between themselves and men around them and so
acquire a certain immunity to the pain of conflicting and tangled events that might otherwise confuse and perhaps even overwhelm them. . . .
[T]he threat of being overwhelmed by difficult social interaction is dealt with by fixing a self-image
in advance, by making oneself a fixed object rather
than an open person liable to be touched by a
social situation."

There is a sort of in-the-office professionalism, by
no means totally undesirable, that calls for a perso-

na, that is wearing a professional mask: the lawyer is to be detached, objective, unemotional, and in control of the client, herself, and the situation. The norm of objectivity and detachment isolates the lawyer from her client's feelings, but first and more insidiously, it isolates her from her own. Detachment can, and often does, become a morally destructive process in human relationships and also a bad working habit: Feelings are how we know who we are, and also how we "read" a situation.

Lawyers (and physicians) naturally attempt to protect themselves from the deep feelings that arise in the work with clients and client concerns. Maintaining a facade of impersonal coolness avoids a sticky confrontation between the deeper self of the lawyer (a sense of self that goes beyond work and professional life, a sense of self that is often not expressed in one's professional life) and the real self of the client (the person beyond the client and her legal problem). Hence, the lawyer relates to the client in terms of function, as an instrument for problem solving.

MacDonald's Sam found that his professional life and what might be called his legal persona had taken over his private self. His legal persona dominated his whole personality. Sam the lawyer ate, breathed, and slept law. He talked like a lawyer, thought like a lawyer, and dressed like a lawyer. The psychological identification was complete. In such a case, as John Noonan notes, the legal persona "become[s] indistinguishable at a psychological level from other disguises of the self. . . . [A] judge [and lawyer] may speak and even think of the law as an invisible companion telling him what he must do." The danger that we mean to identify is the danger of the legal mask slipping into place, and fitting so well, working so well, that we forget we have it on. Sam found that had happened, and the result was that he became rigid and inflexible and unable to listen to what people said to him. He felt this most keenly (after he came to see what he had done) in his relationship with members of his family, but it had undoubtedly happened—and probably long before—in his relationships with his clients and with people he worked with in his law office.

One way that we cover over our feelings and needs is in the development and use of a persona. The persona (and the ego with its many defenses) makes us adaptable, constantly adjusting to the flux and flow of the world. But the persona is a problem, because it pushes so much aside (everything unusable, unwanted, shameful, fearful). The urge to make ourselves presentable to the world (to be liked and respected, to build up our self-esteem), an urge we realize in and through the persona, is reinforced by the demands and expectations of our society. Genuine and sustained reflection is absent in the lives of busy, overworked lawyers, and in the lives of most professionals. We are submerged in everyday activity, whether in industry, government, church, education, or family. The pressure to do our job and the relentless pace of our lives do not permit contemplation. We move in established grooves. In such a world—and this is an irony—methods of self-awareness are identified as *therapeutic,* as medical, as a cure for illness, and as the special province of psychologists, psychiatrists, therapists, and counselors.

Lawyers are blind to their own personae, to the evasions and manipulations accepted by lawyers but held in disdain by clients and others outside the profession. The persona is one way we deal with the injustice perpetrated within an adversary system of justice but held sacrosant by lawyers. One of the reasons that we distance ourselves from clients is to silence them from speaking of shameful matters that we have learned to accept, to adapt to, and live with by way of denial. The persona has a back side, a part of the self that Jung perceptively called the shadow. The "shadow" contains all those elements of the personality which the ego condemns, those aspects of our psyche which are intellectually, emotionally, and socially unacceptable. The shadow, Erich Neumann tells us, is "the expression of our own imperfection and earthliness, the negative which is incompatible with the absolute values" that we attempt to live out in our lives and our professions. The shadow "roots the personality in the subsoil of the unconscious, and this shadowy link with the archetype of the antagonist, *i.e.,* the devil, is in the deepest sense part of the creative abyss of every living personality." Other psychologists and counselors confirm Jung's insight. Erik Erikson found that "identity formation normatively has its dark and negative side, which throughout life can remain an unruly part of the total identity. Every person and every group harbors a *negative identity* as the sum of all those identifications and identity fragments which the individual had to submerge in himself as undesirable or irreconcilable or which his group has taught him to perceive as the mark of fatal 'difference' in sex, role or race, in class or religion." (Emphasis in original.)

Freud's theory of repression makes it obvious how the persona and the shadow elect to go their separate ways, conscious energy flowing toward the persona and the unconscious holding back those experiences and feelings which are rejected in conscious life. The division of labor between the conscious and unconscious realms is functional and allows us to put aside what is socially unacceptable (every society designates behavior and thought that are shameful and to be held in disdain). But the division of labor is, in Freud's words, "overdetermined"; like all adaptive behavior it tends to be overused, and used in circumstances far beyond its functional need.

C. G. Jung made it an explicit part of his theory and therapeutic practice to engage the patient in a process of recognizing the shadow and bringing it into conscious life. Jung was always careful to avoid the suggestion that bringing the shadow to conscious life was an argument for hedonism or social irresponsibility. To the contrary, Jung saw the confrontation with the unconscious as one of the most difficult tasks in human life, a confrontation that makes those who undertake the journey more, rather than less, socially responsible. Erich Neumann, one of Jung's followers, made this insightful comment on the confrontation with the shadow: "The self-experience involved in the journey of depth psychology (the first stage of which is the encounter with the shadow) makes man poorer in illusions but richer in insight and understanding; the enlargement of the personality brought about by contact with the shadow opens up a new channel of communication, not only with one's own inner depths but also with the dark side of the human race as a whole. The acceptance of the shadow involves a growth in depth into the ground of one's own being, and with the loss of the airy illusion of an ego-ideal, a new depth and rootedness and stability is born."

Ultimately, as Sam also found out, the 24–hour-a-day legal persona became a neurosis. It became that because the lawyer role was invested with status and prestige, and the mask fit. He had not managed to integrate his professional role with his other parts of himself. Sam imagined himself as one of those self-actualizing individuals whom Abraham Maslow described as able to "assimilate their work into their identity, into the self, *i.e.,* work actually becomes part of the self, part of the individual's definition of himself." This kind of self-definition, and integration, is both desirable and dangerous. In any case, most of us don't get that far; what we do is switch back and forth: The diverse and conflicting professional roles of the law and the conflicts and contrast of professional and private lives create a world of constant change— from lawyer to person to lawyer, from bereaved clients to aggrieved clients to pushy clients to worried and passive clients.

The Greek god Proteus could escape those who would question his prophecy by assuming the form of various animals and even fire and water. The "shape-shifting" of Proteus is not, in the view of Robert Lifton, a Yale psychiatrist, and others, merely a story from Greek mythology but an archetypal motif in our own lives. Lifton characterizes the Protean style as "an interminable series of experiments and explorations, some shallow, some profound, each of which can readily be abandoned . . . ." In essence, the Protean style is the wearing of many masks as a way to live with the psychological shifts that accompany the roles, situations, and worlds in which we find ourselves. When we admit to the fragmentation in our lives, and experience the wearing of masks to help us adapt to diverse roles, we imitate the Greek god Proteus. Lifton observes that "while he [the Protean personality] is by no means without yearning for the absolute, what he finds most acceptable are images of a more fragmentary nature than those of the ideologies of the past. And these images, limited and fleeting though they may be, can have enormous influence on his psychological life."

The paradox for the Protean person lies in the quest for identity in the chaos of flux and change. Erik Erikson, reflecting on the ambiguity and conflict in the Protean personality, captures the paradoxical quality of this Protean energy, of a god who "knew the past, the present, and the future of all things, and it was in order to avoid having to tell that truth that he assumed the pseudo-identities of animals and elements of nature. Only when caught napping and held down before he could escape into different beings was he forced to be himself and tell what he knew. So there was a real and lasting Proteus in the original Protean personality, a tragic core-identity in the multiplicity of elusive roles."

The Protean quality of playing diverse roles, of wearing different hats, and masks is both a liberation and a danger. Erikson, questioning the Protean style, asks: "But what if role-playing becomes an aim in itself, is rewarded with success and status, and seduces the person to repress what core-identity is potential in him? Even an actor is convincing in many roles only if and when there is in him an actor's core-identity—and craftsmanship. Comparably, there may well be some character types who thrive on Protean possibilities, even as there is, by definition, a developmental period (namely, youth) when the experimentation with a range of roles and alternating states of mind, can be a way of personal growth. What is described as a Protean personality today may, in fact, be an attempt on the part of adolescent personalities—and America has always cultivated these—to adjust to overwhelming change by a stance of deliberate changeability, of maintaining the initiative by playing at change so as to stay ahead of the game. . . . Those who are gifted in this game, and therefore, truly playful in it, may with luck make it an essential part of their identity formation and find a new sense of centrality and originality in the flux of our time."

The story of Proteus connects with our own lives, lives in which it becomes increasingly difficult to avoid wearing masks. If we cannot avoid the masks we can tell the truth about them and be aware that there is a self behind them.

LAWYER NEEDS

Lawyers as persons have personal needs, needs they seek to satisfy in their professional lives. We are often unaware of how these needs affect the practice of law and our ability to perform effectively and with human caring in a professional role. Even our ideals create needs that may in fact aggravate the role-identity conflict; recent research suggests that idealistic professionals are the ones most likely to suffer burn-out.

Leete, Francia, and Strawser, in a systematic investigation of lawyer needs and the extent to which they are satisfied in the practice of law, used the "need hierarchy" developed by the late humanistic psychologist Abraham Maslow. The need hierarchy looks this way (from most fundamental up to "highest" need):

I. Security Need: the feeling of security in my position

II. Social Needs

    1. The feeling of self-esteem obtained from my position

    2. The prestige of my position within the firm (that is, the regard received from others in the firm)

    3. The prestige of my position outside the firm (that is, the regard received from others not in the firm)

III. Autonomy Needs

    1. The opportunity for independent thought and action in my position

    2. The authority connected with my position

    3. The opportunity, in my position, for participation in the setting of goals

IV. Self Actualization Needs

    1. The opportunity for personal growth and development in my position

2. The feeling of self-fulfillment obtained from my position (that is,
the feeling of being able to use
my own unique capabilities, realizing my potentialities)

3. The feeling of worthwhile accom-
plishment in my position

It is important in using Maslow's psychology to
understand that needs as he saw them are arranged in a hierarchy. It was Maslow's theory
that needs on the lower end of the hierarchy (security, social needs) must be satisfied before higher
needs (autonomy, self-actualization) can be satisfied. He recognized, as do these lawyer-research-
ers, that this is a matter of more or less. It is
possible, in other words, for a person to satisfy
needs for autonomy after he feels largely satisfied
with his levels of security and social comfort; but
it is not possible for him to feel autonomous if he
has insecure feelings about his social position and
self-worth.

Leete, Francia, and Strawser considered lawyers
on three sets of variables—(1) solo practitioners,
partners, and associates; (2) lawyers in small
towns, medium-sized towns, and cities; and (3)
small firms, medium-sized firms, and large firms.
Here are a few of the things they found out about
lawyers:

—Compensation is a significant concern
among solo practitioners and lawyers in small
communities, but it is not a major concern of the

profession generally. This suggests the validity, among lawyers, of the first principle of job-enrichment psychology: Earnings cannot be made high enough to satisfy all important human needs.

—Lawyers in small communities tended more than those in other communities to feel that their needs for social position, autonomy, and self-actualization were met. They were least satisfied with their compensation, but this concern did not block other satisfactions.

—Lawyers in middle-sized communities were significantly less satisfied with their social position and their autonomy, while the small-town lawyers were happiest on this count.

—Lawyers in large firms felt highest satisfaction with compensation, but relatively low satisfaction with social position and autonomy. Both of these dimensions were also sources of relative dissatisfaction for lawyers in small firms.

—Solo practitioners felt high satisfaction in all dimensions except compensation. Partners in law firms were more satisfied on that dimension and as satisfied on the others. Associates in law firms were less satisfied than either solo lawyers or partners in all dimensions except one; they were more satisfied in the matter of compensation than solo lawyers were.

—Overall, lawyers felt less satisfaction of their security needs than businessmen do, but their level of dissatisfaction was not high enough to interfere with satisfaction of higher needs. On those higher needs (social needs, need for autonomy, self-actualization), lawyers tended to fairly high levels of satisfaction; they felt more satisfaction of their need for autonomy than business people do.

TOWARD SELF–UNDERSTANDING

The intellect, that is, merely "thinking" about ourselves, as we know from Freud, is seldom sufficient to learn the truth about ourselves. While it may not be possible to rid ourselves of *all* self-deception (a fact that will persuade many not to make the effort), it is possible to be more aware of ourselves as professionals by constantly observing (and uncovering) the deeper layers and aspects of the self. It is during this uncovering, this locating of the various aspects and dimensions of the self that we come to understand the path we have taken, the way we do our work, the way we are in the world with others, the way we are in relation to all else.

Our motivations for actions and the foundations for our beliefs have a basis and serve purposes of which we are, in part, unaware. While we see ourselves in our own actions, thoughts, beliefs, fantasies, and dreams, the problem is that we do not see ourselves as clearly as we would like. We have not learned to be as honest with ourselves as we would like. Yet, each of us has the capacity to reflect on the way his own life works, and on the philosophy that each of us imposes on his own life and the lives of others. The paths we choose show up in the way we talk and listen to clients, in the kind of counseling we do.

To the extent that we eschew reflection and the effort to see ourselves more clearly, our ideas, theories, and dreams, even our lives, are submerged in the world. The emphasis on present needs, on doing rather than being, make our persona, our philosophy of life, and our moral perspective more and more inaccessible to awareness. A lawyer can easily practice law and engage in a course of conduct that seems to involve no significant moral choices. You can live a life oblivious to ethical choice, oblivious to the conduct that shapes and ultimately defines your own character. How does this happen? How do we let a persona, a philosophy, and even social and ethical illusions, guide our lives? To what extent is the philosophy we live out with clients hidden from us—hidden as we go about being-in-the-world as lawyers? We argue that the ultimate philosophy of counseling is seeing more clearly how we make a world in our interaction with those we serve, those who seek our help and expertise.

How do we let a persona, an implicit philosophy of life, and even social and ethical illusions, guide our relationships with clients? A good counselor becomes aware of illusions, those of the client and her own. It is the exhortation we find scattered throughout philosophy—to lead an examined life—that is the theme of this chapter.

The task is to lift the veil of ignorance that obscures the philosophy we live out in our talking and listening to clients. What we need most is possession of what is closest to us—insight into who we are as we work, the way our work shapes and distorts our character. Socrates taught that philosophical truth comes only from persistent reflection and meditation which cast light on the darkness of self. To follow Socrates we must learn to do our own thinking, to value reflection, and to learn from our own inner world, even as we learn from our clients; in both cases we must choose to listen.

In the counseling we call psychotherapy, the problematic nature of our attempt to exist in the world with others is an issue. When we seek therapy and psychological counseling, something has gone wrong in relation to others, to ourselves, to the way we imagine ourselves in the world with others. But for the mess that lives fall into, that is, the pathological condition of our being with parents, spouses, children, friends, and colleagues, there would be no such thing as psychological therapy, no need for counseling.

Freud and Jung insisted that the way to understand others is to understand ourselves. Freudian and Jungian analysts undergo the same therapy they later undertake with their patients. The doctor (psychiatrist, therapist, counselor) sees the possibility of healing (understanding, listening) in light of her own experience of being heard, understood, and healed.

We bring Freud and Jung into our discussion here because they provide a working theory of human motivation that makes clear the importance of being aware of how the unconscious affects our personal and professional lives. Freud and Jung are of continuing relevance to the lawyer, because lawyers have a need for self-awareness, a need they resist. Freud and Jung showed that our lack of self-knowledge, and our failure to initiate a program of self-scrutiny, is not caused by laziness so much as by resistance. Established beliefs and patterns of thought and interaction resist change; that is a point we can accept without appeal to Freud and Jung. But these giants of psychology make this resistance to self-scrutiny, and to psychological development, a focal point of their theory: Resistance is a powerful force that stands between the ego and our awareness both of everyday life and of the unconscious and "internal" world that affects our everyday decisions, our personal and professional interactions, and our relationships with clients.

Even if the lack of motivation is overcome (and how is it that one overcomes a resistance that is itself unconscious?), there are serious obstacles to self-scrutiny identified in Freud's and Jung's teaching. The difficulty in gaining access to unconscious motivations may prove the undoing of even the most dedicated. The psychoanalytic explanation for the difficulty lies in the "repressive forces" that keep unconscious material unconscious. Psychological repression serves as a watchman who refuses to allow an impulse to move from the unconscious into conscious awareness.

Resistance is not limited to the obstacles thrown in the path of the analyst prying into deep recesses of the patient's mind. (Freud observed that "one hardly comes across a single patient who does not make an attempt at reserving some region or other for himself so as to prevent the treatment from having access to it.") Resistance serves the individual as a censor to avoid conscious awareness of emotional experiences that have been lodged in the unconscious. Freud found that resistance to unconscious material seriously cripples insight and understanding and indicates that an individual's "critical faculty is not an independent function, to be respected as such; it is the tool of his emotional attitudes and is directed by his resistance."

A word more about resistance: Given the intellectual and psychological resistance in the service of repression which censors and blocks unconscious motivations from awareness, it becomes clear that the obstacles to insight through self-scrutiny are extraordinarily difficult to overcome. However, these resistant, protecting, unconscious motivations do not doom the process of self-scrutiny. In fact, it is the appearance of the resistance that signals the existence of that which has been denied, the very thing (thought, feeling) that would, if it could, create a conflict. Therefore, the resistance, rather than posing an insurmountable problem, serves as an indicator that material is being repressed. At this point, in psychotherapy, the resistance itself is pursued.

The first point of this excursion into psychoanalytic theory on resistance is a point about our ability to keep the uses of the lawyer role under the control of the moral self. The point is that self-scrutiny has an emotional complexity that cannot be dissipated through intellectual decision. Conscious effort is not enough. The second point is that self-scrutiny is worthwhile: All of us fear the unconscious; some of us are unwilling to experience the painful and unsettling awareness of a deeper self. Some of us even believe that digging around in the unconscious is dangerous. The testimony of the experts is that the danger is rarely serious. Karen Horney finds such harm or danger "so rare as to be negligible. Observation in every analysis shows that patients are well able to protect themselves from insights they are not yet able to receive."

The typical reader of this book, who, we hope, is willing to engage in self-scrutiny and a study of the legal persona outside the psychoanalytic setting, does not have the advantage of "working through" unconscious conflicts and repressed drives and thoughts with an analyst. The question then is whether insight from self-scrutiny is possible outside a psychoanalytic setting where one is encouraged and guided by a psychoanalyst (Freudian), an analytical psychologist (Jungian), or a psychotherapist. Horney, who has dealt at length with the obstacles to self-scrutiny and the potential of self-observation, gave a tentative yes in response to this question. We believe that self-scrutiny is possible. We encourage our readers, as we encourage our students, to seek to do that with friends and classmates and teachers. We worked out the contents of this book largely to provide hints and encouragement for such an exploration.

Lawyers and law students—and those who write for them—undertake the study of law and psychology in order to understand the people we deal with professionally—clients, brothers and sisters at the bar, judges, juries, etc. We argue throughout this book, however, that one of the principal lessons for counselors is the importance of learning about ourselves. This lesson about self-awareness is of greater significance for lawyers as they tend to avoid their own feelings; lawyers tend to fool themselves about the psychological importance of the elements of the counseling relationship which are in front of and within them. It is for some reason easier to talk about a not-present, not-timely (and therefore unreal) client psyche than to talk about one's own. This is a weakness that is characteristic of almost all discussions of interviewing and counseling skills.

SELF–UNDERSTANDING AND
CREATIVE PROBLEM–SOLVING

Danzig-Nevis International has developed a series of exercises on self-evaluation that center on
obstacles which keep us from being creative in our
work.   These obstacles to creativity are important
to lawyers because there is an area, beyond hard
choice and collaboration, for the expertise, knowledge, and craftsmanship of the lawyer.   In terms of
content, this function is a matter of formulating
solutions to problems.   Solutions depend upon creativity.   Creativity depends upon self-discovery,
and self-teaching.   Here is discussion of the blocks
to creativity, and some adaptations of it to a lawyer's life:

Block One: *Fear of Failure*.   Someone who has
dissolved or reduced this block is able to take risks,
to assert her creativity, to take chances on pain or
shame, and to seek change.   Our profession is built
on adventurous lawyers—Horace Binney, for example, who vindicated charitable trusts in the
United States by arguing, from 16th century English court records, that the Supreme Court should
reverse itself; Louis D. Brandeis, who built his
career on challenges to concentrations of wealth;
Thurgood Marshall, who was able to reverse the
trend to racism in public education by convincing
the Supreme Court to overrule its own clear prece-
dent.   Here are some clues—signs that this block is

interfering with one's capacities as a problem solver:

I am not willing to seek help in those more or less routine situations where I could make it alone but I could make it better or faster with help.

I don't seek to learn something if I feel, from past experience, that I have relatively low talent for that kind of learning (for example, I do not like to study language or repair cars, or sing a song). I prefer to limit myself to what I'm good at.

I don't want people to know about my mistakes. I would rather hide from them.

It is hard for me, in my fantasies, to see myself as a hero. My imagined triumphs are private, and quiet, and tend not to be celebrated.

Block Two: *Reluctance to Play.* A lawyer who has overcome this block tends to think of her work as play, as intrinsically enjoyable. She sees humor—not grim humor, but ironic humor—in many of the things she and other lawyers do, in the solemn pretensions of the profession. She doesn't worry about seeming to be silly; she is, at times, and enjoys it. A friend of ours, Terrence Kelly, of the Colorado Bar, was making a difficult argument to a three-judge federal court in Denver. He had exceeded his time. The presiding judge said, "Mr. Kelly, don't you think you ought to give the other side a chance?" Kelly, who has a superbly creative sense of play, looked at the bench, and at opposing counsel, and said, "Gee, your Honor, I thought by now they were convinced." He not only de-fused the occasion, he captured it.

Block Three: *Resource Myopia.* A lawyer who has overcome her resource myopia knows how to use the resources around her and within her. She tends to encourage others to develop new skills and to grow. (Poorly paid secretaries in law schools should, as a condition of their employment, be given an option to learn from the teachers whose work they type. If law schools do not demonstrate this kind of commitment to resources and skills development where will it be learned?) She has a knack for delegation where delegation works best. She has a sense of her own strengths and limitations; she is not afraid to refer cases, but she is also not afraid to stretch herself to do something new, or to do better something she has done before.

Block Four: *Over-Certainty.* Lawyers who are not over-certain in their lives with clients have mastered the ability to be flexible. They have less routine in their lives and are less likely to think of clients (or problems) as having labels or categories. As a result, their problem-solving is not stereotyped; a lawyer who is not blocked by over-certainty, for example, might solve a civil-rights riddle with antitrust law; she might solve collection agency oppression with the rules on unauthorized practice of law. (The growth of the common law is, for the most part, traceable to flexible advocates.)

A lawyer who is blocked by over-certainty tends to persist in professional behavior which does not get the job done; she tends to be guided by unfounded assumptions.

Block Five: *Frustration Avoidance.* Unpleasant experiences—such as frustration—can be creative if we are willing to let them be creative. A lawyer who is blocked by his own need to avoid frustration may tell himself:

I will make a decision, even if it is a wrong one, then continue to worry.

It is a waste of time to argue with someone whose mind is made up.

There is no point in continuing to watch a boring play, or to read a dull book, or do an unrewarding task.

Block Six: *Custom Bound.* One way to examine the extent to which custom blocks creativity is to ask where my values come from. From tradition? From myself? From others? And to what extent are these values functional for me? One way to look at lawyers as problem solvers is to see that lawyers in our society have a hand in social and institutional change. The issue is whether adherence to custom—to, if you prefer, unexamined values—makes it hard to accept and implement and use change in a creative way. If I am being blocked by custom, what are the messages I'm giving myself?

Incomplete sentences bother me. So do split infinitives and dangling prepositions.

I believe that the rules are changing too fast for our own good.

The great lawyers are all dead.

Block Seven: *Impoverished Fantasy Life*. It is possible to ignore or distrust parts of my mind, of my life, which are real and may even be pressing— my dreams and day-dreams, and images, and visions of glory. Browning could have been speaking to lawyers when he said a person's reach should exceed his grasp. And much of one's reach is a matter of psychic life. And yet, there is a pervasive belief that if one looks at what is deep inside himself he will see guilt and shame and ugliness, that being our true selves will unleash a "psychic Nazism." It is hard to say "I'm okay," and fearful to look at the beauty and playfulness and courage that is within, that deeper sense of self that it is possible to befriend. What do I say to myself that impoverishes fantasy life?

Just give me the facts, ma'am.

I don't have dreams or can't remember them.

I can't imagine what it would be like to be somebody else, to do anything else.

I would never take a trip to India.

Block Eight: *Need for Balance*. An inability to live with chaos and disorder and ambiguity often cuts a good lawyer off from problem solving resources in himself and his client. Andrew Watson has identified in law students an unusually high need to master the environment, to line things up, organize, impose structure. Many law students become anxious as they find that very little in the law is settled and what is settled is being challenged. But seeing one's own life and the law as a process, as undefined, is often a way to release creative energy. It is probably why so many great lawyers in the common law system have been history buffs and have tended to explain law more in terms of its development than in terms of its inherent logic. What do we say to ourselves which lets the need for balance become an obstacle to creativity?

I don't like to see people without appointment, and when I do see people I don't want to be interrupted. (A character in the play "A Thousand Clowns" hurls this charge at his lawyer: "If the world were coming to an end, you would learn about it on the telephone.")

When I'm in a meeting I like the agenda to be clear; it bothers me to hear discussion when there is no motion on the floor.

I believe the judge should be in absolute control of what goes on in his courtroom.

I dislike poetry which does not rhyme, atonal and Oriental music, stream-of-consciousness fiction, and modern buildings.

People should be on time and things should be where they belong.

Block Nine: *Fear of the Unknown.* Lawyers like
to know what they're doing; this is the problem-
solving side of Andrew Watson's theory that lawyers have a high need for order. The unknown
might be disorderly. An example of this need, this
habit of mind, is the old aphorism that a good trial
lawyer never asks a cross-examination question
unless he knows what the answer will be. If one
pursues that rule in office practice she will be a
solipsistic counselor; she will work only from her
world and avoid the world that the client brings
into the law office. How does a lawyer operate
when blocked by fear of the unknown?

I prefer to use established and proven forms
for wills and pleadings; you never know what
will happen if you start tampering with what
works.

If it ain't broke don't fix it.

Proposals such as "no-fault" insurance, simplified divorce laws, and new and quicker ways to
administer decedents' estates are destroying the
legal profession and harming the public.

It is no part of a lawyer's job to play psychologist for his client.

Block Ten: *Reluctance to Exert Influence.* Lawyers would not, at first blush, appear to lack a
willingness to assert themselves. But the profession is more varied than the stereotypes suggest.
Many lawyers and law students are in fact blocked
by a fear of seeming to be too aggressive or too

influential. And many of us who are often asser-
tive also often fail to press a point of view, possibly
on the theory that silence is more comfortable or
"cooler." There is, in fact, some special learning
to be gained from feedback which reflects how we
come across when we keep our mouth shut. How
do we allow our reluctance to exert influence to
control our creativity?

I hate scenes. If someone is annoying me—in
a theater or at a party—I usually just leave.

There is nothing I can do to change things.

It is better, in meetings or work groups, to
avoid disagreements and, when that fails, to
smooth them over.

You can't fight city hall.

People who complain are neurotic.

Block Eleven: *Reluctance to Let Go*. It is possible to try too hard, to work too long, to forget how
valuable and rejuvenating it is, once in a while, to
just walk away. It is especially tempting to forget
that the best resource in problem solving is oneself,
and that in the interests of getting the job done we
still need to protect and preserve that resource.
This block has other dimensions, too—the tendency
to get nervous about what we do and the attendant
neglect of the people we are doing it with; anxiety
about getting things done so that we cannot let
ideas incubate or ripen or, maybe, just go away; so
much need to control the action that we sell short
capacities in other people. What are the secret

messages we send ourselves which block us by making us reluctant to let go?

I have to have reasons for what I do. It is not enough, for me or for anybody else, that something feels right.

If at first you don't succeed, try, try, again.

Never leave for tomorrow what can be done today.

If people want my advice, they should listen to what I say.

Block Twelve: *Impoverished Emotional Life.* Feelings are facts. A client's feelings have to be built into the relationship and into the results of working together. They are part of the raw material of problem solving. The lawyer's feelings are also facts. It takes energy to hold them back; solutions that ignore feelings are somehow incomplete, weak, less workable. Awareness of self and others is a precious professional asset. What do we say to ourselves that causes us to ignore emotions?

Anger, silly joy, and that sort of thing is not . . . (cool? mature? rational?)

I am surprised to learn how strongly people feel.

I seldom . . . (cry? burst out in anger? shout for joy? sing out loud?)

Block Thirteen: *Unintegrated Yin-Yang.* Synergy is one way to express this idea. The object is to move things away from the poles of opposition—to see that contrasting points of view, for example, can contribute to a good solution; that conflict can be used rather than suppressed. If anything is clear in the substantive law it is that circumstances alter cases, that few things are perfectly clear. From a philosophical point of view, it is possible to see professional life as a dualism, a we/they, win/lose game. It is also possible to look for and find a wholeness in the world, and that perception may be what I need to relax and let myself be creative. When do we block creativity by polarity?

I either like someone or I don't.

Some people are just plain bad, but I also know people who are really saintly.

Children should be seen and not heard.

Students should learn, teachers teach.

A lawyer's time and advice are his stock in trade.

A person has to have strong values, and he has to stick to them.

Block Fourteen: *Sensory Dullness.* We walk on carpets, and sit in padded chairs, surrounded by artificially cooled or heated air, and listen, if we're very unlucky, to piped music that we are not supposed to notice. An environment can numb the senses. How does it feel—to walk on freshly-cut grass, to smell a pie baking, to taste the subtlety of a fresh, raw vegetable? To awaken to an experience like one of these is to find a new vista on resources, and on how we adapt to an environment. How do we turn off our senses?

I am uncomfortable when it is . . . (hot? cold? windy? noisy? dark?)

Popular music (or classical music or country music) all sounds the same to me.

My office is where I work, not where I live.

I don't touch other people.

I don't feel good when I . . . (am dirty? am sweaty? am in old clothes? don't have my hair combed?)

* * *

The counseling disciplines nourish and preserve a stubborn dogma about creativity—a hope that the average among us is creative enough. Creativity in Shakespeare's and Mozart's range may be a gift of God, but the stubborn dogma can bear that fortuity; we need not be driven mad about it, as Salieri was. We can, despite the inexplicable occasion of genius, still insist that there is enough creativity in each of us to make life better for ourselves and those who need us. The agenda, then, is to locate and remove the habits and hangups that keep a lawyer from working at her or his creative best.

BIBLIOGRAPHY

The literature on self-awareness is voluminous. Virtually every book store in the country has a section containing psychological self-help books which promote self-awareness of one variety or another. Some of these books are better than others. Some of them are well written and some of them are not. Some psychology self-help books are helpful; others may lead the reader astray.

In this bibliography we have included a few self-help books and some references which readers will recognize as "pop psychology." Many of the references, however, are to solid academic and scholarly books written for a general audience. We have drawn on the ideas in many of these books as a basis for our own. We include a variety of different theoretical and philosophical approaches to self-awareness, and a sample of books written over the last fifty years. A lawyer-counselor will find some, if not all, of these references, useful: Goldman, Vital Lies, Simple Truths: The Psychology of Self-Deception (1985); Kopp, Even a Stone Can Be a Teacher: Learning and Growing from the Experiences of Everyday Life (1985); Lasch, The Minimal Self: Psychic Survival in Troubled Times (1984); Trungpa, Shambhala: The Sacred Path of the Warrior (1984); Percy, Lost in the Cosmos (1983); May, The Discovery of Being (1983); Ferrucci, What We May Be: Techniques for Psychological and Spiritual Growth Through Psychosynthesis (1982); Houston, Life-Force: The Psycho-Historical Recovery of the Self (1980); Fried, The Courage to Change: From Insight to Self-Innovation (1980); Schumacher, A Guide for the Perplexed (1977); Dass, Grist for the Mill

(1977); Kohut, The Restoration of the Self (1977); Deikman, Personal Freedom: On Finding Your Way to the Real World (1976); Bergen, The Cold Fire: Alienation and the Myth of Culture (1976); Lifton, The Life of the Self: Toward a New Psychology (1976); Lilly, Simulations of God: The Science of Belief (1975); King, For We Are: Toward Understanding Your Personal Potential (1975); Kilpatrick, Identity and Intimacy (1975); Murphy, Outgrowing Self-Deception (1975); Sampson, Ego at the Threshold: In Search of Man's Freedom (1975); Zaleznik and De Vries, Power and the Corporate Mind (1975); Assagioli, The Act of Will (Penguin, 1974); Katz, Preludes to Growth: An Experiential Approach (1973); Browne, How I Found Freedom in an Unfree World (1973); Trobert, Learning From Experience (1972); Shostrom, Freedom to Be (1972); Van Dusen, the Natural Depth in Man (1972); Harper, The Existential Experience (1972); Hamachek, Encounters with the Self (1971); Horney, Neurosis and Human Growth: The Struggle Toward Self-Realization (Norton Library, 1970); Stevens, Don't Push the River (1970); Schutz, Joy: Expanding Human Awareness (Evergreen Blackcat ed. 1969); Klapp, Collective Search for Identity (1969); Fingarette, Self-Deception (1969); Jourard, Disclosing Man to Himself (1968); Watts, On the Taboo Against Knowing Who You Are (Collier, 1967); Warner, Self-Realization and Self-Defeat (1966); Assagioli, Psychosynthesis (1965); Fingarette, The Self in Transformation (Harper Torchbook, 1965);

Jourard, The Transparent Self (1964); Strauss, Mirrors and Masks: The Search for Identity (1959); Wheelis, The Quest for Identity (1958); Bergler, "The Mirror of Self-Knowledge," in Psychoanalysis and Culture 319 (Wilber and Muensterberg eds. 1951); Bois, Explorations in Awareness (1957); Horney, Self-Analysis (1942).

On self-awareness for lawyers see Elkins, "The Legal Persona: An Essay on the Professional Mask," 64 Virginia Law Review 735 (1978); Watson, "Know Thyself and Thy Client," 1 Learning and the Law 23 (1974).

We pay more attention to self when we stumble or go astray, get sick, or start doing odd things. In recent years, there has been much talk about the phenomena of burn-out, an experience of exasperation, depression, anger and despair that makes professional work difficult, if not impossible. On burn-out, see Maslach, Burnout: The Cost of Caring (1982); Potter, Beating Job Burnout (1982); Pines and Aronson, Burnout: From Tedium to Personal Growth (1981); Freudenberger, Burn Out: The High Cost of High Achievement (Bantam, 1981); Edelwich, Burn-Out: Stages of Disillusionment in the Helping Professions (1980); Woolfolk and Richardson, Stress, Sanity, and Survival (Signet, 1979); Selye, Stress Without Distress (Signet, 1975).

On lawyer and law student stress, see Barber, Surviving Your Role as a Lawyer (1983); Davis, "How Lawyers Can Cope with Stress," 3 Virginia

Bar Association Journal 15 (Summer, 1977); Taylor, "Law School Stress and the 'Deformation Professionelle'," 27 Journal of Legal Education 251 (1975).

One of the ways to avoid burn-out and to increase the imaginative range in which we practice the art and craft of lawyering is to see the creative potential in professional life and bring more creativity to our problem solving. The literature on creativity is a rich source for lawyers who seek to view themselves as artists as well as technicians. See Progoff, The Dynamics of Hope: Perspectives of Process in Anxiety and Creativity, Imagery and Dreams (1985); May, The Quest for Beauty (1985); Gedo, Portraits of the Artist: Psychoanalysis of Creativity and Its Vicissitudes (1983); Goldberg, The Intuitive Edge (1983); Kopp, The Pickpocket and the Saint: Free Play of Imagination (Bantam, 1983); Gawain, Creative Visualization (1982); Perspectives on Creativity and the Unconscious (Proceedings of Jungian Conference, Miami University, 1980); Kris and Kurz, Legend, Myth, and Magic in the Image of the Artist (1979); Arieti, Creativity: the Magic Synthesis (1976); Low, Zen and Creative Management (Anchor, 1976); May, The Courage to Create (Bantam, 1976); Watzlawick, Weakland, and Fisch, Change: Principles of Problem Formation and Problem Resolution (1974); Adams, Conceptual Blockbusting: A Guide to Better Ideas (2nd ed. 1974); Spector, The Aesthetics of Freud: A Study in Psychoanalysis and Art (1972); The Creative Experience (Rosner and Abt eds. 1970); Barron, Creative Person and Creative Process (1969); Creativity and Learning (Kagan ed., Beacon paperback, 1968); Gordon, Synectics: The Development of Creative Capacity (Collier, 1968); Barker, Brain Storms: A Study of Human Spontaneity (1968); Moustakas, Creativity and Conformity (1967); Neumann, Art and the Creative Unconscious (Harper Torchbooks, 1966); Koestler, The Act of Creation (1964); Philipson, Outline of a Jungian Aesthetics (1963); Art and Psychoanalysis: Studies in the Application of Psychoanalytic Theory to the Creative Process (Phillips ed., Meridian, 1963); Kubie, Neurotic Distortion of the Creative Process (1961); The Creative Process (Ghiselin ed. 1952); Schneider, The Psychoanalyst and the Artist (1950); Osborn, Your Creative Power (1948).

REFERENCES

Binney, The Life of Horace Binney (1903); Leete, Francia, and Strawser, "A Look at Lawyers' Need Satisfaction," 57 American Bar Association Journal 1193 (1971) (discussion of Maslow); Jung, Analytical Psychology (1968); Noonan, Persons and Masks of the Law (1976); Neumann, Depth Psychology and a New Ethic (Harper Torchbook, 1973), and The Origins and History of Consciousness (Princeton University Press, 1970); Freud, The Complete Introductory Lectures on Psychoanalysis (Norton, 1966); Sennett, The Uses of Disorder: Personal Identity and City Life (Vintage,

1971); Erikson, Life History and the Historical Moment (1975); Lifton, Boundaries: Psychological Man in Revolution (Vintage, 1969); Rosenthal, Lawyer and Client: Who's in Charge? (1974); Saxe and Kuvin, "Notes on the Attorney-Client Relationship," 2 Journal of Psychiatry and Law 209 (1974).

CHAPTER TWELVE
EPILOGUE ON LEARNING

LEARNING ABOUT PEOPLE

Whatever use you may have made of this book, we expect that you will not have come away from the reading (and the exercises) with the sense that you now know all you need to know about legal counseling. We have provided some ideas and reflections on the work of lawyers with clients, but this is only a beginning. Law school is a beginning, a long arduous one, in understanding law and how it works—what lawyers do with the law and do to people with the law.

If you have read this far and, with the help of other readers and maybe a teacher, have experimented with some of the ideas and skills presented, you will have come a long way. We understand that you may not yet see yourself as a skilled counselor: it may be comforting to note that the graduates of non-legal counseling programs often share a similar feeling of being unskilled. This feeling of not being there yet, not having gotten quite enough, is understandable and valuable. If you take that feeling into your relationships with your clients, most will understand that you are a learner (although a few will not), and you will have a different sense of your work (your listening and talking) with clients than a lawyer who ignores the counseling dimension in professional life. Knowing that you have something to learn is exactly the kind of attitude that gives rise to good listening ("active listening") and to talking with a client rather than talking at him.

The ideal next step in learning about counseling would be to learn more about people, and to begin with yourself. You are your own best resource in learning about people. You and your own experiences are a textbook. The exercises that we have provided in the Appendix are examples that we have taken from the textbooks of ourselves and our students. We have labeled them exercises, but they are nothing more than an opportunity for you to think about and to reflect on your own experience, your feelings and your fears, your own wonderment about who you are and what you are becoming.

Much learning from your own textbook, from yourself, can be done alone—by a process of discourse or dialogue with yourself. Much of psychology developed that way, particularly the introspective depth psychology of C. G. Jung. Much of Freud's theory on normalcy is introspective; he was his own principal subject in The Psychopathology of Everyday Life and The Interpretation of Dreams. The philosophical psychology of Aristotle, Aquinas, Nietzsche, and William James is from introspective thinkers who did not merely think, or even think and then write; they thought and wrote in conversation with themselves, learning from what they wrote, experienced, and dreamed, and then writing what they learned. Jung's analyses of his own dreams are remarkable instances of this—as are Freud's little detective stories on why he left his umbrella at home, or how he came to use the wrong word in a conversation. To wake up with a feeling of sadness from a dream; to find that you are depressed for no reason; to realize that you are sexually attracted to one client and always angry with another, that you feel powerless and out of control with still another, are the experiences from which your own psychology of lawyering can be made.

Much of literature is worked out this way, too. Trollope's making flesh-and-blood people out of the lonely daydreams of his wretched youth is an example. "There is a gallery of them," he said, "and of all in that gallery I may say that I know the tone of voice, and the colour of the hair, every flame of the eye, the very clothes they wear." His characters were with him when he went to bed, he said, and as he woke from his dreams. They were alive because they were real; each of them told Trollcpe about people, as people told him about his characters and as both told him about Trollope. And thus C. P. Snow called Trollope one of the greatest *natural psychologists*.

A dialogue with oneself is, therefore, one way to begin learning more about people from the best

possible source. There are several forms and disciplines for this:

—journals and diaries;

—letters, which have the advantage of invok-
ing another person with both her reactions and
what you imagine her reactions will be;

—fiction, which has in all the great storytellers (and many lesser ones) been a way to pull
things off the shelf and to get a look at them;

—descriptions of dreams and daydreams,
which often reveal feelings one does not readily
admit, and which are, in Jung's view, a major
source of intuition (seeing around corners). We
are in the world with our dreams as much as we
are with our plans and conscious goals. Dreams
are an aspect of reality and of our lives that gets
ignored in the pursuit of other more dominant
aspects of everyday reality. Counseling depends
on understanding how some aspects of our experience—process, nonverbal communications, feelings, dreams—are discounted, devalued, ignored,
driven underground, while other aspects of reality are treated as the only real reality.

Counseling as exemplified in psychotherapy and
psychoanalysis broadens this principle of dialogue
with self to dialogue with an accepting, reflecting
other person. In both the Freudian and Jungian
views of analysis, the therapeutic encounter allows
the use of another person to learn about and resolve the mysteries in oneself. The helping person

is a safe opportunity to do with human help what Aristotle and Aquinas did through writing. This use of an accepting other is at the heart of Rogerian "client-centered counseling" and the principle behind the companionship and introspective lawyer model advocated in this book. Everyone has had the experience of using a friend for a sounding board, and learning as one talks. Seeing that sort of thing happen to others is one of the joys of the kind of counseling that we find it possible to do with clients, with students, and with each other.

One of the most powerful, immediate, and provocative means of making a study of oneself is to work in a group that makes what happens in the group the subject of study, that, as the researchers say, generates its own data. The object of such groups (T-groups, encounter groups, human-relations groups, sensitivity groups, problem-solving groups, virtually any small group that focuses on process as well as content) is to provide information about how we interact, who we are as we try to make our way in the world with other people. The idea of a T-group (T stands for training, and the training that is envisioned is training in the skills of interpersonal relations) is that the group's task or agenda is the process of how the group works, how each member of the group interacts within the group. The claim is that such an agenda is the most immediate and accessible and the least costly way of discovering how each member of the group relates to the people in his life outside the group. Another idea in the work of T-groups is that being surrounded by accepting, supporting people (that is, other people who share the goal, who seek to learn about themselves) will free you (and them) to be candid—to be candid most of all to yourself. When the agenda of the group is no-agenda, that is, when a group does not set as its purpose some specific task, goal, or problem to be solved, then we become for each other a screen on which feelings are projected and can be examined. The idea that a group is educational (in contrast to being a place of encounter for the sake of encounter) means that the "process" of the group is assimilated and brought back into the group, so that members of the group can "see" what is happening, to themselves and to others.

T-groups were, during the late 1960s and throughout the 1970s, a significant teaching device for learning the skills of interpersonal relations and a means of personal self-development. Both of the authors have participated in various small groups, received training as group leaders, and have used small groups (and what is called small group process) as parts of our law school courses. While T-groups receive less public attention today, and were never made an integral part of under-graduate and graduate programs in psychology, such groups continue to exist and are used in the training of business leaders, managers, teachers, psychiatrists, clergy, and others who work with people and realize the need to know more about themselves and their relations with others. Experiential learning in T-groups focuses on the "here and now." We know of no other educational tool that provides the kind of learning that takes place in an agenda-less small group in which people come together to learn from their own immediate experience.

MORE ON JOURNAL WRITING

We have suggested that there is a way of talking and listening to clients that is guided by seeing the client as a story, and seeing ourselves as having a story that we tell with our lawyering, and in our relationships with clients. People need to tell their stories as well as live them. We tell a story in our work, in the briefs we write, the cases we try in the courtroom, and in law office conversations with clients. Our counseling, as we practice the art of good talking and listening, is a matter of telling and listening to stories. Many people seek a telling that is more truthful, more revealing, than the storytelling reflected in their day-to-day work. Compare, for example, the storytelling you do at a cocktail party with the stories you tell your lover.

This is how one student expressed that need: "In legal writing it is possible to steer wide of anything that matters to you as a person, but the attraction for such analytical writing passes quickly. I need to face my feelings; that need becomes a craving. Until the craving is satisfied by writing—really writing—my dreams become wild, my attention to detail lags, and my restlessness insures my unhappiness." And so we have, over the years, turned to writing, and asked our students to write: journals, long letters to friends, and even fictional accounts that will capture the meaning of the world as we have experienced it. We need this kind of writing, the kind of writing we find in journals, letters, and novels, to give expression to our lives. And when our lives are too full, crowded and busy to do this kind of writing for ourselves we turn to the writing of others, to those who have found the time, who have responded to the need to say something imaginative (and truthful) about life, about the world in which they live (and the world in which we live).

There are many reasons to keep a journal, and many ways in which to do it. We (the authors) have worked with journals over the years, writing our own, and asking our students in law school to keep journals as a way to learn about themselves, about how becoming a professional matters in their own lives.

Doing a journal is difficult. If it were easy, everyone would do it. Knowing that introspective and personal writing is good for you, that you can learn about yourself, and begin to better understand the conflicts and joys experienced as a law student and lawyer, is apparently not enough to prompt a person to actually keep a journal. The fact that so few lawyers and others in public life and leadership positions keep journals and do the kind of introspection that we suggest here is an indication not only of the difficulty of doing a journal but of an attitude toward introspection. Abraham Zaleznik and Manfred F. R. Kets de Vries, in their book on corporate leaders, Power and the Corporate Mind, argue that "Leaders, who orient themselves to power and action, are usually indifferent to the notions of psychic truth; instead, they care about practicality and feasibility." They suggest that truth, what we might call psychological truth, "can be sought only on the edges of depression, the potential for helplessness that must be acknowledged in the process of arriving at the understanding of goals and the manner of their pursuit. Depression is too painful for most people to endure, so they involve themselves in activity and, occasionally, in a preparanoid search for antagonists, danger, and obstacles that reality seems to be erecting for them to overcome. The consequence is insensitivity and lack of awareness, which diminish the capacity to perceive and communicate."

The habits of journal writing and introspection are discouraged in the reality of a world dominated by the routines of everyday life. And it is the routines of everyday life, the meetings with clients and other lawyers, the court appearances, the papers to be drawn up and filed, the brief to be written, that keep us busy, our lives crowded with practical matters. Who has time to think, much less write, or keep a journal that seems to serve no purpose other than his own peace of mind? Busy people who long ago quit reading textbooks have no time for making a textbook about themselves. The busy lawyer tends to justify his life by telling himself, "I don't have time to do anything else." And it is exactly this kind of experience, of being rushed, of not having time, that becomes an integral part of our relationship with clients, that impoverishes our counseling, that gives our lives the feel and the "texture" that they have. This experience, of lawyering and everyday life, and the conflict it creates and the frustration and burn-out it ultimately produces, can itself be made the subject of our journals, an entry-way or opening into a deeper understanding of who we are and what we have become as lawyers, how we have found a place for ourselves in the world, or how we continue to search for that place.

One of the authors of this text (Elkins) has worked with this experience of "being rushed" and used journal writing to explore this aspect of his own everyday reality. What follows is a meditation, a philosophical reflection, on this experience.

* * *

I am intrigued by the possibility of experiencing the world as it is. I know that such experience is rare, and must be cultivated. Perhaps it is impossible, beyond my ability. And even as I write this last statement I see that it is a statement of pessimism, if not cynicism—perhaps even a statement that I do not believe. I remember Albert Camus's statement in his essay on the myth of Sisyphus:

> The mind's deepest desire, even in its most elaborate operations, parallels man's unconscious feeling in the face of his universe: it is an insistence upon familiarity, an appetite for clarity.

> * * *

> This heart within me I can feel, and I judge that it exists. This world I can touch, and I likewise judge that it exists. There ends all my knowledge, and the rest is construction.

I am surrounded by my world, with all that it is, and with all those actions of which I am a party and those of which I am a stranger. The world as it is—what could this mean? The physical world. Descriptions of places. Rock. Mountains. Water. Ocean. Sky. But does the world come to us as rock, as the mountains which I see in the distance as I write? No, I suspect the world comes to us, is given to us, first in imagination, first in that time when we emerged from womb, Mother, Earth.

There are times when we are so very present to the moment that nothing else seems to exist except the consciousness of that moment. I sit down to drink my morning coffee and embrace that moment as if there was never to be another. The day ahead has not, as yet, become a reality. The dreams that came during the night have been forgotten, yet leave a psychic residue, so that I can still feel the dreams' presence. And so for that brief moment, early in the morning of the day, I am suspended in time, conscious of the night which preceded my waking, and the light of day that lies ahead. It is a simple and truthful time, a moment to be in the world, and with myself. I surrender to the simplicity of that moment and my own existence. In that moment I see how life is both simple and whole.

The moment, the consciousness that I have experienced, will pass. During the day I will lose myself in doing, in the ritual of everyday life, in those routines that can be taken for granted without harm. And while I fear the delusional qualities of these routines, they too desire celebration. Both the moment of simplicity and a day of ritualized performance are forms of awareness, each a celebration of life.

How am I pulled away from the rare moments of clarity, of direct experience, of simple being? What happens to such moments? Why are we unable to maintain a simple being-in-the-world? Just as there are digressions in conversations, there is much to take me away from the "experienced moment." The day calls. I respond to its demands. I answer the call of Necessity, of Work. I enter another world. It too is a world that I make, that I constitute with my choices—a world in which I sometimes, but by no means always, feel at home. But my real home as a human being is that place where I am more myself, more likely to be direct and unadorned, that moment when I can still remember the reverie of dreams, have just begun to make my way into the beginning of a new day. To make a life of such moments is to build a life where one lives, a life that shelters and provides a harbor, a place for awaiting the fate that befalls one on the open sea journey.

The social world in which I live as a law teacher, like the world of lawyering, is like an open sea, with virtually unlimited possibilities, a world in which I am pushed and shoved about, where I "make it," "get taken," and "am broken." It is a world which I enter, which I have chosen, but only with trepidation and the presence of an anger that tells me all is not well.

Life has all too few moments when it is possible to be fully present, quietly attentive to that which is most immediate and direct. Such moments elude capture. As the primal mind becomes a modern one (assuming such a transformation as this could ever occur), we begin to search out and work (and pay) to capture such moments. We search for moments of quiet simplicity, of realness, of truth and authenticity. There is an urge to find in our social existence, in life writ large, some way to capture the quality of human experience, the flakes of fire of a life lived in attentive aware moments.

Contemporary life insures that we have few moments with ourselves. The day is filled with demands, schedules, work, doing. Our lives are caught up in the structure that we erect around us. We take a job and invest our work with an authority that makes it a master and we its slave. We answer to our work, and then ourselves. We give up the freedom to experience life's quiet moments. In a different time, perhaps in more primal cultures, such moments were carried into the day. While there is much foolish romanticizing of the "primitive," I have no doubt but that at some early time in our evolution as cultural beings the ability to experience the present moment was more easily sustained (and evoked in sacred ritual) than it is today. Or perhaps, that is one of the fantasies that I project onto the past, and imagine as a quality of the primal mind. Necessity existed for the primitive as it does for me. And that some part, for many a substantial part of life, is devoted to the sustained effort to survive in the face of Necessity (and its facelessness), a fate that we share with our ancestors.

Everyday life becomes its own reality, a reality that colors, usurps, and finally dominates all else. The prosaic and mundane are ever present. Everyday reality becomes a crusty overlay, a thick impenetrable layer of rocky topsoil that cuts us off from the meaning of our own experience. I can let the world define me, accept what I see and am told, play along, take it as it is. There is always someone to suggest what must, or should, or can be done. Necessity is everywhere.

The Necessity that I battle—work, routine, boredom, procedures, unfairness, inequality, injustice, detachment, compartmentalization—makes everyday life real. The reality of my everyday life is like an ore which must be processed and transformed if it is to yield a useful metal. It is from the "felt sense" of everyday life with all its routines and patterns, the ore of ordinariness, the working out of what happens as I live from one day to the next, with all its perversions, that I extract the story that constitutes my own life. Our lives are revealed, made visible, in our stories.

In the faceless world we have created we now find a resurgence of interest (a new reverence) for the traditional forms of everyday life which sustain us: farming, gardening, childrearing, housebuilding, eating, running; activities that suggest human scale forms of energy, work, and communities. The need to recreate the ordinary and everyday lifeworld, to give new meaning to our work, to the routine, the habitual, the mundane, and the prosaic, gives rise to new perspectives and new disciplines, to new ways of contemplating and imagining our world, new ways of talking about the place of human beings in the world they create.

* * *

In this writing the author has tried to say something about the world and how the world is experienced and then reconstituted in his own life. This philosophical reflection is one way of seeing the world, a seeing that is personal (introspective) and political (a criticism of how things work).

Journals work in many ways, reflecting for the most part less of a philosophical statement than the one we have presented here. Journals are paradoxical, on the one hand unique to the writer, and, on the other, an expression of hopes and dreams, failures and fears that each of us experiences in his daily life.

When we asked our students to write journals, to use them to learn about themselves, we did so because the felt experience in one's life as a student is a significant feature and not merely an adjunct to the substantive knowledge that is being taught and learned in law school. By writing about their experience of writing, their feelings about doing a journal, students gave us feedback, and practiced the art of reflection. Feedback is a counseling skill, and is integral to journal writing, and it is something that we can teach ourselves (and each other) to do. Thus, a journal shared with your teacher is a form of feedback, as a journal that you write and then later reread is a way of giving yourself feedback. The feedback that you give yourself and the teacher says something about what happened (content), but it is also a statement about process, about how what happens to you matters to you, about your "felt experience." And if that is not real, and important, nothing is.

When students write about doing journals they speak, often, of journals as a kind of therapy. This is the way one student explained it:

I write to survive. Whenever I feel a lot of pain, I write to some unknown individual, just spewing out my rage and pain. It has a cathartic effect. Sometimes when my feelings and thinking are at odds with each other, I attempt to make decisions through stream-of-consciousness writing. I make a deliberate attempt to write everything about a feeling or thought. After a week or so, I reread my writing to see how the situation has changed.

Doing a journal is thus a way to deal with pain, disappointment, confusion, conflict, and failure. These experiences, the ones we hate so much to admit, the ones we dread having, the ones we hope will just go away, are the kinds of experiences that journal writing helps us experience more fully. (The same is true of happy feelings, of course.) The journal claims the experience as one that can be admitted, owned up to, explored, even appreciated.

A journal is a way of keeping a record, and a place for seeing that one is moving in the desired direction. For some students, writing is a way to stay on an even keel; it keeps them on track, moving in the right direction, helps them be more effective and realistic. One student says: "I am depending on the journal to keep my thought processes keen, even in the tide of overwhelming amounts of case material and demand for one-lane thought." But the ego which gets into journal writing, and it is the ego that worries about being effective and realistic, of setting goals, and achieving them, also has a penchant for ignoring aspects of our lives that don't get expressed by being on track, by the linear movement from goal A to goal B to goal C. There are needs and purposes in professional life that are sacrificed in the making of goals and in achieving them, in doing what our teachers and our clients ask us to do. Goal-oriented achievement poses no small danger, even as it gets us to where we have chosen to go (when we actually choose a path). One student writing on this point recognizes that law school is a great adventure and one that calls for sacrifice: "This journey is probably the greatest adventure I have ever embarked upon. This [journal] is a record of my development, a living account of the adjustments and sacrifices that I have made to accomplish a goal that was set so long ago." The journal is a way of seeing what our purpose is and where we have been—if not where we are going. One student writes:

I want to see myself in my journal. I have saved my writings for over ten years. By re-reading these writings, I can see many facets of my personality. I can read about how I express anger, love, worry, hopes, dreams, and pain. I can compare how I feel now with how I felt ten years ago. I can evaluate the changes. My collection of writings keeps me aware of what I have been through, and helps me focus on my goals.

Another student writes:

My journal is still full of questions for me to resolve. Hopefully, every time I am in doubt my journal will be a barometer to show me how far I have veered from my course, or how well I have obtained my objectives.

A journal works as therapy, when it works (sometimes nothing seems to work), because it gives whatever is troubling us, pulling us down, or moving things too fast or too slowly, a chance to speak for itself. The ego crowds out the many voices of our lives that don't fit easily behind the persona, into the demands that our clients (and the world) make upon us. The therapeutic value of journal writing that students (and we the authors) experience comes from getting back into awareness these voices trampled on in the rush of everyday life. One student writes:

Without regard to the purpose of this journal, the process of drafting it over the semester has been a valuable experience in itself. I have thought about things in depth, whereas without the journal, I would merely have let them pass. I have questioned and criticized, whereas without writing the journal, I would have been apathetic. But, most importantly, I have forced myself to take a step back from "all of this" [law school] and try to gain a perspective of it, whereas without writing the journal, I would not even have attempted this. In essence, the journal has been very beneficial to me, even if I have not created a "purposeful" or "good" journal.

Journals and introspective writing help us see what is truly important in our lives and how the apprehension, anxiety, anger, and fear as much as our happiness, contentment, *and* achievement are inevitable and valuable in our lives.

Journal writing is an "outlet," or as one student dramatically puts it: "This journal has given me an outlet to plug all my frustrations and problems and ideas into. It has been my psychiatrist." Another student speaks of the journal as a way of seeing and understanding her own life:

This has been an excellent outlet for me and my frustrations and tensions. I write down my problems, insecurities, feelings and then come back and read what I have written and it gives me a different and clearer perspective of the situation. Sometimes just by the actual "writing" physical tensions are released and frustrations calmed. It has been an excellent way for me to look deeper and find out new things about myself.

To counsel another person, to attend to her problems, the concerns and fears that are related to her problems, it is necessary for the counselor to "see" and reflect on what is happening in her own life. The work that a lawyer does, the listening and talking we do with clients; the way our encounters and interactions with clients are imagined, conceived, and executed cannot be divorced from the feelings, fears, failures, hopes, and dreams of the person who is the lawyer. Only if the lawyer were able to view herself purely as a technician, only if her professional work were purely routine, would it be possible to study and understand, to learn and perform the lawyer role without it having an effect on who she is as a person. A student writes: "This journal has made me confront myself as a person. If this writing serves no other purpose, that is enough." One effect of learning law, knowing law, and practicing it out in the world is that it makes one kind of person rather than another, bringing satisfactions, pleasures, and also fatigue, alienation and disenchantment. This subjective dimension of professional life, unexamined in legal education, makes lawyering worthwhile and fulfilling or simply work to be tolerated.

Journal writing is a way to explore, to discover, to see how the goals we make for ourselves in turn bring with them restrictions and limitations:

My law school writing is, for the most part, different than my personal or imaginative writing. I am expected to accurately record and analyze divergent facts. While analysis can be creative, it is nonetheless no real part of myself. As a law student I am only reacting to factual situations or to theories already formulated by others. At most I am creating theories from separate, smaller groups of ideas already formulated. Legal writing strives for succinctness. While necessary for clarity, brevity removes one's spirit from the work. When clarity is the only emphasis, writing has no soul.

Legal writing can, however, be seductive at times. When I am tired or would rather not face up to the world or my feelings, I find it easier to analyze than create.

Another student comments:

Writing for an assignment has always been difficult for me. I've been afraid to sound like myself—for fear that what I'm saying isn't worth listening to. I must sound authoritative and often I find myself using words that I would never use in conversation. I'm still not sure if writing is supposed to sound like me or not. I've concluded that if the assignment involves research on a particular subject, I should never sound like me.

I remember handing in a writing exercise in high school that was returned to me with every "I" and "me" circled in red ink, along with a comment that these words were used far too often in the essay. It had a profound effect on me. I'm still somewhat paranoid about personal pronouns in my writing.

In Law School all I've written are memos and a brief for the Legal Writing course. It's something you do by writing, but it isn't writing. The memos were the easiest—research and write—"it could be this, it could be that"—no feeling, no emotion permitted. The brief permitted the expression of some emotion through the need to be persuasive. This was "me" talking and it involved somewhat of an investment. I wrote alone in the apartment all weekend. I found it a painful process—almost like labor. It felt as if I had delivered this baby, and now a baby expert was going to look at it and he might tell me it was ugly—or, worse, that it was dead!

And another:

School causes us to write for our teachers, others, instead of for ourselves. We learn that we cannot write, that we are not worthy of writing for ourselves. This process continues in law school.

When I have a writing assignment, I panic. Will it be as good as the professor wants it to be? It's so hard to write for oneself when grades and jobs depend on pleasing the professor. Why are we all so caught up in pleasing others with our writing?

I associate methodical, sterile, "correct" writing with becoming a lawyer. When I write for law school, my writing is not original, it is a conglomeration of other people's thoughts and writings on yet other people's thoughts. Everything I write down has to be footnoted! Law school has made me more confident in terms of writing correctly, but not creatively.

As a woman, I write more about love, pain, coping, and relationships. It is hard to imagine a woman writing a book about fishing.

When I recently began to keep a journal, I sat down with nothing particular in mind and simply began to write. No typographical errors to correct, no misspellings, no delay in putting ideas into words. It felt good.

In journals there is often a sense of discovery, the surprise that there is more going on in our lives than we have been willing to admit. We imagine ourselves as we go along—particularly so in a demanding educational regimen: We think we know who we are. Journal writing questions this imagined self and the prescribed roles and accompanying self-identity that takes place in learning law and being a lawyer. We discover ourselves in writing, and the self we find is often one that has been in hiding. As Joan Didion, the novelist, puts it, "Writing is the act of saying I."

One of the consistent themes in counseling, one of the things that bring a lawyer to imagine himself or herself as a counselor, is a curiosity about the lives of his or her clients. When we see the need to understand another person from his perspective, then we realize that the only manner in which that will be possible is to know something of our own perspective. Students express something of what Didion meant; they are, in their journals, writing to say I, writing to know who this I is. One student says:

Writing is important to me now to help understand exactly what my thoughts are. Sometimes I don't even know what I'm thinking or feeling. When I write I begin without a goal or idea in mind. I simply start out with a blank page and begin with a few general comments. Then come the thoughts, and before I know it my most closely guarded secrets are there on the page. It is as if I cannot help myself—my innermost thoughts slip so easily from my mind to my pen that I am hardly aware of it. Afterwards I feel refreshed, whole. I know that if I tried to explain my thoughts to others rather than write about them, my words would be tempered by my perception of their reactions, or their needs. Only in writing am I completely free, completely open.

Another says:

My writing has enabled me, for the first time, to begin to look at myself honestly. Sometimes this is very hard to do, since I still struggle with who I am and what I want from life.

I have begun a journey, through writing, wherein I discover diverse sides of myself. So much territory remains undiscovered. I am beginning to risk expression that I never would have dreamed possible. I feel that I am growing and developing as a person in many new ways. I am no longer afraid of my writing. Rather, I look forward to being able to express myself, not only for release, but as a tool for reflection on who I

am. My writing has taken on a whole new
meaning. I am writing for me and it feels good.

A third student says:

Doing the journal has come at a good time for
me [the first semester of law school]. It has
helped me through a stressful and lonely period,
a time in which the only key to survival was a
dependence on the development of a source of
inner strength.

Writing concretizes dreams, hopes, fears, frustrations, anger, confusion, and love. The writer
takes that which is amorphous and ephemeral
and makes it real. Validation of the personal
voice can open avenues of expression and potential for change which stimulates the emergence
of a whole inner self into an external world
previously off limits.

Learning law as a student, practicing it as a
lawyer, teaching it as a teacher, depends more
than we have previously recognized on what we
think and imagine of ourselves as persons. The
continual exposure to law and legal thinking affects our inner world, the subjective world of
images, emotions, feelings, and fantasies. Law and
legal thinking, the talking and listening we do *as*
lawyers, shape our view of the world, and become a
world-view. (See Chapters Three and Eleven.) In
exposing ourselves and our inner world to the
truth of writing, we "see" the shape of this person
we are becoming, the person present in all our
doing. When education (learning law) and the

work of ordinary Wednesday afternoons (the practice of law) focus exclusively on skills and knowledge—the problem to be solved, the next client to
be seen—then we lose sight of the human dimension of our craft. One way to retain and recover
the values that are pushed aside in the rush of a
busy day is to write about our "felt experience."
Law is not something merely to learn, use, and do;
it is something to experience. It is the experience
of working with our minds in the company of
clients, and of other lawyers who call our skills and
knowledge into question, that makes our work both
doubtful and pleasurable, alienated and meaningful. By consciously focusing on our experience of
the world in journals, we students and lawyers
develop a sense of our own identity shaped by
reflection and introspection, an identity that is
grounded in the concern and caring for what happens to ourselves and to the clients we represent.
In writing about what matters to us, what we have
succeeded in doing and what we have failed to do,
things we understand and things which remain a
mystery, about the lives we see our clients living
and how we become a part of their lives when we
serve them as lawyers (often enough, unintention-
ally), our lives take on a new depth and authenticity. It is this "inner experience" that Robert
Redmount suggests is "the core of . . . inquiry
into professional conduct."

Journals are a means by which we connect our
knowledge and our work with our subjectivity, our

sense of self. A journal validates subjective experience, brings it into view, makes it valuable. Subjectivity surrounds our learning, our knowing, our doing. Journals bring the subjectivity that is always, already there, back into conscious awareness. The journal is one way that we relate knowing to being, to the excavation of the story that we are already living.

BIBLIOGRAPHY

Binder and Price, Legal Interviewing and Counseling: A Client-Centered Approach (1977); Shaffer and Redmount, Legal Interviewing and Counseling Cases (1980); Watson, The Lawyer in the Interviewing and Counseling Process (1976).

The literature on small groups and small group process is extensive: Back, Beyond Words: The Story of Sensitivity Training and the Encounter Movement (2nd edition, 1987); Blumberg and Golembiewski, Learning and Change in Groups (1976); Lieberman, Yalom, and Miles, Encounter Groups: First Facts (1973); Lakin, Interpersonal Encounter: Theory and Practice in Sensitivity Training (1972); Slater, Microcosm: Structural, Psychological and Religious Evolution in Groups (1966); Berne, Principles of Group Treatment (1966); Schein and Bennis, Personal and Organizational Change Through Group Methods: The Laboratory Approach (1965); Bion, Experiences in Groups (1961).

On the use of small groups in legal education, see Grismer and Shaffer, "Experience-Based Methods in Legal Counseling," 19 Cleveland State Law Review 448 (1970).

For a critical perspective on small groups, see Malcolm, The Tyranny of the Group (1975).

On journals and diaries: Rainer, The New Diary (1978); Progoff, At a Journal Workshop (1975); Nin, The Novel of the Future (Collier, 1970). Examples of the craft of journal writing include: Bentley, Winter Season: A Dancer's Journal (Vintage, 1984); Henry, Toughing It Out at Harvard: The Making of a Woman MBA (1983); Koller, An Unknown Woman: A Journey to Self-Discovery (Bantam, 1983); Truitt, Daybook: The Journal of an Artist (1982).

For autobiographical writing that provides a model for journal and diary writing, see Rodriguez, Hunger of Memory: The Education of Richard Rodriguez (Bantam, 1983); Wishman, Confessions of a Criminal Lawyer (Penguin, 1982); Pirsig, Zen and the Art of Motorcycle Maintenance: An Inquiry into Values (1974).

REFERENCES

Zaleznik and De Vries, Power and the Corporate Mind (1975); Jung, Analytical Psychology (1968); Redmount, "Attorney Personalities and Some Psychological Aspects of Legal Consultation," 109 University of Pennsylvania Law Review 972 (1961); Rogers, Client-Centered Therapy (1951).

APPENDIX

THE COUNSELING PROFESSIONS

There are occasions in your practice of law (as in the work of virtually every professional who deals directly with people) when you will need help in dealing with the problems confronting the client, or help with a problematic client, or, we hope on fewer occasions, help with the problems you have created for yourself and your client. One of the realities of contemporary society is the division of labor in the helping professions. Few lawyers will be willing to help their clients resolve all the problems (especially protracted psychological ones) they bring with them to the law office.

In this section we describe various mental health professionals for the purpose of giving you some idea about who clients can be referred to for further help.

Psychiatrists are medical or osteopathic doctors who have specialized in psychiatry; they operate the way other medical specialists operate (on referrals from other medical or osteopathic doctors) and tend to practice on the medical model. (This last is a very broad generalization; there is growing diversity in psychiatry on both assumptions and methods.) Almost all psychiatrists have the M.D.

or D.O. degree; some have specialist certification in the field of psychiatry and some do not.

Psychoanalysts are usually psychiatrists who use psychoanalytic methods—that is, the methods of depth analysis devised by Freud and his followers. There are a few "lay" analysts who do not have the medical degree. "Psychoanalysis" is sometimes used to describe Jungian psychotherapy, although Jung and his followers preferred the term "analytical psychology" to describe his method; some Jungian analysts are medically trained and some are not. The Jungian method, in its purest form, is, as psychoanalysis is, time-consuming, intense, and often expensive. One distinctive feature of both Freudian and Jungian psychotherapy is that the analyst has himself been "analyzed," has received the treatment that he now provides his client.

Psychologists, except where the term is used in its most general sense, when it describes anyone who works with others using psychological and counseling theories, are specialists who are not medically trained. Clinical psychologists, whose practitioners are licensed in most states and who engage in a broad range of counseling, therapy, and testing, are trained at the Ph.D. level in universities and, typically, have undergone periods of internship in mental institutions or as counselors. Some psychologists limit their practices to the administration of psychological and personal development tests. Most clinical psychologists now provide psychological services on a private-patient (or "client") basis, on a model similar to that followed by medically trained psychiatrists. Psychologists are likely to be more diverse and eclectic in the methods they use than psychiatrists; they do not prescribe medication but sometimes have consulting relationships with physicians who prescribe medication on the psychologist's recommendation.

Psychotherapy is a generic term which usually means therapy short of long-term psychoanalysis. There is a wide array of methods of psychotherapy, ranging from the non-directive methods of Carl Rogers to the highly technique oriented Gestalt work (pioneered by the legendary Frederick Perls) and the TA (transactional analysis) theories of Eric Berne and Thomas Harris. Most psychotherapeutic methods have in common a discursive setting in which professional and client talk about the client's problems.

Psychotherapy is sometimes practiced by persons with the "Ed.D." degree and by persons not trained at the doctoral level. Typically these practitioners have credentials at the master's degree level in psychology or social work, and they usually practice within an institution in which they are supervised by persons trained at the doctoral level. Many community mental health clinics do their work through psychiatric social workers and psychologists trained at the master's degree level.

Marriage counselors are trained at the doctoral or master's degree level, in non-medical schools of counseling, and practice in institutions, in agencies, and in private offices. Many of them are also trained (and certified) as clinical psychologists. The American Association of Marriage and Family Counselors says, about one of its members, that she "has met rigid education and examination requirements, and is licensed by the state in which she practices where regulated by law; is knowledgeable in areas of human growth and development, behavior, family dynamics and interaction; is skilled in counseling techniques and processes; is committed to a stringent code of ethics; is experienced—she has served at least two years in supervised clinical internship; is an active member of a professional association serving marriage and family counselors; and welcomes your inquiries about her methodology, background and experience."

Clergymen are also counselors. The traditional clergyman relied on experience and the grace of God for his human-relations skills, and was often ill-served from both sources. (But, then, much the same could be said of the traditional lawyer.) Seminary and divinity-school training now includes development of human-relations skills, and many religious congregations now include among congregational clergy professionals who are certified in psychology or marriage counseling and ordained to the ministry or rabbinate. A useful conduit to such persons, and to clergy who are not formally trained but are regarded as competent in counseling, may be a local agency that acts in social matters for the church; examples: Catholic social service organizations, the Council of Churches, the Ministerial Alliance, or Jewish community organizations.

APPENDIX

EXERCISES

Some of these exercises are for groups, and some are for individuals working alone; but most can be used alone or with a group. The titles we give to each of them are meant to suggest the point of each exercise and the portion of the test with which it fits. Group exercises can be done in class or out of class, with supervision or without supervision. In most cases all that is required by way of preparation is that one member of the group read the exercise, locate materials that are needed, and understand what the general idea behind the exercise is. In some exercises the person who directs the exercise will not then be eligible to join in it because of information that has to be kept secret at first. In most cases these exercises can be done in one law school class period or less.

Note: The exercises which have not been designated as group exercises can be done entirely alone, perhaps as a subject for written reflection in a journal, or with a partner. The introspective part of the exercise can be used without journal writing in class meetings, in a group or series of groups. For example, after 15 or 20 minutes of working alone, group members discuss, in pairs, their work on these questions. Then pairs join and, in quartets, discuss the questions raised in the exercise. (When this sort of progression moves from pairs to quartets, each member of the group can introduce his or her partner to the other pair in terms of the substance of the questions. This device helps emphasize the importance of listening.) The quartets can later become groups of eight, each of which takes as a task the prescription of goals and ideals most likely to form good legal counselors.

EXERCISE ONE: IMAGINING OURSELVES AS LAWYERS

Close your eyes and imagine yourself as a lawyer. Try to picture the office where you work, the kind of clothes you wear, the kind of activities that you are doing. Try to record all of the images that come to mind; *take your time.*

—One way to do this is to lean back and daydream and tell another person what you see.

—Another way to do it is to fill out one day's worth (or two, or three) of your journal as a practicing lawyer, a journal that records your work for billing purposes and as a record of what you do.

—What you're after in this case are images: What you look like; what other people in your lawyer's life look like; the furniture and decoration in the place you work; the noises, the smells, the sights. You should come out with a catalogue of images.

To what extent do your images reflect stereotypes of lawyers—that is, what other people think of lawyers? (That is, what you think other people think.) To what extent do these images reflect your own notions about lawyers? To what extent do these images say something to you about yourself, not as a lawyer, but as who you are?

EXERCISE TWO: PERSONAL CLIMATE

We intend nothing mystical or puzzling with our concept that "personal climate" surrounds a relationship. The way we feel when we are with particular people, in certain places, is a sort of climate, an environment. The attorney-client relationship which is the primary focus here is one of many kinds of familiar relationships. Even in professional relationships, though, there is likely to be no single pattern that describes how we relate to our clients.

One analogy to "personal climate" in law-office relationships is the "personal climate" in the law-school classroom. Pick out one of the courses that you are taking in law school. Apply the various factors that we have outlined in the text (Chapter Three) to the "climate" of the law school classroom.

How does the view of the law that each of you takes into the classroom affect the "personal climate" there? Is the teacher's view of the law different from your own? How does the difference affect your learning? What kind of assumptions do each of you make about the law?

Does the teacher seem to have a general philosophy (a sense or theory of human nature) that provides a framework or structure of his or her teaching? If you do not immediately perceive such a general perception or philosophy, does that mean the teacher does not have one?

It is sometimes argued that even those who contend most vehemently that they have no philosophy do nevertheless have one. Do you agree with the assertion? And if that is the case, is it possible for a teacher to teach without reference, in some way, to such a philosophy? Or for a lawyer to practice law without one? What kind of teaching would that be? What kind of lawyering?

Now reverse the situation. Ask each of these questions concerning general philosophy in relation to yourself and your learning as well as the teaching *you* do in class.

How do you and the teacher view lawyers? Does your view of who lawyers are and what they do have an effect on the climate of the law school classroom? Is it something of this sort that makes some classes seem practical and some theoretical? What kinds of assumptions are made by teachers who take radically different approaches? Is it, then, the view the teacher has of lawyers that brings her to teach a class in a particular way? And is it, then, your view of yourself as a lawyer, and as a student of law, that determines whether you appreciate (and can be critical of) what the teacher is doing?

And finally, what is the teacher's and your view of your student situation? What does the teacher think of students? How are your regarded by the teacher? as a student? a colleague? a friend? a companion? a pest? an enemy? How is the teacher's view of you communicated? That is, how does it become part of the "personal climate" of the classroom? And how do you respond? What are your feelings about the dynamic that has been created, and in which you participate (with others)? How do you view yourself as a student? What metaphor would you use to describe your view of yourself: Player? Sponge? Roadblock? Pest?

The object of all these questions is to suggest a way to study counseling. The situations that we are already in, the relationships that we already have, are a laboratory for learning. What we have to do is to pay attention to them. Learning to be a counselor involves making use of these situations for the explicit purpose of learning more about ourselves and how we relate to others. Human-relations skills are those we use every day, skills we can learn more about, skills that can be improved as we become more conscious of how we experience something as ordinary as the relationship you have with each teacher, in each course in the law school.

The lawyer you will be, and the manner in which you relate to your clients, will not be so radically different from who you are now, the way you relate to others now, and the way you are learning to relate to others from the relationships you see around you. When you leave law school you will undoubtedly try to get away from being a student and adopt a stance more appropriate to being a lawyer and a professional person. Does that mean that you will reject the perceptions and philosophies you see now, or act toward your clients as your teacher now acts toward you?

By reflecting on these questions about your teacher, her relation to the law, to the classroom, and to you, you have been exploring how professionals relate to others. And when you see yourself as a student in relation to a teacher, and in a particular course, you have come close to putting yourself in the position of a client vis-a-vis a lawyer. What sorts of working relationships will you have with your clients, if they feel toward you as you now feel toward your teacher(s)?

EXERCISE THREE: CONTENT AND PROCESS

Part A

Most lawyers and law students have a fairly easy time understanding what content is. Process is more elusive. Part of the reason for the difference is that we are usually more aware of the content level of our interactions than we are of the process level. The way we live, the way we are educated, and the way we come to think about the world and ourselves is focused on (1) what we do, (2) how we do it, and (3) how we experience the doing, that is, how we feel about ourselves and the way our actions take on meaning. In philosophical (and theological) terms, we are more attuned to *doing* than to *being*. When we meet someone we do not know, there is a strong temptation, one that is hard to resist, to ask: What do you *do?* Knowing what a person does lets us make assumptions about him and about who he is, based on the work he does, the position he holds. This interest in what a person does is an example of the way we focus on content.

Another example of the distinction between content and process comes from the way we relate to our dreams. When you recall a dream, or write it down, you are focusing on content, a description of the images that appeared and the actions that took place in the dream. Freud called this descriptive element of the dream its "manifest content." But the content of dreams doesn't tell us very much, or at least it usually doesn't tell us what we want to know. The problem is that the content of dreams most often doesn't carry a literal message. The dream doesn't tell us what we want to know about ourselves (generally speaking) until we get beyond content. If the dream is to have any meaning, if it is to be understood, at least in relation to our own lives, then we have to explore what Freud called the *latent* aspect of our dreams. The latent part is what we would call process.

In the terminology that we borrow, this deeper level of the dream works as a process that is out of awareness. When we look at the process level of the dream, how it is working, what the images might mean to the dreamer, the feelings that the dream evokes, and the way that the dream returns throughout the day, then we are at the process level: The process is the dreamer's relation to the dream. The dream has more meaning when its manifest content is placed in the context of the underlying process that brings the dream into being.

See if you can find examples in your conversations and relations of this distinction between content and process. Which do you *know* more about in the situations in your own life? How do you explain the fact that you tend to pay more attention to one than to another?

Part B

In Exercise Two you were asked to focus on the "personal climate" of a law school classroom and your relationship with one (or more) of your teachers. If you tried to respond to all the questions raised in that exercise you made use of what you know about the teacher, what you know about yourself, and what you are able to describe about the way the two of you affect one another; that is content. It is what you imagine to be the views and philosophy of the teacher and of yourself that affects the way you learn. Some, although perhaps not all, of your responses to those questions about personal climate come from your own feelings about what happens (to you) when you are in the presence of this teacher. The feelings—yours and the teacher's and those of other students, and perhaps even other teachers—operate, for the most part, out of sight; they are not an explicit part of the classroom learning. They are process. Feelings tend to point toward the process level of an interaction and of a relationship.

Review your responses to Exercise Two and see if you can find how your evaluation of the "personal climate" of the classroom draws on content and how it draws on process.

Note: Parts A and B of this Exercise can be used in groups and sub-groups; see our suggestions before Exercise One.)

Part C

Using your knowledge of the content and process distinction, see if you can describe a conversation (either one in which you were a participant or one that you observed), an interaction (with a friend, a stranger, the Dean, your spouse), or a situation in the classroom. Choose for this exercise a conversation in which you think you can distinguish content and process.

Remember that process is a response to the question: What is really going on here? Process reflects the "personal climate" of the conversation. Be careful that you do not view process as only a matter of motives. Process is more a question of "how" than a question of "why." For example, if, as you describe this conversation, you ask, "Why did he say that?" you will not necessarily move from the content to the process level. The process level is more likely to be reached when you ask about feelings, rather than reasons: How was he feeling when he said that? How did I feel when I heard what he said?

The distinction that we are making here is sometimes seen as one between the objective and the subjective. Content tends to be associated with what is objective, process with what is subjective. We know that objective and subjective are not rigid categories of human experience; neither are content and process. But making the distinction enriches counseling. Seeing how the distinction works in your own life, in the way you learn law, in the way you talk to your friends and describe what is going on around you, helps you get beyond the merely verbal distinctions. Good counselors train themselves in the art of taking feelings into account. Awareness of the distinction between content and process is a device for doing that.

EXERCISE FOUR: COMPETITION: INITIAL THREATS TO A WORKING RELATIONSHIP

In the text we have identified two initial threats that pose a danger to a good working relationship between attorney and client: competition and professional domination (often called "paternalism"). Competition and paternalism are not things that just happen in professional relationships; nor are they inevitable. Competition and paternalism are learned. You learned a lot about competition and paternalism before you came to law school and it is likely that you are learning about them now, in law school. One way to understand competition and paternalism as threats to a working relationship with clients is to unravel the complex history of your own learning about competition and paternalism.

As a law student you are now in a competitive world, for law schools are places of intense competition. It is possible—even likely—that you chose to come to law school because you are a competitive person. Do you see the competition that is going on around you, now? Do you see how you fit into this competitive world? What do you do that helps it work? How do you respond to this competition? How does it make you feel? How has it affected your experience of law school?

Competition is commonplace in our culture, so much so that most of us have become accustomed to winning and losing, of being winners and losers. Competition can be the spur of "doing a good job" and, for many, the motivation to reach levels of personal achievement that would not have occurred without the push of competition. There is, at least on first appearance, nothing inherently wrong with competition. Much of what we see and hear as we grow up in America says that competition is good for us—and this in a culture that otherwise exalts cooperation, community, and loving our neighbor. Competitiveness, in American culture, is often talked about as if it were a virtue. But the experience of many law students (and of outside observers) is that competitiveness has become such a focal point of the academic structure of legal education and the social interaction of law students that the virtue is in danger of becoming a vice. The concern of many students (and teachers) is that competitiveness tends to usurp other virtues (caring for others, for example) and can blind one to the intrinsic worth of the activity in which one is involved.

Return, now, to the questions in the second paragraph of this exercise and see if you can describe how you and your feelings fit into this competitive academic world. Then it will be useful to talk about this with a friend. After that the information—the data—you have assembled about competition will be valuable material for a group or class discussion on (1) competition as a threat to working relationships with clients; (2) competition as it relates to paternalism in counseling; (3) strategies and techniques in working with clients; and (4) strategies and techniques for making constructive use of competition in solving problems. (See also Group Exercise Sixteen.)

EXERCISE FIVE: COUNSELING THEORIES

We have identified four approaches to counseling in Chapter Five: Companionship, Non-directive, Directive, and Interpretive. They are not meant to be all inclusive, nor anything other than handy references for your use in understanding how counseling may differ according to the model, orientation, philosophy, theology, and perspective of the counselor. Remember in Exercise Two your consideration of the assumptions and expectations that you and the teacher carry into the law-school classroom, of the general views that each of you has about law, about students, and about being in school, as well as the philosophy that each of you has about human value. Psychological counselors often discuss the assumptions, expectations, and even philosophies they carry into therapeutic relationships.

Given our cursory statement, in the text, of each of these orientations, which do you suppose you will (or do) follow? Which comes closest to the way you work with people? Can you identify what it is in the description of each approach that makes you feel (relatively) comfortable with that orientation? Reverse the process: Select the orientation which you identify with least. What is it in our description of this approach to counseling that bothers you?

In this book we have attempted to offer an eclectic view of counseling by drawing on a number of psychological theories. We (Elkins and Shaffer) however, make clear our debt to the work of Carl Rogers for helping us see that the client is his or her own best resource in problem-solving. Rogers's "non-directive" school of counseling is more than just a technique or a working theory for counselors. It is also an *educational* theory, one that has influenced our teaching of counseling and of other courses. (See, for example, Carl Rogers, *Freedom to Learn*, 1969). We have also learned a great deal from the "Gestalt" psychology of Frederick Perls; from Eric Berne's "transactional analysis"; from Freud's theory of the unconscious; from Jung's theory of psychological types and his writings on the persona; and from Hebraic (Judaeo-Christian) theology.

We offer these comments to suggest that the student interested in counseling will want to find out more about different "schools" of counseling and the diverse philosophical and theological sources of counseling theory. We have found that a "school" of counseling theories and practices turns out to be more than merely a set of principles or a prescribed way to do therapy. A theory of counseling is also a theory of education, a theory of growth, and a theory of the person. It says something about how we learn and how we change. Professionals, lawyers included, tend to view themselves as learners, as life-long students. They are required by the demands of legal institutions and clients to change, to react to new situations, to new problems, to new people. (Many states now have mandatory continuing professional education which, sadly, is too often limited to content and ignores process issues in professional practice.)

A theory of counseling is also a world-view, a philosophy; your answers to the question in the second paragraph of this Exercise will help you see what philosophy you are living out; it will be practiced as you work with clients. A counseling theory (for example, Carl Rogers's "non-directive counseling") is not only a philosophy for professional relationships but can also be the basis for a philosophy (or theology) of life.

Return to the basic counseling orientation that you most identified with, and the one you identified with least, and see if you can find out more about them. Read something that one of the founders of each of these "schools" wrote. (See the bibliography in this book.) As you learn more about the school that you find most interesting, try to learn more about the one with which you have the least affinity. (It is important that you read something that was written by the principal figures in these schools of counseling. Psychology books that describe psychological theories, whether of Carl Rogers or Sigmund Freud, tend to bland description or biased dismissal.)

EXERCISE SIX: DEFERENCE

Given the society we (you and the authors) live in, it is likely that you have spent time in doctors' offices, their waiting rooms, and their examination rooms. We ask in this exercise that you recall an occasion when you were in a doctor's office, as a patient, and you talked with the doctor about some "problem"; that is, you described physical sensations and feelings that focused your concern on your body—sensations and feelings that suggested to you that something had gone wrong. These sensations and feelings are seen by the doctor as "symptoms" of the problem—if not the problem itself. Please stay with the memory part of this exercise until you have an experience firmly in mind; if you have a choice among experiences,

choose the one that was most extensive or troubling—perhaps the one that came most immediately to your mind.

When you visited the doctor as a patient, there
occurred the kind of talking and listening that we
(in this book) have viewed as counseling. How did
the talking and listening take place in the doctor's
office? Who initiated topics of conversation? Does
it work to call the talking and listening a *conversation?* What other words might work? Lecture?
Reprimand? Interrogation? Does it work to think
of what happened as counseling? What other
words might work? Explanation? Instruction?
Consolation? Intimidation? Did you take the doctor's advice? Do you return to that doctor? How
has your relationship with the doctor changed
since then?

Patients have historically paid deference to the
physician—"The doctor knows best." Think about
your relationship with physicians, with your family doctor. How do they work? Do you pay deference to the physician? How does the deference
work? Prior to this exercise, have you given
thought to deference to professionals, like physicians, and how deference works? What does it say
about deference to professionals that you have not
given thought to it, that you have not consciously
experienced that deference?

How does deference work? How does it feel?
How does it help the physician get her work done?
How does it get you what you want from the

physician? How does it help to figure out what it is that you actually want? Is the deference working for you (is it in your best interest) or for the physician (in his management of the illness or disease, the ability to keep the office running, and his peace of mind)? Or is it simply a matter of "The doctor knows best"?

Does it matter to the establishment of deference that the physician is a man and the patient is a woman (or vice versa)? What can you say from your own experience (or from what you know or have read) about the way deference in relationships with physicians affects the health care of women?

EXERCISE SEVEN: CLIENT SELF–DETERMINATION AND MORAL CONCERNS

Part A

You represent the husband in an acrimonious divorce action. Your client, Dr. Martin Arrowsmith, has no desire to continue supporting his wife, Leora, in the manner to which she has grown accustomed in the ten years that they have been married. Dr. Arrowsmith says that he expects his wife to get custody of the children, that she is much closer to the children (a girl aged four and a boy aged six), because his work has resulted in his wife being primarily responsible for the children during their early years. You pause over this point and talk to Martin until you are satisfied that he really does not want custody of the children.

Martin is afraid that his wife's outrage over the fact that he is leaving her for a younger woman will result in an effort to make him suffer as much as possible financially. Martin seems particularly worried about his financial interest in a pharmaceutical business that a large supermarket chain is considering for purchase.

During the interview, Martin suggests the possibility of seeking custody of the children and using custody as a "bargaining chip" in the settlement negotiations. He wants to get matters settled with Leora and insure that his interest in the pharmaceutical business is not encumbered in any way. Leora knows of Martin's interest in the business but does not know that a potential sale is in the offing. Leora is a recovering alcoholic, and after spending three weeks in a residential alcoholic treatment facility (when the children were two and four), she has refrained from drinking. Martin tells you that he knows his wife wants to avoid a custody fight at all cost, but he does not elaborate.

* * *

This is the sort of law school problem that you might meet in an ethics course, or a family law course, or a business planning course, as well as here, in the counseling context. What might make the counseling context unique is that the best place to begin talking about it here is probably your own feelings about it:

(1) How do you feel about Dr. Arrowsmith? About this "case"? About his "problem"?

(2) Does it, as Phil Donohue might say, "bother you" to use the threat of a child custody battle as a "bargaining chip"?

(3) What do you see as the counseling *issues* involved in working with this client? For example—for *you*—is rapport going to be an issue?

(4) If the issues include what the profession regards as ethical issues, what guidance is provided in the Code of Professional Responsibility and the Model Rules of Professional Conduct?

(5) Consider the following observation of Warren Lehman in "The Pursuit of a Client's Interest," 77 *Michigan Law Review* 1078, 1079, 1091 (1979): "Doubtless many clients, thinking they know what they want—or wishing to appear to know—encourage the lawyer to believe he is consulted solely for a technical expertise, for a knowledge of how to do legal things, for his ability to interpret legal words, or for the objective way he looks at legal and practical outcomes. It is as if the lawyer were being invited to join the client in a conspiracy of silence; the point of the conspiracy is that in silence neither shall question the assumption that the means can be truly separated from the end and that the end is the client's sole problem and solely his. Such an idea of the lawyer's job seems to relieve him of the ethical responsibility that might be his were he to assume a duty to comment on the wisdom or virtue of what his client is about. I do

not think the burden of commenting upon the client's purpose can be so easily avoided. The interaction of lawyer and client is a moral event, whether morals are explicitly broached in conversation or not. The question is not whether the lawyer can or ought to comment, but what message does he convey.

* * *

"The only thing the lawyer can do for his client is be free himself, which means free to be honest in saying exactly what he thinks and feels, to confront himself. It is transcendence for a lawyer to say to a client: 'I am fearful of influencing you unduly in this matter. The tax saving is there. It may be important to you to save the money. If so, by all means defer the gift. But money saving is not everything. One should hardly organize one's life around a revenue code. I will think none the less of you whether you choose to defer or not. Some people, I suspect, may be embarrassed—odd as it may sound—to ignore an apparent financial advantage, for to do so sounds irrational. Let me assure you, I would respect more highly a [person] who will do now what seems right to him now. What sounds rational is not always humanly reasonable. . . .' The important thing about any such message is not that it be calculated to neutralize the legal-rational bias, the legal influence, but that it be honest and not intended to manipulate. Sometimes a side benefit of the speaker's honesty is a shock in the listener that shakes him loose and helps him be free."

Return now, to your client, Dr. Arrowsmith, and to the question asked in the early part of this Exercise on your feelings about him. Assess those feelings as they bear on your relationship with him. After you do this alone or with a friend (or first alone and then with a friend), or with a small discussion group in class, the information you generate may be useful in seeing how counseling is (and is not) a moral activity.

EXERCISE EIGHT: ACTIVE LISTENING

The client is a lecturer in sociology at a local university. He has had recurrent, frequent, and recent clashes with the head of his department and has reason to believe that his contract will not be renewed. He explains this, and adds that he wonders whether there is anything a lawyer can do to help. You know this much from your secretary, who talked with him when he made the appointment to talk to you.

Part A

What follows is a series of statements by the client during the course of an interview. We interrupt the interview to pose a list of options or alternatives for possible responses by the lawyer. Select the response that you would be most likely to make to what the client has said.

C–1: "I don't know what's the matter with that place. You walk across the campus and don't even see anyone you know. You can walk into offices and they give you the cold shoulder. Faculty members are not treated with any respect at all."

I will:

1. indicate my understanding of the client's bitterness.

2. convey the idea that attitudes typically taken toward young teachers at large universities might understandably cause him to feel bitter and rejected.

3. get the client to continue talking so that I can get a better idea of what he has to deal with.

4. lead the client to consider that his present worry about unemployment may be in part the result of his own attitudes.

5. indicate to the client that this doesn't sound like the kind of problem that a lawyer can deal with effectively.

C–2: "It wasn't this way where I taught before. It was tough there, but you had your job and you did it. I had a fifteen-hour teaching load some semesters. I could have let the classes slide, but I never did. I always prepared thoroughly."

I will:

1. lead the client to explain in more detail what the memory of his old college means to him.

2. gently point out that the present situation is different and that memories of the old college are irrelevant.

3. try to convey the feeling (my feeling) that I mean to sympathize with how difficult the new situation has been for him.

4. let him know I recognize his feelings, that in his old college his hard work was appreciated.

5. help him to recognize that his feelings of bitterness are probably due to the fact that the university he now teaches at is much larger and that therefore there is bound to be less of a sense that others depend on him.

C–3: "You see, there are teachers all around me who do so little, and do it so poorly, that it makes you sore. There are a lot of teachers who let the teaching assistants do all the work. It makes me boil, just like it used to when I was a kid and my big brother would sneak away on Saturdays and leave me all the work."

I will:

1. get the client to realize that criticism of others is not a solution to his problem.

2. try to convey an appreciation (my appreciation) of how he sees the situation as one in which he has been taken advantage of and not appreciated.

3. tell him: "You have difficulty working with people who complain about others."

4. explore further how this situation reminds him of his childhood, with the idea that he might need psychological counseling.

5. reveal my own feelings about his feelings of being taken advantage of (which are . . .)

C–4: "You know, it's a funny thing, but when I go in to talk to them about this contract thing I feel shaky all over. It's the silliest damned thing. Why should I do that?"

I will:

1. help the client to minimize his concern over this problem of feeling shaky all over.

2. try to help the client connect his feelings of rejection with his anxiety about going in to the head of his department to talk about the contract (so that he will understand his feelings better).

3. express as directly as I can that I can see how his reactions must puzzle him and cause him concern.

4. ask him if he has given thought to some things he might do to deal with his anxiety.

5. ask him to talk more about his relationship with the department chairman and his colleagues in the department, to determine if they might be terminating his contract for a good reason.

C–5: "I think it would be a screwy thing to do, really, but I think sometimes that I will write to the old college where I was teaching and see if they will take me back. It would be a lot easier than fighting over this mess here. It would be good to see some of the old crowd back there. But it would be a silly thing to do."

I will:

1. point out to the client that it sounds like he is ambivalent about pursuing legal action.

2. ask for more information about what he wants to do in this case, including his feelings about possible legal action.

3. tell him that he has some escapist attitudes and that these attitudes will simply interfere with my ability to help him in his legal case.

4. help him see his present situation is really not as bad as he now thinks it is.

5. suggest to the client that I am probably not going to be willing to represent him.

C–6: "I can go live with my mother, if I have to. She doesn't have much; I've been sending her money for years. I never know just what to do about that. It seems to me that I had a right to what I earned. I didn't live very high; I sent home two or three hundred dollars a month. What do you think? Does that seem fair to you?

I will:

1. help the client see that his relationship with his mother has nothing to do with his legal case and my representation of him.

2. help the client see that his present ambivalence about what to do about his contract is related to his ambivalence about his mother.

3. encourage him to talk more about his situation with his mother.

4. try to reduce his anxiety and uncertainty by telling him that I am sure he has always done the right thing with his mother.

5. tell him that what matters is that he feels he did the right thing, regardless of whether I or anyone else feels it was right or wrong.

C–7: "When I'm feeling discouraged, I wonder if there will be anything for me to do next year. Maybe I've lived my life. Maybe I should just drop out, or maybe what I've got to live for is second rate in comparison with what I have had."

I will:

1. convey to the client the idea that, if he continues to look at his future this way, it will be more likely to become true, and that it would be better to put his mind to the problem at hand.

2. try to elicit more information about what he will do if he loses his job.

3. point out that one alternative seems to be going back to his old position.

4. indicate that I understand—or that I am trying to understand—that he feels disillusioned.

5. point out that his discouragement is a natural result of his present stressful situation, and therefore that he should try not to worry about it.

C–8: "I am beginning to wonder if my abilities are even marketable. I am wondering if I am going to have to live on the damages you collect for me. I don't want to go back to my old college, and I can't bear the thought of starting all over at some new place again."

I will:

1. sympathize with the client that the situation looks hopeless.

2. try to help him see that regardless of his immediate situation, he has important talents and abilities that will help him find a position.

3. suggest that he rethink his decision about not going back to his old college.

4. discuss with him the difficulties of getting damages in this kind of situation.

5. help him see that his present assessment of the situation is not accurate, that he has real abilities, and that with a lawyer in the case the university might be willing to extend his contract.

Part B

Now that you have worked through the exercise, choosing the content to your responses in the manner indicated, do the exercise a second time and mark the response that you think would be made by a good counselor.

Part C

As the interview continues, assume that you want the client to feel that you understand him. Your responses now are for the purpose of trying to reflect to the client that you understand how the client feels, or, at least, that you are trying to understand. Choose the response (and in this case we provide the actual words of different possible responses).

C–9: "So, I guess that what I want you to do is to make sure I keep my job. I suppose, though, that I probably will bungle it. Things couldn't get much worse."

1. You want work and yet you feel that if I can get them to give you another contract, something will go wrong anyway.

2. You feel that your lack of self-confidence makes you incapable of holding the job even if you keep it for now.

3. This inability to hold a job has been troubling you and you're turning to me for help.

4. You feel it's almost futile to try to get the job back.

C–10: "Oh, well, I guess it's all sort of hopeless. The days go on. Everyone's planning for next fall's classes except me. My landlord says the papers are full of stories about the shortage of people in my field who have jobs in industry. A manpower shortage. Maybe that's what's wrong with me—a shortage of manpower."

1. You feel that you're not quite up to the fight, is that it?

2. You feel that, if you're not hired again for next year, it will be because of your own shortage, is that it?

3. You feel, do you, that this hopelessness may be something inside you?

4. In other words, you feel pretty inadequate.

C–11: "You know, last year I really thought I was going places. My classes really clicked for a while. Then I had a bad break. Oh, well, you're probably not interested."

1. You feel, do you, that to explain it to me would only bore me?

2. Things looked pretty hopeful for a while but then the bottom just dropped out, is that it?

3. You'd really like to tell me about this but you feel uncertain about going ahead, is that it?

4. I take it you feel pretty disappointed.

C–12: "Well, what happened was that I stood up for a fellow professor in a faculty meeting—a man who was terminated last year. And I spoke up. And what I said was met with stony silence. Like it was in bad taste. So I am getting the skids now. There may be other reasons for my getting the boot, but that reason sticks in my mind."

1. In other words, while you see other factors involved, you are pretty sure that, if you are terminated, it will be because of your exercise of free speech in a faculty meeting.

2. In other words, you feel that there is a connection between your defenses of a colleague and your possible termination.

3. You feel you are being treated unfairly and you just can't get that out of your mind.

4. That's the reason that sticks in your mind, but you feel there may be other reasons.

C–13: "Do you ever have anything grab onto you so you couldn't shake it loose? (Angrily) Well, mister, I have. I've got a habit that if I don't cut it out, I'm going to ruin myself and my career—everything!"

1. In other words, this thing is just driving you over the precipice, unless you can bring it under control.

2. It's a habit you can't shake. It may be ruinous.

3. This thing bothers you quite a bit, doesn't it?

4. In other words, you feel you just don't have enough will power to meet this thing.

C–14: "You see, it all started when I was a kid. We had a club in high school; we used to go out and drink beer. We did that every week. Well, beer got to be quite a habit with me. My folks were German; they didn't think anything of it.

Well, that was okay, but after I got into graduate school I drank more and more, and I've been drinking awfully heavily in the past few years. My colleagues at the other college told me to lay off. If I could quit drinking, I'd be okay."

1. You begin to slip in your work when you start drinking too much.

2. This drinking is something you want to conquer.

3. You feel that you used to drink to drown your disappointment in yourself.

4. It may have started out innocently enough, but now it's become something that's a real problem to you.

Part D

This exercise on active listening and feedback is adapted from an early (1950) treatise on non-directive counseling, by Dr. E. H. Porter, Jr., a psychologist employed in industry. It bears the forbidding title *An Introduction to Therapeutic Counseling*. It is as valuable a source as we know about on reflective counseling (and interviewing); it includes exercises such as these, and systems for scoring responses. It may be helpful for you to apply this scoring scheme to the answers you chose—

—in Parts A and B, to see (i) what sort of responses seemed to you to carry out your own style, and (ii) what sort of responses seem to you to be consistent with a reflective style; and

—in Part C, to see what specific choices of words will work in a determined effort to *be* reflective—to listen actively.

Dr. Porter suggested these as scoring categories for an exercise that resembled our Parts A and B:

—*evaluative* ("the counselor has made a judgment of relative goodness, appropriateness, effectiveness, rightness")

—*interpretive* ("the counselor's intent is to impart meaning to the client, to show him . . . what the client might or ought to think")

—*supportive* ("reassure . . . reduce the client's intensity of feeling, to pacify . . . the client need not feel as he does)

—*understanding* ("to ask the client whether the counselor understands correctly what the client is 'saying,' how the client 'feels' about it . . . how the client 'sees' it")

In scoring what we have adapted as Part C, Dr. Porter sought to show how some choices of words are more reflective, more indicative of active listening, than others. He invited attention to these aspects of the words the counselor chooses:

—*content* ("in large part . . . simple repetition")

—*shallow or partial* ("limited. . . . involving only a portion of what the client expressed or

. . . 'undercutting' or 'watering-down' the feeling . . . expressed")

—*reflection* ("rephrasing in fresh words the gist of the client's expression without changing the meaning or feeling")

—*interpretive* ("goes beyond the meaning . . . adds meaning not expressed by the client")

This explanation of what we and Dr. Porter had in mind in this exercise may help you to go back over your answers and to determine both how much your style is a reflective style and how you are beginning to develop the ability to use a reflective style when you want to.

EXERCISE NINE: FEELINGS

In counseling theory, there are a minimum number of what might be called principles. But there are some, even if few in number, and one of the ones that we have adopted in this book is that "Feelings are facts." Feelings are something that counselors learn to pay attention to, learn about, and learn from. The learning from feelings is learning who the client is and who I am as a lawyer and a person. For the counselor, the learning moves in two directions, from the client to the counselor, and from the counselor to herself. (And, in the case of feedback, the learning moves from the counselor to the client. See Exercise Eight.)

The way to learn about feelings is to work with them, to see what you know about feelings and how they work. It is easy enough to define feelings and emotions (some psychologists and counselors draw a distinction between feelings and emotions; we see no purpose in doing that here), but the important thing is to check and see what you actually know about your own feelings. Most of us make assumptions about feelings—first, that we all have feelings ("I have feelings") and second, that we know what they are, that we can describe and, if need be, name them. We now want to explore those assumptions, to see what assumptions about feelings you have and how those assumptions work. The goal is to find out how your views on feelings will affect your work as a lawyer counselor.

Part A

In the first part of this exercise we would like for you to make some kind of statement about your relationship with your own feelings. Some of us feel overwhelmed by feelings and some of us do not. Some of us are guided by our feelings and some of us try to lessen the impact of feelings on our decisions. The kind of knowledge (certainty) we have in regard to our own feelings varies widely. Some people are more confused about their feelings than others. Some of us seem to know what our feelings are and others do not. We could go on, but the point is simply this: How do you see yourself in regard to your feelings? What do you *know* about your feelings? How do you *see* them working (for you and against you)?

It will be a good idea to write down your answers to these questions (and the questions that you have about feelings). Do this part of the exercise now, before you read the remainder of the exercise. We are going to ask that you use what you write in a subsequent part of this Exercise.

Part B

One of the ways that you can learn about feelings, perhaps the best way, is to see how your own feelings work. One way to initiate the process of self-understanding is by thinking about our feelings, getting an assessment of our own experience of feelings. We have done something of this sort in Part A. This was only a first step. Our feelings happen, we have them, out in the world. Feelings are connected to the way we are in the world, with others. This helps account for the fact that we so often "blame" our feelings on others. (See Chapter Four.) Feelings are often thought of, in our individualistic culture, as personal and idiosyncratic, but they are more than that. We "see" our own feelings and experience them as real. Others see our feelings, and see how we respond to feelings. Feelings are as much out in the world (objective) as they are "my feelings" (subjective).

Select another person in the class whose attitude toward *your* feelings is of interest to you (a person whose views you are curious about). Team up with this person. Talk about the response you wrote to the questions in Part A. Ask this person to tell you (honestly, one would hope) how she or he sees you and your feelings. One way to do this is to ask your partner to *imagine* how you relate to your feelings.

Part C

In the final part of the exercise read the following commentary (statements that we have gathered from various sources on feelings and emotions) and, when you have finished reading, return to what you wrote in response to Part A. How does your relationship with your own feelings reflect an understanding of what is being explained in the commentary? How could you relate to your feelings in a way that would reflect what you have learned from the commentary? Are you motivated to learn more about your feelings?

The statements: A feeling, or emotion, might be seen as a message that contains information that we send to ourselves about an experience. Feelings are an internal communication system. They provide feedback—facts—to us about ourselves and others. David Viscott points out that "our feelings are our sixth sense, the sense that interprets, arranges, directs and summarizes the other five. Feelings tell us whether what we experience is threatening, painful, regretful, sad or joyous." Viscott goes on to make an even more dramatic statement. "Not to be aware of one's feelings, not to understand them or know how to use or express them is worse than being blind, deaf or paralyzed. Not to feel is not to be alive. More than anything else feelings make us human. Feelings make us all kindred." David Viscott, *The Language of Feelings* 9 (Pocket Book edition, 1977).

Feeling lies in the realm of affect, which is often viewed in contrast to the cognitive realm, the realm of thought and intellect. Feeling "is a message to the cognitive processes, to the thinking brain and to our intelligence. . . ." Willard Gaylin, *Feelings* 7 (1979).

"The most intelligent of men [and women] have no particular advantage over others in understanding what they feel. Indeed a high intelligence is often a severe handicap when it is used to rationalize feelings and offer logical, but none the less elusive, detours away from the truth. Everyone knows intelligent people who do not seem to have any understanding of their feelings, and as a result make poor and untrustworthy companions. They distort the world, although at times with a convincing elegance and even grace, but still remain far from understanding themselves," David Viscott says (at 21). Depending upon your psychological orientation, and your awareness of your own feelings, you will at times experience making decisions or taking action based on your feelings. At still other times we act based on feelings without admitting to ourselves that we do so. Feelings, then, can become explanations for choices.

It is from our feelings that we find, Willard Gaylin contends, the means to "judge the importance of our activities. We want to feel pride and joy, but we also want to sense others' delight, love, appreciation, and respect. Emotions, then, are not just directives to ourselves, but directives from others to us, indications that we have been seen; that we have been understood; that we have been appreciated; that we have made contact" (at 9).

Feelings serve yet another function: "Feelings of anxiety, boredom, tension, and agitation alert us to the sense of something wrong, and, more importantly, by the subtle distinctions of their messages they indicate something of the nature of the impending danger and direct us to specific kinds of adaptive maneuvers to avoid, prevent, or change the incipient threat. Feelings of guilt allow us to model our behavior against certain ideals and register when we have moved away from those ideals, or have not yet achieved them," Gaylin says (at 7).

When we say that feelings are facts, we are saying something about the nature of reality, at least reality from a counseling perspective. David Viscott argues that "reality can't be comprehended without taking into account feelings." He goes on to say that "the reality we derive from our perceptions is largely a creation of our own needs and expectations. . . . Thinking is a much more indirect way of handling reality than feeling" (at 13, 19–20).

John Welwood, a psychotherapist who is also knowledgeable about Eastern philosophy, particularly Zen Buddhism, has some interesting things to say about emotions. "Emotions are our most common experience of being moved by forces seemingly beyond our control. As such, they are among the most confusing and frightening phenomena of everyday life. People often treat them as a nuisance or a threat, yet failing to experience them straightforwardly undermines sanity and well-being." Welwood then raises this question: "Can we ever befriend our emotions and accept them as part of us? Why is emotion so hard to come to terms with in our culture?" In our very rational, even rationalistic profession?

Welwood sees feeling and emotion as "what arises in response to letting the world in." Welwood's idea is contrary to the prevailing notion that emotions and feelings are private and idiosyncratic to the individual. If the emotion is the way we experience the world, that is, the way we let the world in, then our feelings are about being in the world. They are fundamental to any connection with other people.

Welwood suggests this approach to thinking about emotions: "The first step in taming the lion of emotions, in transmuting their fierce energy into illumination, is to befriend it by letting it be, without judging it as good or bad. Running away from a fierce animal or trying to suppress its energy only provokes attack. . . . Although emotions may seem to have us in their grip, as soon as we turn to face them directly, we find nothing as solid or fixed as our judgments or stories about them. . . .

"We usually try to keep them [emotions] from flowing through us because they threaten the control we try to maintain. Since ego by definition is the activity of holding on, 'I' cannot let go, 'I' want to ward off anything that threatens this hold. What is possible, however, is to let the emotions wash through me, and, in so doing, wash the controlling part of me away from them. If I can really open to the actual texture and quality of a feeling, instead of trying to control it or churn out story lines for it, 'I'—the activity of trying to hold myself together—can dissolve into 'it'—the larger feeling process itself." John Welwood, "Befriending Emotion," in *Awakening the Heart* 79–90, at 79, 81, 86 (J. Welwood ed. 1983).

Welwood's view is also reflected in the work of James Hillman, a Jungian analyst who has worked out a substantial revision of Jung's ideas (a revising that is most often referred to as archetypal psychology). Hillman says, "It is through emotion that we get the exaggerated sense of soul, of honor, of hurt, of anxiety, of our own person. In emotion we get the awareness that we are not alone in ourselves, not in control over all of ourselves, that there is another person, if only an unconscious complex, who also has something—often a great deal—to say about our behavior. . . . We fall into emotions, moods, affects, and discover a new dimension which, much as we wish to rid ourselves of, leads us downward into depths of ourselves." James Hillman, *Insearch: Psychology and Religion* 53–54 (1967).

EXERCISE TEN: HARD CHOICES AND COLLABORATIVE DECISIONS

Consider each of the following law-office cases. Assume each of them occurs in your office. The issue here is: what kind of counseling issues might be involved in each of these cases?

Case One: Herbert "Huck" Finley, age 18, is charged with breaking and entering a pool hall, a felony. Huck is being held for trial as an adult. The prosecutor says he will accept a plea of guilty to simple trespass, a misdemeanor, in view of the client's youth, the fact that this is a first offense, and the crowded condition of the docket. In your initial interview with Huck, he said he was nowhere near the pool hall at the time in question, and that he has never broken and entered a building.

Comment: Huck says he did not do it, but he can avoid a prison sentence if he now says, officially, that he did. How would you respond to the counseling dilemma presented here? How does the counseling dilemma present a moral dilemma? How does the distinction between hard choices and collaborative decisions work in this situation?

Case Two: Anna Faren is distressed because she has discovered that her husband, Andrew, had an affair with another woman. She is hurt, feels betrayed, and thinks other people know about it and are talking about her. She fears for the welfare of their three children, but admits that Andrew is (or was) a good husband; she is talking to you about divorce.

Comment: Anna has to decide (choose) when enough is enough, when final is final, in the most intimate (and fateful) association a normal person has. How can you help Anna make the choice?

Case Three: Margaret Cross has nearly a million dollars (although it doesn't show), is 68 years old, loves her husband Lewis, and has two adult, well-provided-for children. She realizes that Lewis, who is ten years younger, will probably outlive her. She wants him to enjoy his widowhood, but she thinks there ought to be something left over for the children and, even if there isn't, wonders a bit about Lewis's wise use of "her" money.

Comment: Margaret is making choices that will have much to do with how her husband spends his widowhood—perhaps 15 or 20 years, or more—and she is implicitly making choices about who makes the choices. What is a lawyer to do to aid Margaret Cross in getting what she wants and needs out of the choices that she is about to make?

Case Four: Charles Cross, Margaret and Lewis's son, is 31, happily married, and the father of four children, the eldest of whom is ten. He realizes, when he talks to you about a will, that he and his wife Ruth may both die before the children are adults. Lewis and Margaret could take care of the children if they were orphaned. Care by Ruth's parents would be impossible (one is dead, one an alcoholic), but Ruth's brother and his wife could take care of them. There are also friends who might take care of the children.

Comment: Charles and Ruth are making choices, in the abstract, hypothetically, that turn on factors that began to be built into their lives before they learned to sit up, and they are making choices, hypothetically, without facts, that would throw them into deep anguish if they were able to decide them on all the facts. How can a lawyer help Charles and Ruth?

Note: This Exercise is aimed primarily at testing understanding of the distinction we make in Chapters Seven, Nine and Ten. It may be useful in group or class discussion, but, we think, more so if members consider it alone, after reading one or more of those chapters but before discussion begins.

EXERCISE ELEVEN: A SENSE OF PLACE

Part A

Plan a visit to a law office. Many law students do not see the inside of a law office until they are invited to one for an employment interview. The points we make in Chapter Eight are best demon-

strated from inside a lawyer's office. In an interviewing and counseling course you will probably
have occasion to engage in simulations and exercises in which you interview each other and individuals outside the law school community. In this
Exercise, schedule an interview with a lawyer, in
his or her office. Tell the lawyer that you are
interested in the physical location and arrangement of lawyers' offices and how law office ecology
affects the interaction between lawyer and client.
Write a report of what you learn by entering the
lawyer's territory and using the observations you
have made after reading Chapter Eight.

Part B

Plan a law office for yourself. If you feel flam-
boyant, express the idea of your office abstractly or
symbolically—with crayons, pictures from
magazines, water colors, cut-outs, or whatever. If
you are graphic and precise, draw a floor plan for
it, or a chart that will show how people are to
move in it.

Then make cutout silhouettes of a desk, three
chairs, and a small table with a lamp on it. Then
arrange this "furniture" by moving the cutouts
around, within the dimensions of your office. Two
possibilities (two of many) using a graphic-and-
precise floor plan:

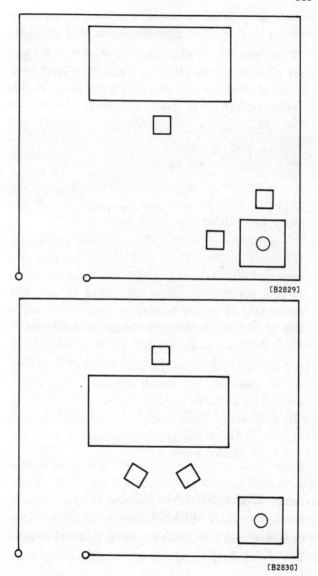

[B2829]

[B2830]

Part C

When you finish the plan, in Part B, or using your memory of the office you described in Part A, ask yourself about how you will arrange the people in this law office, in three situations:

—interview of an old friend, a middle-aged woman you've known since you were a child, who wants to talk to you about her will.

—interview of one of your firm's business clients who is older than you are, important to the firm, and whom you have never met.

—a conference with a distinguished and senior lawyer in another firm; you are on one side of a case and she is on the other; the time has come to talk settlement. She just called to say that she would be happy to stop by your office while she is in your building for another meeting.

Note: The report we suggest for Part A, and the plans and discussion we imagine for Part B, can be done in class or as group projects. The office drawings or collages (Part B) can be reviewed in small groups and then placed in a location so that everyone in the class (group) can look at and ask about each person's ideas.

EXERCISE TWELVE: LAWYER INFLUENCE

Consider the two following interviews of a contracts client, by different lawyers. The client pur-

chased an office building through a real estate
broker.   At the closing of this transaction, the
broker who had earned a commission from the sale
said he would also keep an eye out for a renter for
premises in the building that became vacant in the
future; the buyer said she would appreciate that.
Six months later, one office suite fell vacant and
the broker referred a renter.   The broker then
asked for a broker's commission on the rent.   The
buyer resisted and she and the broker then agreed
on a compromise figure.   At that late date, the
buyer consulted a lawyer—ostensibly to find out if
a roughly drawn promissory note would do to pay
the settlement.   The two interviews are set out
below.

The object of this Exercise is to find out how you
would describe the counseling dilemma (the moral
dilemma, if that's what it is) presented in these
interviews.   As you read the interviews be conscious of your feelings, and of the source of your
feelings.   For example, do your (moral) feelings
about making and breaking promises affect your
view of this client, of what the client wants to do,
and of what you would do to help the client?   How
is the *moral* aspect of the decision approached by
these two lawyers?

FIRST LAWYER INTERVIEW

C: I have no written agreement.   It's all oral.

L: Well, first of all this is a point of law, as I
     understand it.   For him getting you the ten-

ant for that length of time there would have
had to have been a written agreement, and
without that written agreement, under the
Statute of Frauds, you wouldn't be bound.
Now at times we don't want to try to stress
that, because it might cause unnecessary litigation. If there really was an agreement,
which it doesn't sound like there was, between you and Mr. Baer, it might be wiser
just to save you and Mr. Baer time, to work
it out without having to rely on the techni-
cality of the Statute of Frauds.

C: So, how do I work it out? I tried to work it
out here with a note. If you help me, I won't
have to pay him.

L: I would say the first thing I would advise
you to do is to see if there are any grounds—
such as perhaps, in the agreement to buy the
building, which might have contained a
clause that Mr. Baer should be your agent in
finding tenants.

C: I'm pretty sure it did not.

L: I think that if you wish to avoid litigation,
your oral agreement with Mr. Baer for $5000
is substantially below six percent, and if we
found out exactly what percentage commission he should have, even if it was five
percent, you would still be ahead with $5000.
. . . . I think there are two possible courses
of action right now. I think one would be to
tell Mr. Baer that we're not going to pay any

money, and if Mr. Baer suggests that he is going to file an action against us, on what grounds does he think he can do that. The other course of action would be that if you don't wish to get involved in the chance of litigation, to try to write a note of the type you have here.

C: In other words, you think I should negotiate more with him.

L: I think the first step you should take is to talk to him and try to negotiate. . . .

C: Would you like to talk to him too?

L: Yes.

SECOND LAWYER INTERVIEW

C: I had a verbal agreement with him, but I don't know if I really have to. However, I assume I do. I don't know. I don't want to get legally involved if I can help it. Do I have an obligation to pay?

L: When he first told you that he had done this, there was no obligation to pay at all.

C: And I could have told him good-bye, and leave me alone.

L: There was nothing he could do about it.

C: Well, what are you telling me then? That I should pay him or that I shouldn't?

L: Well, I'm not saying that you should pay him or not pay him, on the basis of that.

But I think that's something that, in making your decision, you have to consider—not just your legal obligations, but also other compensations, which are up to you to decide how significant they are to you. You see, the point is that we don't know how difficult it would have been for you to get somebody to become a tenant in that building, and, after all, he did go out of his way to get somebody in that building, and that person is now paying for leasing. So you're getting a benefit conferred to you, right now. Now, it's true that you may not technically be liable to him, and we're not saying that that shouldn't be an important consideration to you. Obviously.

C: Well, all right. I said before I suppose I have to pay him. How about this note now?

We would say to each of these lawyers: The one thing that is not possible in this situation is not to react. Some of us may think we can say, "Okay, whatever you want," but we cannot. Each of us is bound to have feelings in such a case, and the fact that you have feelings is bound to be picked up by the client and to matter to him. Your feelings *should* matter to you as well. The client may not perceive your feelings accurately, but he will pick up something. The lawyer who is aware of his or her feelings is likely to feel moral disapproval, or rebellion, or panic, or a lack of control over the situation or a need to protect the client from himself. The way you feel in these situations as a lawyer, and as a person, depends on the kind of relationship you have with the client and how each of you expresses feelings and moral impulses. We know that expression of moral feelings is not easy, and there is little in legal education and training that prepares you for the task. It is something you will have to practice, a skill that you will have to learn in the law office. It is an essential skill in the craft of counseling.

Do you agree with us?

Try this: You and a partner (in or out of class) role-play the situation. See how much lawyer influence is present when you role-play the lawyer. Is it possible to decide on a preferred level of influence and then carry out your decision in talking to a client?

(Note: This exercise is adapted from an in-class exercise devised by Professor Louis M. Brown for use in a first-year contracts class.)

EXERCISE THIRTEEN: PROFESSIONAL AUTHORITY

Louis Auchincloss is a renowned novelist and a Wall Street lawyer. Auchincloss begins one of his stories, "Equitable Awards" (which appears in a collection of work entitled Narcissa & Other Fables, 1983), with a scene in the law office of Miriam Storrs. What follows is the beginning of an interesting story, and an instructive one for the student of counseling:

Gwendolen Burrill sat facing her lawyer
across a broad desk, the very bareness of
which, except for an unspotted green
blotter and a black pen stand that was
obviously never used, suggested that its
occupant, in the business of offering simply a brain full of ideas, operated more
efficiently without encumbrance. But
the stripped neatness of the desk,
matched with the bleakness of the cham-
ber, chaste except for a large, dull print
of Bowling Green in the 1840s, depressed
Gwen, making her feel that her own
rather faded attributes—curly chestnut
hair streaked with gray, skin more
smooth than pink, a decayed girlishness
that showed its forty-six years—were being harshly exposed, laid out, so to
speak, one by one, on a long board, to be
picked up appraisingly and then, presumably, put down again.

(L–1)   "Let me explain how the nineteen eighty
divorce law works, Mrs. Burrill. It is
based on the theory that marriage is a
kind of business partnership. The court
will assess the value of what you as a
wife have contributed to this partnership and award you accordingly. And
the division will encompass not only income but principal. In your case I'd go
so far as to suggest that we're justified in

asking for a fifty-fifty split right across the board. Half of your husband's total wealth, and, of course, a full half of his earned income until your death or re-marriage."

(C–2) "But how," Gwen protested, "can you argue that I contributed to his success in his law firm? He's slaved away there, day and night, for the last twenty years! Just the way you all probably do here."

(L–3) "And how could he have done that if you hadn't been doing your part? Mr. Bur-rill has been able to give himself totally to his profession only because you have lifted the weight of his private life off his hands. Who looked after the home, the children, the vacations, the entertain-ments? Who freed him of all his petty cares, even his major ones? Why, Mrs. Burrill, I'll bet you even bought his shirts!"

(C–4) "It's true. I did."

(L–5) "And now that you've given him half your life, now that you've lost your chance for a professional career in which you might have done at least as well as he, are we to let him cast you aside like an old shoe? Excuse the expression! I'm afraid I got carried away."

(C–6)   Gwen smiled as sweetly as she was able, but it was less to spare the lawyer's feelings than to hide her own pain. Old shoe! but of course, wasn't that just how this young woman would regard her? Miriam Storrs, juris doctor, couldn't have been more than thirty, probably less, and she had none of the masculine tailored firmness that women of Gwen's mother's generation (and some of Gwen's) liked to associate with their career-oriented sisters, smugly deeming it the price they had to pay for their success in a man's world. But Miriam Storrs was blonde and even possessed of rather baby-blue eyes, and the fineness of her figure was only too apparent under that silly white dress with the flowered hem.

(C–7)   "Excuse me for asking a personal question, Miss Storrs. Are you married?"

(L–8)   "Oh, yes. My husband's a doctor. A pediatrician."

(C–9)   "And do you have children?"

(L–10)   "Not yet, but we hope to."

(C–11)   Gwen sighed. What a useless, idle creature she must seem to such a couple! A life wholly dedicated to domesticity— and a domesticity that had come to this!

(C–12)   "Do you like divorce work?"

(L-13) "A case like yours, yes."

(C-14) "Because you consider me a victim of male chauvinism?"

(L-15) "Not really." Miriam's demeanor of bright professional sympathy faded a bit, and Gwen had a sudden glimpse of how her counselor might look to an adversary in court. "I assume you chose your own life and chose it freely. But you gave up certain opportunities when you did so, and your husband accepted that sacrifice. He shouldn't be allowed now to renege on his part of that implied contract. He must make you whole."

(C-16) "How can that be done?" Gwen shrugged sadly as she rose to go. "But, of course, you mean only to the extent possible. Very well, I'm in your hands. I leave it all to you."

Pause now, to note your reactions and your feelings. Can you imagine yourself as a lawyer in a similar situation? How do you see yourself responding to Gwendolen Burrill? Would you respond as Miriam Storrs did? Answer carefully, considering each exchange and how your response would have differed from Miriam's?

What kind of psychological issues (issues for counseling) do you think will emerge for Miriam Storrs, the lawyer, as she talks and listens to her new client, Gwendolen Burrill? Of what significance, psychologically, is it that Gwendolen's husband is a lawyer? And of what significance is it when you also learn in the interview that Mrs. Burrill's father selected and made the arrangements for his daughter to visit Miriam Storrs?

Consider your feelings about Gwendolen Burrill as she is presented by Auchincloss in the scene. Do you have immediate, strong impressions, or feelings? How do you account for these feelings? And if you do not have such feelings, given what you have read and now know about Mrs. Burrill (or will you call her Gwendolen?) can you imagine that your view of her and your feelings about her might change over time? Of what psychological significance to the relationship is the fact that Miriam Storrs is a woman? That she is substantially younger than her client?

And of what significance to the outcome of the case, and your, and Miriam Storrs's, representation of Gwendolen Burrill, is this business of the way Sidney Burrill has practiced law? Gwendolen says: "He's slaved away there [in the law firm], day and night, for the last twenty years! Just the way you all probably do here." Do you see this remark as an attempt at humor? An effort on the part of Gwendolen to establish rapport with her lawyer? How would you respond to a client who made such a remark?

During the course of your representation of Mrs. Burrill, you will, of course, learn more about Sidney, her husband. After leaving Miriam Storr's law office and the discussion about a divorce, Gwendolen reflects on how her parents had not been opposed to her marrying a lawyer, but that their idea of a lawyer was someone who would make his name and then go "into government, or diplomacy, or some sort of higher education.

"But Sidney, with that pale skin, that dark, faintly unshaven look, those staring red-lined eyes that seemed to search for a problem and a solution in the simplest things, with his way of losing himself and the world in work, could never break away, or perhaps even want to break away, from those cool, aggrandizing clients who were shrewd enough to know, without ever being big enough to tell him, how indispensable a tool he was to their daily machinations." And when you learn that Mrs. Burrill sees her husband in this way, what do you imagine as the outcome of this perception on her feelings toward her husband and toward Miriam Storrs, her lawyer? Toward *you*, her lawyer?

During the course of the relationship Mrs. Burrill reveals the following information concerning her perceptions and feelings about her husband and his work, and her relationship with him. Assume that you learned each piece of information as Auchincloss presents it in the story and in the order we present it here. How does each disclosure affect your feelings toward Mrs. Burrill? How do you imagine each disclosure will affect your relationship with Mrs. Burrill?

(1) Mrs. Burrill's parents "had never thought him [Sidney] good enough for her."

(2) "She had not suspected his [Sidney's] almost compulsive habits of work before they were married. She knew that he labored hard, but then so did all the other young lawyers among her new, post-college friends. She considered that she labored fairly hard herself. She was a secretary in a publishing house and shared an apartment with her former Vassar roommate."

(3) "Sidney seemed to have inherited a brain from nowhere and to be quite willing to place it a hundred percent at the service of his employers. He never looked beyond his firm; he never questioned its right to use every bit of Sidney Burrill for its general purposes. He was like a faithful hound that needed but a single master, and that would probably be just as content with a second if anything should happen to the first. But the very exclusiveness of this loyalty created in him an odd independence about other things. Sidney was, as Gwen boasted, a free soul—outside his firm. He had no prejudices, no boredoms, no tiresome idiosyncrasies. He was gay and easy with people at parties; he liked to drink and, as she soon discovered, to make love. She had no doubt, when he first became serious about her, that she would be to his heart what his law firm was to his mind. But it had not taken many months of marriage to teach her that if she had his love, his time be-

longed to others. And the years simply confirmed this."

(4) "She remembered thinking that things would be different when Sidney attained his ambition and became a partner in his firm. Then he would take more time off, and they would do things together. But her father had warned her against this illusion. 'Lawyers and businessmen in Sidney's league can't afford to slacken the pace,' he had told her, rather complacently, as it now struck her. 'They might make the unpleasant discovery that they had prepared themselves for nothing else in life.' "

(5) "When he [Sidney] wasn't working, he could be charming: affable, amiable, open-minded, funny and interested in all the little things that were going on around him. In the country he loved to identify birds and flowers and to take the boys [Sidney, Jr., and Fred; at the time of the Miriam Storrs interview, both sons are in college] on long walks. The intensity that he brought to his law practice was also available for the mixing of a cocktail, the solution of a crossword puzzle, or the fixing of defective plumbing. The trouble with these periods of relaxation was only their briefness."

(6) Sidney, in turn, "was perfectly aware of the problem that his industry posed for her, and perfectly frank in the remedy that he always put forward. 'You should get a job. You've much too good a mind to waste it all day.' "

(7) Mrs. Burrill has had discussions, some quite emotional, with her husband about the kind of clients he represents. When she relates a statement that her father had made about Sidney's clients being a "nest of pirates," Sidney exploded: 'I think your old man has one hell of a nerve to slam people who make a go of it in fields that he was too dainty to put a toe in! [Gwen's father was a political scientist.] How the hell does he think the money was made that lets him sit on his ass and write beautiful prose about wicked governments? And it isn't even as if he had enough to make you independent of me! By the time he kicks the bucket and Uncle Sam has taken his cut, you may be thanking your lucky stars for your grubbing husband. . . .' "

(8) Mrs. Burrill realizes that "perhaps she should have been taught a little more respect for the men who had to make the money. The trouble might have been that she had been brought up to be unworldly without being wholly unworldly, and that she had not been one of those able to work out the necessary compromise."

(9) " 'All last night, I kept thinking of what you'd said about how I'd contributed to Sidney's career. About my looking after the children and entertaining for him. But it's not true! We could have afforded a nurse, and both boys went off to boarding school when they were fourteen. And as for entertaining, I was never warm and cozy with

Sidney's clients the way I was with my own friends.' "

(10) "There's something else. I had an affair. . . ." Gwen's affair was with a tennis pro that she met at the club that she and Sidney belonged to when Sidney was sent abroad to run the French office of the firm. When the tennis pro left the apartment after their second meeting in the apartment, Sidney came home from the office with an inflamed sore throat and saw the tennis pro, whom he recognized from the club, in the lobby of the apartment. Gwen confessed to the affair, before Sidney said a word about seeing the club tennis pro in their apartment building. Sidney took the news well and there was, following the incident, a brief renewal of romantic interest on the part of both Sidney and Gwen in their relationship.

(11) After Gwen and Sidney returned from France the relationship fell apart rather quickly, but without any dramatic incidents. "Sidney slept in the boys' bedroom and rarely came home for dinner. Finally, after an extensive business trip to the West Coast, he moved to a hotel directly on his return and wrote her that he would be staying there indefinitely."

(*Note:* We envision this exercise as useful for class discussion, after each member of the class studies it.)

GROUP EXERCISE FOURTEEN: SELF–UNDERSTANDING AND SELF–DISCLOSURE

Much of the training that goes into learning to be a counselor focuses on feelings. Empathy, the ability to put yourself in the shoes of another, to understand how he feels, and openness to and awareness of your own feelings are fundamental and basic *skills* in counseling. But immediate feelings are not everything. Counseling a client is influenced by what we bring to the relationship as well as what happens in face-to-face interactions. The past becomes the "trigger" of certain (sometimes predictable) feelings. (See Chapter Three and the discussion there of countertransference.) The past has as much to do with feelings as the present. The past makes some feelings common, some occasional, and some unlikely. And it is also true that our feelings, what we are actually experiencing at the moment, or the feelings we have in being with another person, make us the kind of persons we are becoming. There is a kind of mutual, reciprocal, overlapping of person and feelings, feelings and person, past and present and future.

In order to focus on something concrete, *i.e.,* something that can be learned and taught, something that is relatively easy to talk about, counselor education focuses on feelings rather than persons. In this exercise we shift emphasis: we want to put feelings in the background, and to focus on you as a whole person. One way to do this is to see yourself as a person with a history, with a life that exists over time. It is, after all, your life, your entire life, that you bring with you to law school (past, present, and future), and take with you into your encounters and interactions with clients.

Activity: For this exercise select another member of the group with whom you will feel comfortable discussing significant events in your life, a person whose life is of interest to you.

When you have selected your partner, each of you will need three pieces of 8½″ by 11″ unlined paper. Working separately now, tape the three pieces of paper together, end to end, so that you each have a scroll of paper, approximately 33″ long. Beginning at the far left edge of the scroll draw a line that depicts your life and indicate along that line those events in your life that you now see as most significant in making you the person you are today. Use upward and downward movements of the line to reflect the upward and downward movements in your life. In using the terms "upward" and "downward" we follow what we take as conventional, that to be "up" expresses delight, happiness, joy, contentment, pleasure, exhilaration, and over-all feelings of well-being. When we are "down" we are displeased, unhappy, discontented, alienated, disenchanted, "blue," depressed, despairing. Use the upward and downward movement of your life-line to express these "feeling states" over the course of your life.

We recognize that doing the chart has called for delving into the past, and it is often our past that we hide from. Drawing the life-line chart and discussing it with a partner requires self-disclosure. Therefore, you will want to enter the discussion with your partner with awareness that the conversation makes each of you vulnerable and that self-disclosure can be threatening. During your discussion you may want to focus specifically on how and to what extent the discussion (and the exercise) is threatening.

After you have completed your life-line chart, exchange charts with your partner. Spend a few minutes reviewing your partner's chart, noting those events in your partner's life that help you understand what you already know about your partner. Also make a mental note of those events indicated on the chart that are not reflected in what you now know of the person.

Finally, after you have spent some time reviewing the chart that your partner has drawn, discuss those aspects of the chart that seem to one or the other of you to be significant in the kind of counselor that each of you will be as a lawyer.

When the group reconvenes discuss the exercise and whether it has shifted the focus from immediate feelings to yourself and others as persons with a life history, a story that extends beyond the present. What other means could be used to focus on persons and stories in contrast to immediate feelings?

Subsequent activity: At this point in the discussion divide the class or group into small groups of three or four people each, and see if you can devise a classroom exercise that helps each of you as member of the group to focus on each of you as a person who has a story, a past and a future. One question which you will want to consider in devising the exercise is the extent to which you will have the participants share with others in the group information about their lives.

Continuing the discussion in the large group, or upon reconvening the group after working on the subsequent activity of devising a new exercise for the group, discuss the question of self-disclosure and how you approached it in your discussion with your partner, and in the subsequent activity group. How did the small groups deal with the self-disclosure issue? (See Group Exercise Seventeen.)

GROUP EXERCISE FIFTEEN: GROUP PROBLEM SOLVING

The purpose of this exercise is to gather information on, and then to discuss, whether problem solving is more efficient when groups work together than it is when an individual works alone. The assumption in the exercise is that a group works best when it has a collaborative spirit ("rapport"). The first phase in the exercise is a get-acquainted, group-building, collaboration-establishing phase;

the second phase is problem solving; the third phase is discussion, both of problem solving and of the beginning of relationships (including relationships between professional people and their clients).

Part A

Each member of the group has five small index cards and a pencil. Each is asked to write on one of the cards a description of himself, in terms of what she or he does or is. (For example, one card says "law student"; one says "parent"; one says "private pilot"; one says "Jew"; and one says "little sister.") This is done alone. Several groups can work at the same time; each group should have more than three, fewer than seven members.

When each member of the group has finished the cards, the group discusses them: Each member of the group in turn reads her or his cards to the others, says a bit about each card and how important that identification is. (Variant: If there is enough time, this first discussion can be in pairs; each person talks about himself, from the cards, to a partner; then the pairs get together and each person introduces her or his partner in terms of the cards and their discussion of the cards. For example, "This is Sam. Sam is a new husband and his marriage is very important to him. He also makes model sailing ships and was a paralegal before he came to law school. And, Sam is a law student now. . . .")

Part B

The group is now to undertake a task. The rule of the task is that the group must reach a consensus on its solution: It is not allowed to split the difference on disagreements; and it is not allowed to decide by majority vote. The group's decision must be agreed to by each member of the group (at least partially). There are thirty minutes to complete the task, once the group begins.

Each member, first, considers the following list of occupations in America and has five minutes to decide the relative prestige of each occupation. Each member ranks the occupations from "1" (highest in prestige) to "15" (lowest):

_____ Author of novels

_____ Newspaper columnist

_____ Police officer

_____ Banker

_____ Supreme Court justice

_____ Lawyer

_____ Undertaker

_____ State governor

_____ Sociologist

_____ Scientist

_____ Public school teacher

_____ Dentist

_____ Psychologist

_____ College professor

_____ Physician

After each member has decided on a list ranking, the group begins its work. The group has thirty minutes to agree on its ranking.

Part C

Discussion. The most immediate subject is how the group worked together and how it reached (or failed to reach) a consensus. This involves issues about leadership, compromise, strategies for making decision (including techniques of persuasion), how people felt as the group worked, roles members played, etc.

(This exercise was adapted from Pfeiffer and Jones, A Handbook of Structured Experiences for Human Relations Training, vol. II, 1970).

GROUP EXERCISE SIXTEEN: TRUST

The purpose here is to explore what it means and how it feels to have to trust another person—as each of us is required to do when we need dental work or when our car won't start, or when we are threatened by the law.

The group divides itself into partnerships (of two). Each partnership decides who is to be the leader (the trusted person) and which the led (the person who has to trust). The person who is led is blindfolded and then led by the leader on a "trust walk." Around the building, across the street, into the park, etc. Leading is done by barely touching the person on the elbow, by holding hands, by placing hands on shoulders from behind, by letting the blindfolded person take the leader's arm, or by verbal directions. After approximately ten minutes the partners should exchange roles.

After the walk(s), each partnership can talk about their experiences in each role. This conversation—or "processing" as the human-relations trainers call it—is important.

A variant on the exercise, before the "processing" group conversation, would drop the exchanging of roles—so that the leader remains leader throughout the walk—and add a period of conversation between the two partners *before* (but not instead of) the group conversation. In this one-on-one conversation between partners (which, notice, is more like a lawyer-client conversation than the group conversation is), the partners alternate active-listening interview practice. *E.g.*, the person led asks the leader, "How was it to be a leader, to be trusted and depended on like that?" And the leader begins to answer, and the person led—who is now an interviewer—avoids any further questions and keeps the interview going by reflecting what the leader—who is now the interviewee—says about the experience of being depended on. (Active listening is in principle simple, but it takes practice, as you will find. In principle, what the interviewer says to the interviewee is, "What you are saying is _____ about _____. Do I have it right?" The best active listeners learn to do this with non-verbal sounds and gestures as much as with words. The key is to reflect feelings.)

GROUP EXERCISE SEVENTEEN: PRIVATE INFORMATION

The purpose of this exercise is to explore the situation of people who have to disclose relatively private information to other people—the situation of patients, clients, counselors, students, and, generally, almost anybody who is required to take a subordinate and disclosing posture in order to get help.

The group divides itself into three uneven subgroups. The division is according to answers to this question: Would you be willing to allow others in the group to look at the contents of your purse (wallet) (checkbook)?

Group I are those who answer yes.

Group II are those who answer no.

Then the members of Group II are asked a second question: Would you be willing to look into the purse (wallet) (checkbook) of others?

Those who answer no are added to (remain in) Group II.

Group III are those who answer yes.

Now, for the action:

(1) Group III examines the contents of the purses (wallets) (checkbooks) of Group I. Group

II are observers. Talking is allowed and encouraged. The examination should take about five minutes.

(2) The group assembles for discussion. Group II reports on its observations and then the group talks about the experience of giving and withholding private information and of being in the situation where such disclosure is expected to order to get help.

(Adapted from Pfeiffer and Jones, A Handbook of Structured Experiences for Human Relations Training, vol. II, 1970).

GROUP EXERCISE EIGHTEEN: PREJUDICIAL LISTENING

The purpose of this exercise is to explore the task of listening, to see how hard it is to listen with comprehension (as opposed to hearing only words).

The group divides itself into trios and each member of each trio takes an assignment as Member A, Member B, or Member C. What each trio is going to do is talk about one, two, or three topics for about twenty minutes. Here are the ground rules:

—Topics of conversation are chosen from the topic list (below) by the member who is going to talk.

—Before any member begins to talk about her topic, she must summarize what has been said to that point by the other members. The other members may interrupt this summary to correct mistakes and prevent misunderstanding.

—After Member A has talked for six minutes, Member B has his turn to talk (after he summarizes what Member A said). In each case the member can choose his own topic from the topic list.

—While Members A and B are talking, Member C is the referee—who makes sure the ground rules are observed. When Member C begins his summary, Member A becomes the referee.

—When each member has talked (i.e., after about 20 minutes) the trio assignments are completed and the entire group assembles to talk about ("process") the task of listening.

The topic list:

(1) Professional training, especially that in law schools, is too narrow.

(2) Education at all levels, including professional schools, should expand its curriculum and training, in morals and ethics.

(3) Lawyers have no more responsibility to see that justice is done in our society than do plumbers or stockbrokers.

(4) The University's endowment funds should not be invested in the securities of American companies who do business in South Africa.

(The trio may, before it begins, pick a topic not on this list, provided all members agree.)

The group conversation (after the trios finish their work) should give ample opportunity for each member to report on these questions:

—Did you find that you had difficulty listening?

—Did you find that you had difficulty formulating your own thought *and* listening at the same time—so that you forgot what you were going to say, you were not listening, you rehearsed what you were going to say.

—When the other members summarized what you said were they accurate?

—Did you find it difficult to express what you wanted to say about your subject?

—Was the manner in which the other members put their views affecting you ability to listen to them? (The more you can say about this the more useful your answer will be to the other members of your trio.)

For each question, consider the factors that led to your conclusion.

(Adapted from Pfeiffer and Jones, A Handbook of Structured Experiences for Human Relations Training, vol. I, 1969).

INDEX TO
AUTHORS CITED

INDEX TO
TEXT REFERENCES TO EXERCISES

References are to Pages

*

INDEX TO SUBJECTS

†